The Calling of Fatherhood

Andrew D. Finnicum

WestBow
PRESS
A DIVISION OF THOMAS NELSON

Copyright © 2012 by Andrew D. Finnicum.

All rights reserved. No part of this book may be used or reproduced by any means, graphic, electronic, or mechanical, including photocopying, recording, taping or by any information storage retrieval system without the written permission of the publisher except in the case of brief quotations embodied in critical articles and reviews.

WestBow Press books may be ordered through booksellers or by contacting:

WestBow Press
A Division of Thomas Nelson
1663 Liberty Drive
Bloomington, IN 47403
www.westbowpress.com
1-(866) 928-1240

Because of the dynamic nature of the Internet, any web addresses or links contained in this book may have changed since publication and may no longer be valid. The views expressed in this work are solely those of the author and do not necessarily reflect the views of the publisher, and the publisher hereby disclaims any responsibility for them.

Any people depicted in stock imagery provided by Thinkstock are models, and such images are being used for illustrative purposes only.

Certain stock imagery © Thinkstock.

ISBN: 978-1-4497-5885-1 (sc)
ISBN: 978-1-4497-5887-5 (hc)
ISBN: 978-1-4497-5886-8 (e)

Library of Congress Control Number: 2012912563

Printed in the United States of America

WestBow Press rev. date: 8/09/2012

The Trumpet Sounds on . . .

The Calling of Fatherhood

By Andrew D. Finnicum

> *Deuteronomy 6:4-7*
> *"Hear, O Israel:*
> *The LORD our God is one LORD:*
> *And thou shalt love the LORD thy God with*
> *all thine heart, and with all thy soul,*
> *and with all thy might.*
> *And these words, which I command thee this*
> *day, shall be in thine heart:*
> *And thou shalt teach them diligently unto thy*
> *children, and shalt talk of them when thou*
> *sittest in thine house, and when thou walkest*
> *by the way, and when thou liest down,*
> *and when thou risest up."*

To those brave fathers in the first generation who, like my father,
dare to stand in faith and forever change the heritage of their children;

To my children, I pray that you shatter the cycle of the third generation
and find new mountains to conquer for God.

Soli Deo gloria.

Table of Contents

I. Seeing the Vision ... 1
   1. The Father's Heart: "The Pursuit of Godly Seed" ... 3
   2. The Father's Goal: "The Hearts of the Children" ... 13
   3. The Father's Salvation: "Considering Thyself" ... 28

II. Examining the Devastation ... 33
   4. The Cultural Disaster: "A State of Emergency" ... 35
   5. The Church's Failure: "If Your Eye Be Dark" ... 39
   6. The Father's Neglect: "A Garden Destroyed" ... 50

III. Enlightening the Eyes ... 63
   7. The Father's Purpose: "Arrows for the Lord" ... 65
   8. The Father's Discipleship: "These Words Shall Be in Thy Heart" ... 75
   9. The Father's Method: "Teach Them to Thy Children" ... 84

IV. Reaping the Benefits ... 107
   10. The Father's Treasure: "The Heritage of the Lord" ... 109
   11. The Father's Disciples: "The House of the Rechabites" ... 122
   12. The Father's Offering: "A Faithful Steward" ... 130

V. Building the Body ... 139
   13. The Father's Needs: "It Takes a Body" ... 141
   14. The Father's Allies: "When Every Joint Supplies" ... 146
   15. The Father's Obedience: "Submit Yourself" ... 156

VI. Facing the Fire ... 163
   16. The Father's Fight: "The War of the Will" ... 165
   17. The Father's Foes: "Bombarded on Every Side" ... 174
   18. The Father's Victory: "The Battle Is the Lord's" ... 186

VII. Answering the Call ... 217
   19. The Father's Responsibility: "Prepare the Passover" ... 219
   20. The Father's Sacrifice: "No Price Too Great" ... 230
   21. The Father's Response: "Stand in the Gap" ... 240

Author's Apology

My dear brethren,

I am painfully aware that I am not the ideal person to present this vision. The reasons for me to hold my peace and leave these words unwritten are legion. Having grown up in a wonderful Christian home, I cannot pretend to know the battles that first generation fathers will face if they pursue this vision. Many of the giants in my family's heritage were slain before I ever entered the fight.

I am anything but ignorant of my youth and lack of experience. At this time, I am twenty-five, have been married for a brief five years, and all my children are under five years old. I have never raised a teenager. I have never spent a day in public school. It has been well over a decade since I had secular television programs in my home. It is up for debate whether I have yet experienced my first "strong willed" child. Many who read this book will have been fathers longer than I have been alive.

I should not write this book. But I have no choice. God has written a vision in my heart and, like Habakkuk, burdened me to write it down. Like Jeremiah, I would prefer to say nothing and minister only in my own home, but I cannot. There is a burning fire shut up in my bones. I cannot hold my peace because I have heard the sound of the trumpet, the alarm of war. Having been forewarned, if I fail to blow this trumpet clearly, the blood of many will be held to my charge.

This vision belongs to no man. It flows from heaven to men through the pages of Scripture and the Spirit of God. It is a holy calling. Moreover, the vision is always greater than the people that have it.

I was only born because a faithful preacher of Bible principles convinced my parents that God had called them to raise arrows for God. Despite this, I have not always seen the vision of godly homes as clearly as I do now. When I was a sophomore at Liberty University, a professor dared to shake my intentions of family planning to the core.

Once I surrendered that area of my life to God, the preaching of a dearly beloved Anabaptist minister, who is now fighting an untreatable brain tumor, planted a vision in my heart to pursue a godly seed. I have dedicated the rest of my life to fulfilling that vision. I have searched the Scriptures to see if this vision was true. It is.

In addition to a careful survey of the Scriptures, I am privileged to stand on the shoulders of spiritual giants. Throughout these pages, the words of Charles Finney, William Booth, John Wesley, Andrew Murray, and other faithful men confirm that the calling of fatherhood was once much more clearly understood than it is today. The faithful cloud of witnesses that precedes us gives me added inspiration to answer the call.

To all those who have made this book possible, thank you. Special thanks go to my wife, Ashley. Without her patience and faithfulness, this book would never have been published.

Much of what you are about to read has challenged me, humbled me, grieved me, and inspired me. I hope that it will do the same to you. As you read, there may be times that you disagree with my conclusions. Please overlook any errors on my part and receive as much as you can from these pages, and especially from the Scriptures cited herein. I pray that this vision changes your life. I know it has changed mine.

Sincerely,
Andrew D. Finnicum

Seeing the Vision

"And did not he make one? Yet had he the residue of the spirit. And wherefore one? That he might seek a godly seed. Therefore take heed to your spirit, and let none deal treacherously against the wife of his youth." Malachi 2:15

Men and brethren, as we begin an in-depth study into what God has written in His Word concerning our families and our holy calling as fathers, let us humbly petition our Father, the God of heaven and earth, to help us glimpse into His own heart and see the vision that He has for us and for our families. We must come to God with an earnest desire to see beyond our own limitations into the realm of the eternal. Only by God's grace can we hope to see our calling as fathers from God's point of view. But that is the perspective we must have if we hope to fulfill the call that God has placed upon our lives.

The Scripture quoted above gives us a glimpse into where this study will take us. For some, this study of our holy calling will be a new revelation. For others, it will bring an often needed reminder of the truths we hold dear to our hearts. For still more, it will sound a clarion call for repentance and a return to God's perfect plan. In whatever condition God's Spirit finds us as we consider His Word, let us embrace the Scriptures and welcome the searching, slicing, scouring work that only the unadulterated Word of God can do in our hearts and minds.

Let us ask with Malachi, why did God make me one with my wife in holy marriage? As true now as then, there is one overriding answer—that God might seek a godly seed in the earth. This is the holy purpose of our marriage and the great duty to which God calls us the first moment we hold our firstborn in our arms. Let us then search the Scriptures and ask God to fully reveal to us His heart for godly seed. And then, let us petition heaven for the vision necessary to bring our hearts into agreement with God's, so that we, in one holy unity between God and man, may together seek a godly seed.

CHAPTER 1

The Father's Heart: "The Pursuit of Godly Seed"

The Father in Heaven

If the Father in heaven is truly seeking a godly seed, and if He has called us to join with Him in that pursuit, we can be assured that we have a faithful friend and powerful ally. No one seeks like God seeks. The Bible plainly reveals that Malachi does not stand alone in his declaration that God is pursuing a godly seed. Rather, the whole Bible, from one cover to the other, promises, praises, and commands a holy alliance between the Father in heaven and redeemed fathers on earth to produce a godly seed from one generation to the next. God revealed His heart on this matter from the very beginning of the lineage of faith when He swore by Himself to Abraham that He would establish His covenant not just with Abraham, but with his seed after him.[1] God's heart for Abraham's seed overflows into the pages of Scripture repeatedly. God makes a holy covenant "between me and thee and thy seed after thee in their generations," promises "to be a God unto thee, and to thy seed after thee," and assures Abraham, "I will be their God."[2] What greater promise can God make than to be a personal God to our children?

Lest we somehow believe that God's promise to Abraham was unique only to this father of faith, God reveals His heart for godly seed time and again in the Law of Moses. In Leviticus, God explains that the traditions described in the Law are designed so that the generations to come will remember the mighty works of God and follow Him.[3] Indeed, the mighty works of God described in Exodus occurred because "He loved thy fathers" and "chose their seed after them."[4] God gave Israel His commands "that it may go well with thee, and with thy children after thee."[5] Lest we doubt His sincerity, God cries out, "O that there were such an heart in them, that they would fear me, and keep all my commandments always, that it might be well with them, and with their children for ever!"[6] Brethren, what could God do in our homes if we wholeheartedly believed that this Scripture is the heartfelt cry of almighty God? If repetition is any indication of how much God emphasizes something, then the pursuit of godly seed is near and dear to the heart of God. He repeats again that He delights in fathers to love them and "chose their seed after them."[7] Fathers, if the Israel of that day could count on such a promise, should we, who are now the chosen of God, cower in unbelief and worry that God does not care for our children and may refuse to choose our seed after us? Does God change? To ask the question is to answer it, for we know that God does not change and cannot lie.

If, by chance, we think that such a promise ended with the Law, God's heartfelt desire for a godly seed pours out time and again in the pages of Scripture. To David, He says, "I will set up thy seed after thee," and concerning David's son, He promises, "I will be his father, and he shall be my son."[8] David's response should be typical of any godly father who searches the truths of the Bible concerning his own home. David replies, "Who am I, O Lord God? and what is my house, that thou hast brought me hitherto? And this was yet a small thing in thy sight, O Lord God; but thou hast spoken also of thy servant's house for a great while to come."[9] Should we, as Spirit-filled believers, look back on David with shame and envy that God promised David better things than He promised us? A thousand times no! God desires to do more for our families than He could ever do for David, for God longs to work with us to bring our children into the kingdom of heaven and have us watch in awe as He indwells them as the temples of God. No, God has not left us a lesser hope. Rather, "the eyes of the LORD run to and fro throughout the whole earth, to shew himself strong in the behalf of them whose heart is perfect toward him."[10] Let God find such a heart in us, and He will show Himself strong in our homes.

Moreover, if we begin to conclude that such promises are only for the elite heroes of the Old Testament, God shows us time and again that He never intends to leave the children outside of the kingdom. When men of God come before the Lord, they are to bring "their little ones, their wives, and their children" to be a part of it.[11] When God set aside men to be a part of the priesthood, their sons "from three years old and upward" were included in the service.[12] They were sanctified in holiness with "all their little ones, their wives, and their sons, and their daughters."[13] In addition,

God works specifically with our children, for "out of the mouth of babes and sucklings hast [God] ordained strength."[14] When the psalmist saw into the heart of God for the homes of Israel, he wrote, "The children of thy servants shall continue, and their seed shall be established before thee."[15] He declared by the inspiration of the Almighty that God's righteousness is unto children's children.[16] God again promises through the Psalms, "Blessed is the man that feareth the LORD, that delighteth greatly in his commandments. His seed shall be mighty upon earth: the generation of the upright shall be blessed."[17]

As if the covenants, law, history, and psalms are not enough to persuade us that God is seeking a godly seed, the prophets were moved by God to express His heart's desire for our children. Joel, speaking for the heavenly Father, prophesies, "I will pour out my spirit upon all flesh; and your sons and your daughters shall prophesy, your old men shall dream dreams, your young men shall see visions."[18] Zechariah prophesies that when the Lord returns to Zion, "the streets of the city shall be full of boys and girls playing in the streets thereof."[19] As discussed before, Malachi cries out for a holy dedication in our homes and marriages so that God "might seek a godly seed."[20] Indeed, one of the very last promises of the Old Testament is that when the coming of Messiah is close, God "shall turn the heart of the fathers to the children, and the heart of the children to their fathers."[21] Oh God, let there be such a turning again in our day! Turn our hearts to our children, Father. Not to positions, possessions, or power, but to our children! And, then, God, please turn the hearts of our children back to us as fathers, that we might present their hearts to You.

Malachi's cry compels us to face the question of why God must intervene to turn our hearts to our children. Where are our hearts, dear brothers, if it takes an act of almighty God to turn our hearts back to our children? Have we settled for lesser things? These are questions we must answer at the deepest levels, but for now, let us continue to beg a glimpse into the heart of God.

Perhaps, you say, all these Scriptures are not enough. After all, we have only examined the "old covenant." Perhaps, one might argue, God changed His mind and decided to abandon the children of His faithful servants to fend for themselves on a one-way road to death. What then, says the Son of God Himself? As the express image of God the Father, no man could reveal to us the heart of God more than Jesus. So, what does He say concerning our children? He boldly declares that "it is not the will of your

Father which is in heaven, that one of these little ones should perish."²² Let us consider those words carefully. If Christ is to be believed, then we must believe His every word, not just those that we easily embrace. If Christ is who He says He is, then we must come to the realization that if any one of our children walks away from the faith and perishes in the world, it was in direct violation of the will and plan of almighty God. To conclude that God abandoned our "little ones" and threw them to the enemy for their total destruction and condemnation is to deny the words of Christ Himself. Indeed, it was Jesus who brought the Old Testament promises of a godly seed into the New Covenant by quoting one of the very Scriptures cited earlier to the scribes and Pharisees. As Jesus walked by, it was the children who cried out His praises in the temple, and Jesus, referring back to the Old Testament, said, "Yea; have ye never read, Out of the mouth of babes and sucklings thou hast perfected praise?"²³

When Christ's own disciples miss His love for the children, He is much displeased. As those God-fearing parents bring their little children to Jesus for a blessing, the disciples rush in and rebuke them for bothering Jesus with lesser things. Jesus' response reveals the very heart of God and echoes through all eternity a lesson that we cannot afford to forget. In the midst of healings, exorcisms, displays of divine power, and the greatest teaching to ever occur on this planet, Jesus stops everything to bless one little child. "Permit them to come to me," He says. "Forbid them not, for of such is the kingdom of God."²⁴ And then, the Son of God, the divine Creator of all that was, is, and ever will be, kneels to the ground, embraces His greatest creation, lays His soon-to-be nail-pierced hands upon them, and blesses these dear children. He celebrates them with praises, invokes the blessing of His Father upon their lives, and consecrates them to God with solemn prayer.²⁵ Dear brothers, what a picture! The Son of God Himself has stooped low and embraced a child to reveal to us that they are the very heart and soul of the kingdom of God. Let us not soon forget this image. It will serve us well to keep this vision of Jesus near to our hearts as we continue in this study.

Let us praise God for this glorious truth! The Scriptures clearly reveal unto us that God the Father is actively and intentionally pursuing the children that are growing up in our homes. What's more, it is His pursuit of that godly seed that actually causes Him to deal in our lives, shower His mercies upon us, and bring us into a holy marriage dedicated to God. Yet, with all these Scriptures, it may be that the most important one is still to come. The disciples, who were once rebuked for denying children access to Jesus, learned their lesson well. And, when the day of Pentecost was fully come, Peter rose before the people and began to declare the wonderful works of God. Again, this "New Testament" founder reached back into the prophets of old and, quoting Joel, repeats for God, "I will pour out of my Spirit upon all flesh: and your sons and your daughters shall prophesy, and your young men shall see visions."[26] And, then, at the most important time and place that God could ever make a generational promise, Peter shouts into the crowd, "Repent, and be baptized every one of you in the name of Jesus Christ for the remission of sins, and ye shall receive the gift of the Holy Ghost. For the promise is unto you, and to your children [. . . .]"[27] Nowhere could God's promise for our children have been more significant than in the second chapter of Acts, and God prominently repeated His promise to us and our children right there in the middle of the outpouring of the Holy Spirit.[28]

Was Peter right? Was God yearning, even in a New Testament era, to pour out blessings, salvation, and the Holy Ghost upon a godly seed? The rest of the New Testament answers with a resounding "yes." Cornelius feared God with "all his house".[29] The angel's message to Cornelius was that "thou and all thy house shall be saved."[30] Lydia was baptized with her household.[31] The house of Stephanas was addicted to the ministry of the saints.[32] The Philippian jailer believed with all his house.[33] Crispus "believed on the Lord with all his house."[34] Phillip "had four daughters, virgins, which did prophesy."[35] Thus, the testimony of the New Testament church is that God did not abandon the promises of the Old Testament, but rather expanded and enlarged them in His continued pursuit of a godly seed. Indeed, as God's plan progresses, the value of each godly child increases. At one time, God claimed only the firstborn sons. Now, He desires every child to be dedicated to Him. If God had ten thousand John Wesley's or Hudson Taylor's, He could use every one of them today to further His kingdom. Our children are heirs of the promise that we have received from God. Let us draw near to this revelation of the heart of God and join with Him in the greatest pursuit of all time—the pursuit of godly seed.

The Father at Home

Because the Scriptures make abundantly clear that God's heart is fully engaged in the pursuit of our children as a godly seed in the earth, we must now turn our attention back to the dilemma posed by Malachi. Why does it take an act of God to turn our hearts to our children? God must be talking about something deeper than just the inherent, automatic connection between a father and his children. Rather, this heart to heart relationship between father and child is a direct result of the work of God, and we, therefore, can be assured that God has great interest in every part of this relationship. As we look deeper into this issue, let us pray to our Father in heaven to turn our hearts toward our children in a greater way than we have previously known. As Ezra, let us prepare our hearts to seek the Lord, so that He may prepare our hearts to seek the hearts of our children.[36]

Many fathers, especially those who belong to the household of faith, experience a glimpse into the heart to heart connection between father and child when they first hold a newborn, especially their first one. The "first love" that flows between that father and child overwhelms all thoughts about the responsibility and sacrifice that are soon to follow the arrival of a newborn. In that one glorious moment, the trials of the previous nine months, the difficult process of delivery, and the imminent, oncoming sleep deprivation and self-sacrifice are incomparable to the love that flows from that father's heart. While a heart to heart connection goes even deeper than this, there is a grave danger that we fathers will quickly forget the first love we had for our children. As we search the Scriptures, return often in your mind to the love that flooded your heart the first time that you held your child in your arms. Recall the first moment that you dedicated that child to God. Remember the first time your son or daughter said, "I love you, Daddy." Refuse to lose your first love for your children. God's love for them has never changed or diminished. Has ours?

Jesus plainly declared that our hearts will be dedicated to whatever we treasure.[37] When a man sets his heart upon something, it consumes his attention, thoughts, energy, and time. All other people, things, and priorities pale in comparison to whatever has captured the heart of a man. If a man truly sets his heart upon something, he usually gets whatever it is that he wants. He will do anything to get what his heart is set upon.

Consider for a moment the Olympian athlete. The thought of obtaining a gold medal captures the heart of this man in his youth. From the moment he sets his heart upon that goal, literally everything in his life changes to make room for that pursuit. Every area of his life is disciplined to assist in achieving his heart's desire. All other needs, passions, and opportunities are made subject to the one all-consuming treasure of his heart. For centuries, the dedication of these men has been so complete that even the Apostle Paul was moved to use them as the example for a dedicated believer. One need only briefly examine this man's life to realize where he has turned his heart.

Consider also the soldier. Some belief, ideal, or duty so seizes the heart of this man that no price is worthy to be compared with these passions that burn inside his heart. He will cross any terrain, face any enemy, brave any danger, and abandon those people and places he loves most only to fight for the things that have seized his heart. He voluntarily pays the ultimate sacrifice for idea or country, regardless of whether or not it is appreciated by those less-moved individuals who remain at home. One can quickly see in his constant cadence, willing sacrifice, and etched determination that the fibers of his being have been dedicated to a cause he views as greater than himself.

What of us, dear fathers? Where are our hearts? Would an outsider briefly glancing into our lives know beyond any doubt that our hearts were turned by God toward the salvation of our children? Would God, as He certainly looks down from heaven, be persuaded? Our children are one of our greatest treasures. Our hearts should be with them at all times. If our hearts are somewhere else instead of with our children, then perhaps we have forgotten the incredible value these little ones have in God's eyes. Where are our hearts, brethren?

If we fathers are neglecting our families, what is the root problem? Where are our hearts? Have we set them on lesser things that have no eternal importance? Have we pursued materialism, the American dream, debt, career, hobbies, entertainment, ministry, or retirement at the expense of turning our hearts away from our families?[38] Yes, we have pursued all these things and more. And our families have paid the price. Let us repent, brethren, and turn back to our homes. Let us work with God to turn our hearts toward our children.

How do we know whether we have fully turned our hearts toward our children? Our thoughts, words, actions, attitudes, and the way we spend our time all betray the condition of our hearts. Where are we investing our time? Do we long for the moment each day that we have the privilege of being with our children? When we are home with our children, are they a blessing or a bother? Do they delight us, or the do they distract us from "more important" things? Are they an annoyance or an answered prayer? How would our children answer those questions if they were asked?

What is in our hearts will eventually come out of our mouths. How do we speak to our children? What do we communicate to them of their value to us? If our words do not match what God wants our hearts to be, then changing our hearts is the real necessity.

Another gauge of the heart of a man is his wife. A wife who does not desire children, prefers to be out of the home, and finds her family to be an inconvenience is often a symptom of a husband with the same problems. The responsibility lies with the fathers. Many Christian leaders are mourning that women are leaving their God-ordained roles and pursuing earthly goals. These women are only following the example that the men in their lives set years ago.[39]

Some people will oppose this turning, arguing that our modern world does not permit a father to have the time and energy necessary to fully turn his heart toward home. Many men, torn by the gulf they see between a literal reading of the Scriptures and the cold reality of their lives, will say that we preach a standard for the family that is too high to be taken seriously. Dear brothers, the problem is not that our churches preach the family too high. The problem is that we live it too low. As God turns your heart toward your family, if you should begin to feel the stress that many have faced as a result of a double minded pursuit of their children's hearts and the worlds idolatries, please do not blame the revelation that God is breathing into your life. Don't be discouraged. Be convicted.

For God to fully turn our hearts toward our children, there are three things we must consider. First, we must consider the faithfulness of God. As we discussed in the first part of this chapter, God's heart is to seek a godly seed. He wants to seek them in our own homes. He has promised to assist us in this great cause. Because of this, we can allow Him to turn our hearts toward our children with confidence that all the powers of heaven will be assisting us. We must believe the Scriptures of generational righteousness as much as we believe John 3:16 or the basic principles of our faith.

Second, we must consider ourselves. Like so many men before us, if we fully grasp the height, the width, and the depth of the calling of God upon our lives, we will be as grasshoppers in our own eyes compared to the greatness of this vision. What God seeks to do in our homes and what He promises to do in our children is impossible for men to accomplish. If we put our hands to this plow, we must do so with the help of a Father whose strength, love, and patience far exceed our own.

Third, we must consider the value of our children. Our children have the potential to walk with God from their youth, serve Him all their days, and live with Him forever. What could possibly be worth more than that? What earthly pursuit or temporary pleasure could supersede the value of our children living for God? What will we exchange for our souls, brethren? More importantly, what will we exchange for the souls of our children? Every day of our lives, we make that choice. Either we scorn all other offers as nothing, or we trade the souls of our children on the marketplace as surely as any slave trader ever did. In light of this reality, let us cry out to God to turn our hearts toward our children.

---

1. Genesis 9:9
2. Genesis 17:7-9
3. Leviticus 23:42-43
4. Deuteronomy 4:37
5. Deuteronomy 4:40
6. Deuteronomy 5:29
7. Deuteronomy 10:15
8. 2 Samuel 7:12-19
9. *Id.*
10. 2 Chronicles 16:9
11. 2 Chronicles 20:13
12. 2 Chronicles 31:15-18
13. *Id.*
14. Psalms 8:2
15. Psalms 102:28
16. Psalms 103:17-18
17. Psalm 112:1-2
18. Joel 2:28

19. Zechariah 8:3-5
20. Malachi 2:15
21. Malachi 4:6
22. Matthew 18:14
23. Matthew 21:15-16
24. Paraphrased from Mark 10:13-16
25. James Strong, The New Strong's Expanded Exhaustive Concordance of the Bible (2001) Strong's Greek #2127
26. Acts 2:17
27. Acts 2:38-39
28. Andrew Murray Raising Your Children for Christ (1984) p. 253.
29. Acts 10:2
30. Acts 11:14
31. Acts 16:15
32. 1 Corinthians 16:15
33. Acts 16:31-34
34. Acts 18:8
35. Acts 21:7-9
36. Ezra 7:10
37. Matt 6:21
38. Denny Kenaston The Pursuit of Godly Seed (2003) pp. 143-145.
39. *Id.* p. 142.

CHAPTER 2

THE FATHER'S GOAL: "THE HEARTS OF THE CHILDREN"

The Importance of Vision

Once we recognize that God seeks a godly seed in our homes and calls us to pursue and attain that goal with all our hearts, we must look to the Word of God for clear direction on what exactly He wants us to achieve. In this search for greater clarity, we must be like the faithful scribe, Ezra, and "afflict ourselves before our God, to seek of him a right way for us, and for our little ones, and for all our substance."[1] In short, brothers, we need a vision for our families.

What is a vision? Pastor and author Denny Kenaston describes vision as "a mental image imprinted upon the heart by the Spirit of God."[2] We must see it with the eyes of a new heart. This vision is "a spiritual revelation of the mind and will of God" for our families, and it comes from understanding God's Word on this important subject.[3] What do we see with the eyes of our hearts? Kenaston states, "God always precedes the reality of what He is going to do with a vision."[4] What you see now with the eyes of your heart will probably determine where your family will be in five years. For this reason, if for no other, we must have a vision from God for our homes.

A vision for godly homes is vitally important for each father to be able to fulfill the holy calling of fatherhood. God says "Where there is no vision, the people perish: but he that keepeth the law, happy is he."[5] In this context, the word perish has two important meanings. First, the original language suggests the idea of casting off restraint.[6] Thus, when a father lacks vision for his home, he will forsake the restraints that are necessary to produce a godly seed. When men lack spiritual vision, their homes lack spiritual substance and direction. As a result, the children will follow in their father's footsteps and eventually abandon the few restraints that he retained. Second, the idea of an entire group of people perishing suggests the picture of a group of people that is overtaken by the identity of another group. This is the primary way that a group perishes from the earth. They slowly disappear by blending in with some other identity or culture. Either way, unless we fathers do what we need to do, the people that perish for lack of vision will be our own children.

In addition, a vision does far more than just assist us in restraining ourselves. The Lord told the prophet Habakkuk, "Write the vision, and make it plain upon tables, that he may run that readeth it."[7] If we truly have a vision for godly homes written in the tables of our hearts by the finger of God, that vision will propel us toward the goal. That vision will bring purpose to every formerly mundane area of life. It will give us a cause, clearly seen with the eyes of the heart, which makes all of life worth living.

Dear brothers, do not read this book for mere information, knowledge, or technique. While these things are all important, without a vision they will fade from your mind in a few days. Read this book and pray to God that He will breathe into you a holy vision for your home. Ask Him for a vision written so deep in your heart that it will never fade away. Ask for a faith that sees beyond mere sight, that pursues the impossible, and that speaks of things that yet are not as though they already were. And, in those inevitable moments where the vision overwhelms us with the distance we must go to attain it, remember that the vision is yet for an appointed time. Though it tarry, strive for it, and by God's grace you will obtain a godly seed.

Biblical Visions for the Home

If, then, we turn to the Scriptures with open hearts in search of a clear vision of what God desires for our children, we will not be disappointed in our search. The Bible, time and again, paints pictures that inspire us to greatness and makes promises that humble us with God's mercy. Let us first consider this beautiful picture described in the Psalms:

> Give ear, O my people, to my law: incline your ears to the words of my mouth. I will open my mouth in a parable: I will utter dark sayings of old: Which we have heard and known, and our

> fathers have told us. We will not hide them from their children, shewing to the generation to come the praises of the LORD, and his strength, and his wonderful works that he hath done. For he established a testimony in Jacob, and appointed a law in Israel, which he commanded our fathers, that they should make them known to their children: That the generation to come might know them, even the children which should be born; who should arise and declare them to their children: That they might set their hope in God, and not forget the works of God, but keep his commandments:[8]

While this passage is only one of many we will enjoy together, it is a spiritual feast for the father whose heart has been turned by God toward his children. Here is a picture of at least four generations of continued godliness in a family. This father, who sees the command of God to teach and train His children, obeys the call. Then, his children rise up and teach the children which should be born. Then, that generation arises and declares the things of God to their children. What a testimony! Just this one verse should give us enough vision and hope to dedicate the rest of our lives to seeing it fulfilled in our homes. But, there remains yet much more to be seen.

As we turn to another Psalm, God paints us another beautiful picture of a godly home. God says:

> Blessed is every one that feareth the LORD; that walketh in his ways. For thou shalt eat the labour of thine hands: happy shalt thou be, and it shall be well with thee. Thy wife shall be as a fruitful vine by the sides of thine house: thy children like olive plants round about thy table. Behold, that thus shall the man be blessed that feareth the LORD. The LORD shall bless thee out of Zion: and thou shalt see the good of Jerusalem all the days of thy life. Yea, thou shalt see thy children's children, and peace upon Israel.[9]

Here again is a glimpse into how God wants us to see our homes. This godly man fears God and walks in His ways. As a result, his wife is a fruitful blessing to his home. His children grow nearby as obvious blessings of God upon His life. God promises him that he will see his grandchildren at peace in Israel. God is spreading a banquet before the hungry heart of the father who accepts the pursuit of godly seed as his holy calling. And yet, we've only just begun.

God continues this thought in another Psalm, where He seamlessly connects godly homes with other spiritual blessings:

> That our sons may be as plants grown up in their youth; that our daughters may be as corner stones, polished after the similitude of a palace: That our garners may be full, affording all manner of store: that our sheep may bring forth thousands and ten thousands in our streets: That our oxen may be strong to labour; that there be no breaking in, nor going out; that there be no complaining in our streets. Happy is that people, that is in such a case: yea, happy is that people, whose God is the LORD.[10]

What a promise, brothers! Dare we fully see this vision with the eyes of our hearts? God says our sons will grow up as plants, and our daughters will be the cornerstones in the foundation of life, home, and church. Moreover, God directly connects that condition to full garners, thriving sheep, strong oxen, and a happy, contended group of Christians. These things automatically go together. We dare not cling to Scriptures that reference the church, while at the same time ignoring the promises to the family. Rather, let us rejoice together in the goodness of a God who promises us such blessings! Yet, even still, the half has not been told.

God did not leave the expression of this vision only to David. The prophet Isaiah, who we quote without reservation concerning the Messiah and the future of the church, also expressed wonderful prophecies for our homes. He writes:

> Yet now hear, O Jacob my servant; and Israel, whom I have chosen: Thus saith the LORD that made thee, and formed thee from the womb, which will help thee; Fear not, O Jacob, my servant; and thou, Jesurun, whom I have chosen. For I will pour water upon him that is thirsty, and floods upon the dry ground: I will pour my spirit upon thy seed, and my blessing upon thine offspring: And they shall spring up as among the grass, as willows by the water courses. One shall say, I am the LORD'S; and another shall call himself by the name of Jacob; and another shall subscribe with

his hand unto the LORD, and surname himself by the name of Israel.[11]

Brothers, let this prophecy become a defining vision of our homes! Here, God has used the prophet Isaiah to deliver a great prophetic promise that extends to us, today. This prophecy is as certain to be fulfilled as any other prophecy that Isaiah ever wrote. Consider the magnitude of what God is saying in this passage. He first comforts us with the fact that it was He who made us and formed us from the womb. That means that God knows every flaw, failure, and inferiority that could prevent us from attaining a godly seed. Yet, God's humbling promise follows; He will help us because He has chosen us to do this work. Moreover, if we become thirsty for His divine help, He promises to pour so much of His spirit upon us that it overflows in a downpour upon our children. As a result, our children will be like trees planted by the river of water that flows from their godly father's spirit-filled life. God promises that the children who grow up in such a condition will stand and identify themselves with God and His people. Brothers, we do well to be overwhelmed by such a God and such a promise. Let all our doubts, fears, and criticisms be laid to rest in the light of such an abundant vision from God.

As if what God had already promised was not enough, Isaiah continues to prophecy the goodness of God upon our children. He states, "And they that shall be of thee shall build the old waste places: thou shalt raise up the foundations of many generations; and thou shalt be called, The repairer of the breach, The restorer of paths to dwell in."[12] Imagine the magnitude of such a verse! God's desire, no rather God's divine, sovereign will, is for our seed to build up the waste places resulting from centuries of religious perversion of the true church. He calls us to raise up a foundation of many generations.

How many generations do we want our foundation to hold? Are we to be content when our house divides and crumbles after one, two, or three generations? No, we have been called to raise a foundation that will hold many generations of godly children. When we build such a foundation, we become the repairers of the breach and the restorers of the paths. By clear implication, the failure of our foundations to hold many generations would continue the breach and destroy the path. Our God has truly given us a high calling as fathers.

Just as God promised earlier that He would pour His spirit on our seed, He also promises that our seed will keep His Word. He says, "As for me, this is my covenant with them, saith the LORD; My spirit that is upon thee, and my words which I have put in thy mouth, shall not depart out of thy mouth, nor out of the mouth of thy seed, nor out of the mouth of thy seed's seed, saith the LORD, from henceforth and for ever."[13] Brothers, we must see with the eyes of our hearts that God has made a holy covenant with us to preserve the Word of God in our children.

If God is truly making such a great covenant with godly fathers, what is the destiny of such blessed children? Isaiah tells us "they shall build the old wastes, they shall raise up the former desolations, and they shall repair the waste cities, the desolations of many generations."[14] These same people "shall be named the Priests of the LORD: men shall call you the Ministers of our God."[15] God says, "I will direct their work in truth, and I will make an everlasting covenant with them. And their seed shall be known among the Gentiles, and their offspring among the people: all that see them shall acknowledge them, that they are the seed which the LORD hath blessed."[16] God encourages his people, "Tell ye your children of it, and let your children tell their children, and their children another generation."[17] In another place, He says, "all thy children shall be taught of the LORD; and great shall be the peace of thy children."[18] Thus, not only does God have an incredibly important work waiting for a godly seed to perform, He leaves out no child or generation. Rather, all our children are to be taught of the Lord. Then, they are to tell their children, and the faith is passed on from generation to generation.

Thus, God has not hidden away the vision of a godly home in one or two Scriptures that must be pressed and twisted to squeeze out a vision based on loose Scriptural interpretation. Indeed, the truth is quite the opposite. God has openly declared a vision for our homes that is so wonderful that all who read it may begin to run after it with all their hearts.

One final Scripture on this point gives us a key to all that has been said before. What is the goal of the father inspired by such a vision? What is the heart's cry of a father whose heart has been turned by God toward his children? Solomon states it well, "My son, give me thine heart, and let thine eyes observe my ways."[19] Once God has turned the heart of the father toward his children, the rest of the battle is a long fight for the heart of the child. The pursuit of a child's heart is a journey, not just a destination. The battle has only begun when you win the heart of a young child. Anyone can win the heart of a two-year-old. God's kingdom is in great need of men who will fight for and win the hearts of their children throughout their young adult years. This goal requires great effort and determination from the father. The goal as a father is not only to help your child through the battle, but to prepare him to join the battle with you.

When it comes to turning your child's heart toward you, and eventually toward God Himself, insignificant battles can end up being very significant defeats. Consider the story of Achan in the book of Joshua.[20] Achan could not see the significance in refusing to bring the spoils of Jericho into his home, despite the clear command from Joshua. The importance of following Joshua's command was lost on Achan, and so he brought a cursed compromise into his home.

Meanwhile, the significance of the battle at Ai was lost on Joshua and the leaders of Israel. Fresh off the victory at Jericho, Joshua and his group of leaders failed to seek fresh direction from God concerning the battle at Ai. The men told Joshua not to make all the people labor in the battle. Confident in their past victory, Joshua and his leaders conspired together to send a significantly reduced force to Ai in order to make sure that no one was overworked.

At Ai, tragedy struck. The men of Israel fled before the people of Ai, and thirty-six Israelite soldiers died in the retreat. The damage done is often lost on the reader. Soldiers often die in battle; that is the nature of war. However, these men died outside of the covering of God because Achan brought sin into the camp. That night, thirty-six mothers mourned their sons. Thirty-six wives wept uncontrollably at the thought of life without their husbands. Dozens of children struggled to make sense of the fact that their fathers were never coming home. All of this occurred because Achan thought compromise was unimportant. In the end, God rebuked Joshua for failing to detect sin in the camp and revealed Achan's sin to the whole congregation of Israel. Achan, his sons, and his daughters were put out of Israel, stoned, and burned, lest Israel ever again think obeying God was insignificant.

The pursuit of a godly seed is an inspiring vision written out in the pages of Scripture, but it requires incredible amounts of spirituality, effort, and dedication. Fathers must pursue the hearts of their children with all the energy, resources, and focus they possess, and they must obtain wisdom that comes only from God. However, even godly fathers often find that their home is the last place they want to exert additional effort or energy.

Men will suffer many things to get a new contract, promotion, or bonus, but they suddenly become sedentary the moment they walk in their own front door. Even a workaholic can be lazy when it comes to fatherhood. The inability of men to build close relationships with their children is part of the desolation of many generations.[21]

Love must be at the heart of every principle at work in our homes. Yet, love takes a lot of work. Developing thriving heart to heart relationships with our children requires work, focus, and time—lots of time. If you do not like the results you are getting at home, ask yourself how your relationship is doing with that child. You may also need to ask the child how she thinks the relationship is doing. While the battle for your child's heart will last for at least two decades, even the earliest interactions between father and child are of lifelong importance. Let your children talk when they are young and you will build a relationship with them that will keep them talking when they are adolescents.[22] Every child has a natural desire to please their parents. If you recognize this and respond to it, you will reap a blessing of much more obedience later in life. Do not become a "not now" father while your children are young, or you will risk losing their hearts when they are teens.

In all that we do as Christian fathers, we are called to imitate Christ. Because Jesus obviously did not have natural children, our guidance in doing as Christ would do must flow from the spiritual family relationship. In all that we do as fathers, we must consider how the heavenly Father has loved and trained us. This will provide untold insights into our responsibilities as godly fathers. Men, some of the things we have covered in this vision may seem foreign to us. The modern church suffers from at least two generations of absentee fathers and one generation of absentee mothers. Will we stop this plague?

What to Do When the Vision Looks Lost

Perhaps the greatest impediment that prevents us from fully embracing the vision of a godly home as a lifelong pursuit of the heart is the undeniable fact that many children living in Christian homes abandon the faith. Surrounded by the failure to produce a godly seed in many Christian homes, we stagger at the thought that God may have promised us the things quoted previously. The problem, however, cannot be with God. He did not abandon us, and He cannot lie. The great problem in the church is that the fathers have failed to win the hearts of their children. In one of the great tragedies in God's pursuit of a godly seed, King David, who authored much of the vision, later failed God and experienced great hardship in his own home.[23] Let us look in detail at David's darkest hour as a father, so that we might discover how to recover the vision when all seems lost.

The story of Absalom and David is the tragic story of a father who lost his son's heart and paid the ultimate price.[24] Absalom's full sister, Tamar, was abused by their half-brother, Amnon. Realing from the painful results of his own adultery, David was immobilized and unable to render moral judgment on Amnon. Absalom waited two years to see whether David would judge Amnon for his treachery. Both David and Absalom were righteously angry at Amnon, but for two years David did nothing. Finally, Absalom executed judgment on Amnon and took his life.

Fearing his father, Absalom fled, and David mourned daily for his missing son. David longed to go to Absalom and reconcile, but he strangely refused to do so. Joab finally persuaded David to allow Absalom to return to Israel, but David refused to talk to Absalom. Another two years passed. By the time David finally allowed Absalom to speak, the damage was done. Absalom, repeatedly grieved by his father's failure, had turned his heart to other things. Rebellion followed, and civil war soon resulted. When Absalom died in the battle, David mourned uncontrollably and wished that he had died in his stead.

Neither one needed to die if David would have humbled himself and reconciled with his son. The story brings to mind an English proverb, adapted to this purpose. For want of a word a heart was lost; for want of a heart a son was lost; for want of a son a battle was lost; for want of a battle a kingdom was lost, all for the want of a word.

The tragic story of David and Absalom is one of the clearest Biblical examples of what can happen if a father loses the heart of his child. Dr. S.M. Davis explains that the key ingredient in raising godly children is to get their hearts early, keep their hearts, and be extremely vigilant not to lose their hearts, but if you do lose a child's heart, then quickly find out where and when you lost it and execute a plan to get that child's heart back no matter what.[25] The importance of this point cannot be overemphasized. Dear fathers, if you lose your child's heart, you must pay any price short of denying your Lord and your convictions to get it back. Far too many children have been lost because fathers saw rebellion surfacing and concluded that the child was just going through a "testing time." Others concluded that a little rebellion is normal for a toddler or a teenager. Some decided that the standards were just too high. Brothers, rebellion is a heart issue, not a standards issue.

Dr. Davis reminds us that "the heart of every problem is a problem in the heart."[26] The problem that we face in raising children is largely the problem of keeping the hearts of our children while living in a world that is pointing their hearts toward anything and everything other than their parents. We must recognize that "whoever has the heart will eventually have the child."[27] The hearts of our children can be lost, hardened, and stolen, and we have seen all three of these happen in our churches.[28] Many fathers use anger as a tool in child training thinking they will break the will of the child. Anger does not break a will; it breaks a heart.

The key to winning the heart early is listening. If it is important to your child, it is important, period. Dr. Davis explains that kissing your daughter's dolly when she is two is more important to your life twenty years from now than a $20,000 raise. Likewise, listening to your son tell you how his toy truck got stuck in the mud is more important than anything your boss has ever said.[29] What matters to your child must matter to you, or what matters to you will not long matter to your child. Remember, brothers, if God has blessed us with a child, we are fathers first before anything else. No profession, position, or ministry trumps the high calling of God that He automatically gave you when he blessed you with a child.

Only the heart of the father can keep the heart of the child. We cannot expect to keep the hearts of our children unless we give them our own hearts. The heart of a child is just as powerful as the heart of a father. Brethren, we get to play an awesome part in determining where our children set their hearts. Let us not take this responsibility lightly. The hearts of so many children are set upon anything but their father and his God. This is a plague, and, as with David, the responsibility for this plague lies with the fathers.

What plan do we execute if we temporarily lose our child's heart? Dr. Davis presents a roadmap we should consider carefully.[30] First, we must turn our hearts toward our struggling child in confession and repentance. Set the example of reconciliation, just as our heavenly Father set the example in sending Jesus. Second, you must deal with sin in your own life. David's first problem was that he lost moral authority due to his sin with Bathsheba. If you need to confront sin in your child, start with yourself.

Third, separate the child from all negative personal influences. Wrong friends or improper romantic interests often bring spiritual struggles to a young person. Bad company corrupts good manners.

Fourth, separate the child from all negative impersonal influences. Clean your home of wrong music, inappropriate entertainment, and unrestricted internet access. Fifth, replace the bad influences with good influences. If we only clean the house, but do not fill it, something worse may soon replace what was removed. Sixth, pray for and with the child. Many of us instinctively pray for our children during a spiritual struggle, even if we do not pray for them any other time. However, if we have lost the heart of our child, we need to pray for them and with them. Include them in the spiritual battle to win back their hearts.

Seventh, do not push away from them. Remember, David pushed Absalom away and lost any chance at reconciliation. Even through your child may have done things that grieve you, spend hours upon hours with the child, at least one hour per day for six weeks. Eighth, praise anything praiseworthy in the child. Look for anything they do that you can encourage. Celebrate the smallest of victories. Ninth, throughout this process, ask forgiveness for anger, criticism, failure, and inconsistency. These are some of the things that cost you your child's heart in the first place, and they are likely to crop up again during this process.

Tenth, help your child deal with bitterness and hidden sin and forgive anything that surfaces. This will require extensive time and intimate communication. Eleventh, prepare yourself to withstand any persecution against you as you win your child's wounded heart. Many will not understand you as you pursue the heart of your struggling child. Twelfth, commit yourself to long-term change and refuse to stop when short-term change happens. Finally, remember that you haven't lost until you give up. Fight a faithful fight for your child and his or her future generations. This process may cost you a great deal, but any price is minimal in comparison to losing your child's heart forever.

A Heart to Heart Connection

We have talked before about the importance of a heart to heart relationship between fathers and children. The prophet Malachi foretold this vital work of God in the final words of the Old Testament. We have been called to win the hearts of our children for God. To prevail against a world full of competing suitors, we fathers must love and pursue our children more than the world does. If you think that such a call is impossible to fulfill with your current schedule, be assured that, if your children are still at home, the life you have today is the life you really want in your heart. If you wanted a truly different life, you would make the changes necessary to change your life.

Our children long to know how much we love them. We are the primary representation of God's love to our children. As they judge us, they will also judge God. In a survey of American youths, children were asked what three questions they would ask their fathers if they were guaranteed a completely honest answer. The top three questions were "Do you love me? Are you glad you had me? And, are you glad you married my mother?"[31] These are fundamental things that our children should never have reason to doubt.

Grace is a huge part of the heart to heart father-child relationship. Our relationships needs to progress during both moments of our failure and moments of their failure. Both will happen. Grace continues the relationship.[32] The deepest relationships are based on forgiveness, not scorekeeping. We must not keep a mental list of our child's failures. Those failures are a necessary part of spiritual, mental, and emotional growth. For many young people, love is a consistent display of interest, commitment, sacrifice, and attention. We are the adults, the first step always belongs to the father no matter what issue has troubled the relationship. We dare not wait on our children to overcome the troubles that divide our hearts. The first step always belongs to the adult.

We are going to spend much of the remainder of this study on practical aids to raising godly children. However, dear brothers, in the midst of all our protection, preparation, and teaching, we must not forget that the foundation of all these other things is to win the hearts of our children. All our teaching, disciplining, and guiding will reach no farther than the connection between our hearts and theirs.

Author Monte Swan notes that the key to winning the hearts of our children is the often overlooked Biblical concept of romance. The challenge is to parent from the inside out, stay focused on the heart, and turn isolated events into romance-building moments that win each child's heart before any enemy wins it first.[33] Romancing their hearts is no mere new set of rules and bullet points. Rather, romancing their hearts is a new way of thinking about parenting.[34] The missing element in so many father-child relationships is not just doing, but being. Fathers, we must enter the contest for each child's heart with all of our hearts.

We must also guard their hearts well. The idea that our children will "turn out ok" or make it through a certain "season" produces complacent and casual parenting that too often ends in terrible tragedy.[35] In the midst of everyday distractions, family outings, and the quickly passing years, we must keep the focus on our relationships with our children, not the temporary things that draw us together or pull us apart. Winning a child's heart is far greater than any natural accomplishment we will ever achieve. We must learn to major on the majors.

Swan writes that the "heartset" of a child will determine how they handle everything else.[36] Win that battle, and we win everything. Our task as parents is to incarnate the character of God and the fruits of the Spirit before our children in such a way that it compels our children to want to follow us in the Christian life. The pursuit of godly seed begins with the pursuit of a child's heart. It may take spending a whole day with them to get a few minutes of heart-connected conversation. Those moments are worth any price. If our children are complaining about boredom while they are with us, we need to consider whether some competitor has already won their hearts.

Identity flows more permanently from relationship than rules. Discipline will eventually be defeated by desire if desire is relentlessly unchanged.[37] Therefore, it is imperative that we win their hearts. Our children can read our hearts long before they can read words. Our parental power has a less permanent effect than parental love. We must love our way to our children's hearts. If we power our way to obedience without loving our way into heart to heart relationships, heartless compliance to the letter of the law will be deadly to the development of authentic faith. Dear fathers, all the training in the world is only temporary if we do not romance the hearts of our children. At the same time, however, winning the heart is much less powerful if the will has been left unrestrained. Both are imperative to raising godly seed.

On a practical note, most of our "interruptions" are really heart-changing opportunities in disguise. Brothers, does it matter if our errands take three times longer if we win the hearts of our children while we do them? Those heart-connecting moments have far more importance than any errand ever will.

The Scriptures have openly declared the challenging and life-changing truth about the calling of a Christian father. God's heart is fully engaged in the pursuit of a godly seed. His greatest method for achieving that vision is really not a method at all. Instead, God is performing a miraculous turning of the heart of the Christian father toward his children. Then, when the heart of God and the heart of the father are unified in purpose and vision, God turns the hearts of the children toward the father. The calling of the Christian father is to get the heart of his child, keep it from all competitors, vigilantly prevent losing it, and spare no cost or effort to regain the heart in those moments of failure and loss. It is to this great call that God invites us to come.

---

1. Ezra 8:21
2. Denny Kenaston The Pursuit of Godly Seed (2003) p. 39.
3. *Id.*
4. *Id.* p. 43.
5. Proverbs 29:18
6. James Strong, The New Strong's Expanded Exhaustive Concordance of the Bible (2001) Strong's Hebrew #6544
7. Habakkuk 2:2-3
8. Psalm 78:1-7
9. Psalm 128:1-6
10. Psalm 144:12-15
11. Isaiah 44:1-5
12. Isaiah 58:12
13. Isaiah 59: 21
14. Isaiah 61:4-9
15. *Id.*
16. *Id.*
17. Joel 1:3
18. Isaiah 54:13
19. Proverbs 23:26
20. Joshua 7:1-26
21. Denny Kenaston The Pursuit of Godly Seed (2003) p. 126.
22. *Id.* p. 128.

23. It should be noted here that God is not opposed to inspiring an author to write something that he has no experience or qualification to write. Consider Solomon writing the Song of Solomon when he had barely lived a monogamous day in his life.
24. 2 Samuel 13:1-19:10
25. Dr. S.M. Davis "Changing the Heart of a Rebel" available at www.charitychristianfellowship.org/sermons/listing.
26. *Id.*
27. *Id.*
28. *Id.*
29. *Id.*
30. *Id.*
31. Rick Leibee "Leader and His Youth" available at www.charitychristianfellowship.org/sermons/listing.
32. *Id.*
33. Monte Swan Romancing Your Child's Heart (2002) p. 14.
34. *Id.* p. 37.
35. *Id.* p. 70.
36. *Id.* p. 88.
37. *Id.* p. 93.

CHAPTER 3

THE FATHER'S SALVATION: "CONSIDERING THYSELF"

Until now, our study has assumed the existence of a new heart in the father. The time has come for that assumption to end. Dear brothers, as we search for God's heart toward our homes and we ask Him to turn our hearts toward our children, we dare not assume our own conversion no matter what upbringing we may have had. We must examine ourselves whether or not we are actually in the faith.

Maybe you grew up in an ungodly home and you came to the church seeking a change for your family, but you have never actually surrendered your heart to Christ. Or, perhaps, you were raised in a Christian home, grew up in the church, and learned how to play the part without ever experiencing true conversion. Alternatively, you may have wandered as a prodigal son and returned to pursue the blessings of God without ever humbling yourself and repenting before God. Whatever situation you are in, ask God to reveal to you the true condition of your heart.

To seek a godly seed without first obtaining a new heart and a full conversion experience with God is to guarantee a life of misery, anxiety, and failure as you pursue God's vision without God's power and help. But this condition need not exist. God's pursuit of a godly seed begins with His unceasing pursuit of your own heart. If you are not fully persuaded of your own relationship with God, you can be sure that Jesus is pursuing you with a vision and dedication unmatched in heaven or earth.

Real Conversion

The great need for the father's salvation begins with the necessity of real conversion. While men search to and fro for better parenting methods, the eyes of the Lord search to and fro for better men, those whose hearts are perfect toward Him. Any attempt to raise godly children will fail if the parents have not experienced a clear conversion with fruit of that conversion in their lives. The saturation of religious thought, teaching, and experience all around us has cheated many men out of a true conversion. Examining our hearts on this point is vital because many of the New Testament Scriptures listed earlier reveal that conversion in the heart of the father supernaturally leads to conversion in the household. Where do we stand in our relationship with God?

The foundation of the next generation is not what we believe or where we go to church. Virtually every creed and church has suffered from the plague of losing the next generation. No doctrinal statement or dynamic youth program has been discovered that produces the harvest of godly seed. Brothers, the real foundation of the faith of the next generation is not our doctrine, our church services, or our youth programs. The foundation of the next generation is you, as a father, and where you are with God.

How many generations will your foundation hold? Does God dwell personally in your home because He considers you His friend? The almighty God of heaven and earth—He who inhabits eternity and alone possesses immortality—has promised to dwell with the broken hearted and humble father. Let us, therefore, humble ourselves before Him, break our hearts, and pour out unto Him our desperate need for real salvation.

The conversion necessary in the heart of the father is not merely a one time experience of walking down an aisle and repeating a prayer. A godly home will take much more than that. We are talking about a heart, mind, and soul fully surrendered to do the will of God. God is looking for fathers who will give Him their every thought, dream, hurt, goal, and desire in exchange for the promise that God will literally come and dwell with us and in us through the Holy Spirit. Have we yet responded to God in such a way? Until we respond to God's cries and God responds to our cries, we have not experienced real Christianity. This heart to heart relationship must exist between us and God before it will ever exist between us and our children.

Consider Jacob, likely one of the most famous fathers in the Bible. Jacob grew up in a good home. Only two generations from Abraham, Jacob inherited both the blessings that came from his grandfather and the curses of deceit and favoritism that neither Abraham nor Isaac had been able to overcome. Jacob's sin against Esau and Isaac split the family as he fled from his brother's wrath. Through a vision in the wilderness, Jacob returned to a general faith in God. However, despite the apparent blessings of God on his life, Jacob had failed to have the type of experience with God that would forever change his life. Then, through a forced reconciliation with Esau, God prepared Jacob for real conversion.

As Jacob wandered alone, distressed and fearful about his future and the future of his family, God stooped down into Jacob's life.[1] While Jacob searched for answers in the middle of the night, a man appeared from nowhere and attacked him. Jacob summoned all his physical strength and ability to fight for his own survival. As Jacob and the man wrestled throughout the long night and early morning, Jacob realized he was wrestling with God. In this moment, Jacob determined to hold onto God until his life was finally transformed.

Seeing Jacob's determination, God tested him by forcing Jacob's thigh out of joint as they wrestled. Humbled and weakened, yet fully determined, Jacob challenged God, "I will not let thee go, except thou bless me." God's dramatic reply would be the defining moment in Jacob's life. "Thy name shall be called no more Jacob, but Israel: for as a prince hast thou power with God and with men, and hast prevailed." As the match ended and Jacob limped back towards his family, he spoke a testimony that challenges us still today. "I have seen God face to face, and my life is preserved."

Can we join Jacob in this testimony? We must join him if we intend to build a foundation that will hold the next generation. We must lay hold on the promises and the person of God and refuse to let go until we have been completely changed. In that process, God will humble us and test whether we will give up without the blessing. Hold on to God, dear brothers. To be able to raise godly seed, we must have a new heart. To have a new heart, we must surrender every thought and intention of the old heart to God and receive in humility the gift of God.

Through the eyes of the heart, we must see our God. Have our eyes seen the King? We must be able to say, with Jacob, "I have seen God face to face, and my life is preserved." Our lives must be preserved first before we can ever preserve the lives of our children.

We will not be able to clearly see a vision for our homes if our sight is clouded by a grieved conscience. Our vision of God and His purpose in our homes must begin with a clear conscience and a repentant heart. True repentance is described by Paul in his letter to the Corinthians:

> "Now I rejoice, not that ye were made sorry, but that ye sorrowed to repentance: for ye were made sorry after a godly manner, that ye

might receive damage by us in nothing. For godly sorrow worketh repentance to salvation not to be repented of: but the sorrow of the world worketh death. For behold this selfsame thing, that ye sorrowed after a godly sort, what carefulness it wrought in you, yea, what clearing of yourselves, yea, what indignation, yea, what fear, yea, what vehement desire, yea, what zeal, yea, what revenge! In all things ye have approved yourselves to be clear in this matter."[2]

Fathers, we are in desperate need of such repentance! What would the homes of the church be like if the fathers would practice this type of repentance on a regular basis? Let us regularly experience true conversion, repentance, and revival in the midst of our children.

Creating heart to heart relationships with our children—with the purpose of pursing godly seed—must be a spiritual operation. We must have the help of the Almighty. A godly home is an entirely spiritual endeavor, and you dare not even pretend to be a godly father if you do not intend to be a spiritual person.

Fathers, we must be sold out for Jesus. We cannot impart what we do not have. If we want real Christianity in our children, we must possess it first. The greatest influence of our Christianity, whether real or fake, is the influence it has on our children. They will know the strength of our faith, and they will reveal it to the world by their response. God stands ready and willing to help us in this effort if we stay humble and broken before Him.

Enthusiastic "Get to" Christianity

When we experience true conversion and receive a new heart, we can show our children that our obedience to God and our sacrifices for Him are a joy and a privilege. Our children hear our actions far more than they hear our teachings. If we live out a Christianity in our homes that is burdensome, bothersome, and boring, we should hardly be surprised when our children run after other things. If we criticize other believers, express doubt and discouragement about God's ways, and fail to apply God's principles in our family relationships, our children will have no interest in a Christianity that apparently fails to produce a life worth living. In contrast, if we become enthusiastic fanatics about our faith who live out a "get to"

Christianity, our children will rejoice to follow in our ways. Only we can choose which type of Christianity they will see in our homes.

Part-time Christianity will not be enough. We will not produce children the way we envision without ongoing revival in the home. In fact, the greatest influence for godliness in a child's life is a holy revival fire burning in the hearts of the parents. Our call as Christian fathers must be as passionate and compelling as Jeremiah's was when he said, "Then I said, I will not make mention of him, nor speak any more in his name. But his word was in mine heart as a burning fire shut up in my bones, and I was weary with forbearing, and I could not stay."[3] Our call—indeed, our salvation—must be a burning fire shut up in our bones than cannot be extinguished. Ask God to light you on fire with a holy anointing from heaven, and your children will draw nearer to God just to watch you burn.

Children are drawn to passionate beliefs and fulfilled lives. There is no more passionate belief than a real belief in the God of the Bible. There is no more fulfilling life than the one that denies all else to follow Jesus. Yet, many times as fathers, we somehow turn this great life into such a boring, burdensome struggle for meaning that the children run in the opposite direction. What a sin to persuade our children by our actions that Christianity is not a life worth living! It is, instead, the greatest life of all. Let us show that eternal truth to our children through our daily words and action in our homes.

Dear brothers, we must humble ourselves and get hungry and thirsty for God. God's blessing cannot fully reach the children without a father who becomes thirsty for God and receives such a downpour from God that it overflows on the entire home. Your connection to God is the river of water for your young child's tree. How much of God do you want to flow to your children? You are the primary conduit between God and your home. Let our conversion be complete and our Christianity be enthusiastic and victorious. Anything less will serve only to inoculate our children from real faith. Revive us, Lord, for the sake of our homes.

---

[1] Genesis 32:24-30

[2] 2 Corinthians 7:9-11

[3] Jeremiah 20:9

Examining the Devastation

"And it shall be, if thou do at all forget the LORD thy God, and walk after other gods, and serve them, and worship them, I testify against you this day that ye shall surely perish." (Deuteronomy 8:19)

Seeing the great vision that God has imparted for our children, let us now turn our attention to the devastation that exists in the homes of our current age. We are surrounded by a world that is reeling from the results of fathers who abandoned the holy calling of fatherhood for "more important" things. A brief survey of the world around us reveals the dreadful results of multiple generations of fatherless homes. Even most homes that technically have a father present still lack a father who answers the holy call of fatherhood.

After examining the cultural disaster, we will turn our attention to the plague of generational desertion in the church. The Bible has long forewarned that if the people of God forget Him, they will soon perish. The primary way that a group of people perish from the earth is when the current generation is either cut off or consumed by another group. The church is rapidly approaching such a condition.

After examining the church's failure from that panoramic viewpoint, we will commence a more detailed study into the methods and consequences of paternal neglect in the home. As a result, the next three chapters may not be pleasant reading. Yet, they are necessary to impart to us the urgency of our calling as fathers.

CHAPTER 4

THE CULTURAL DISASTER: "A STATE OF EMERGENCY"

It was the proverbial perfect storm. On August 29, 2005, Hurricane Katrina slammed into the Gulf Coast as one of the costliest storms in the history of the United States. In its path lay New Orleans, a city sitting below sea level. As the menacing storm drew closer, the city ordered a mandatory evacuation, but many ignored the warning.

With ferocious winds and massive storm surges, Katrina descended on New Orleans. In the storms wake, the remaining citizens emerged to find a battered, partially flooded city. A new wave of fear swept over the city as looters took to the flooded streets to take advantage of the situation. Then, the levees failed. A series of breaches around the city let in the water that had been held back for so long. With floodwaters reaching twenty feet high in some places, much of New Orleans lay under water.[1] The perfect storm had come, and no one was ready for it.

The tragedy that occurred in New Orleans in 2005 is analogous to the situation faced by the culture around us. In homes, towns, cities, and even the nation, people are building on a foundation that cannot stand the test of time. With some sense of the precarious position in which they build, the secular culture uses the remnants of religion and morality as levees to restrain the inevitable destruction that awaits those who refuse to follow God's ways. However, the levees made from the remnants of Judeo-Christian morality are quickly failing. Barring a miraculous revival, destruction is only a matter of time. Like New Orleans, the culture awaits another perfect storm.

Absentee Fathers

As we focus briefly on the deterioration of the family unit in our culture, some Christian fathers may wonder what relevance the condition of the ungodly has to us. Solomon tells us, "When the scorner is punished, the simple is made wise: and when the wise is instructed, he receiveth knowledge. The righteous man wisely considereth the house of the wicked: but God overthroweth the wicked for their wickedness."[2] Thus, we would be wise to know the calamity besetting the homes that surround us.

An alarming number of fathers are now completely absent from the home. According to the U.S Census Bureau, 21.8 million children live with a custodial parent while the other parent lives somewhere else.[3] This means that more than one in every four children living in the United States lives without one of their parents.[4] Of the children who live with only one parent, 82.6 percent live with their mother.[5] This equates to over 18 million children in this country living without their fathers.

Moreover, many of these absent fathers fail to assist in providing for the basic needs of their children. Less than half of custodial parents receive the full amount of child support that is due.[6] In 2007, almost one in four custodial parents received none of the due child support.[7] In aggregate, 34.1 billion dollars of child support was due in the United States.[8] At least 13 billion dollars was not paid.[9] The total amount of unpaid child support in arrears in the United States is estimated to be over 110 billion dollars.[10] In attempting to collect unpaid child support, our government spends over 5.5 billion dollars of taxpayer money every year.[11]

Father absence has an incredible toll on the children. Since the 1990's, the U.S. Department of Health and Human Services has reported that fatherless children are at a dramatically greater risk of drug and alcohol abuse, mental illness, suicide, poor educational performance, teen pregnancy, and criminality.[12] A full survey of each of these problems is beyond our scope, but substantial literature on each point is available elsewhere.

Absentminded Fathers

While a majority of American children still live in a two-parent home, many of these fathers barely connect with their children. Estimates of how much time fathers actually spend with their children vary depending on the source, but each estimate gives cause for alarm. One source concludes that the American father averages less than ten minutes of time per day with his children.[13] A stunning report from the United Kingdom states that a typical working parent spends only nineteen minutes a day with their children, despite finding time to spend 2.8 hours each day watching television.[14]

The Southern Baptist Convention's research reveals that the majority of children in America spend less than ten minutes of significant and meaningful conversation with their parents each week.[15] Yet, that number included both parents. When they only counted the father, the statistic was measured in mere seconds.[16] Two-thirds of American homes no longer share a meal together during the day.[17] Another source reports that the average father spends a total of eight minutes per day with his children—including meals and watching television.[18]

Where are the men? Where are the fathers? God warned long ago of the symptoms that occur when a people forget God:

> "For, behold, the Lord, the LORD of hosts, doth take away from Jerusalem and from Judah [. . .] The mighty man, and the man of war, the judge, and the prophet, and the prudent, and the ancient, The captain of fifty, and the honourable man, and the counsellor, and the cunning artificer, and the eloquent orator. And I will give children to be their princes, and babes shall rule over them. And the people shall be oppressed, every one by another, and every one by his neighbour: the child shall behave himself proudly against the ancient, and the base against the honourable. When a man shall take hold of his brother of the house of his father, saying, Thou hast clothing, be thou our ruler, and let this ruin be under thy hand: In that day shall he swear, saying, I will not be an healer; for in my house is neither bread nor clothing: make me not a ruler of the people."

The men of our generation are missing. After multiple generations of divorce and conception outside of wedlock, this nation has reaped a harvest of fathers that refuse to be fathers. Many of them no longer even know how. They have rarely if ever seen real fatherhood in action.

As the cycle repeats itself generation after generation, the culture continues its downward spiral. While we can observe this pattern from a distance, its impact is all around us. Moreover, the next chapter reveals that the problems in the culture have crept into the church, bringing the issue of absentee fathers closer to home.

1. "Surge, breach and a 26-foot-deep gouge" Published: Thursday, September 01, 2005, 8:32 PM By Mark Schleifstein, The Times-Picayune available at http://www.nola.com/katrina/index.ssf/2005/09/surge_breach_and_a_26-foot-deep_gouge.html
2. Proverbs 21:11-12
3. Custodial Mothers and Fathers and Their Child Support: 2007 Issued November 2009 by Timothy S. Grall U.S. CENSUS BUREAU
4. *Id.*
5. *Id.*
6. *Id.*
7. *Id.*
8. *Id.*
9. *Id.*
10. Financial Overview for Five Consecutive Fiscal Years, available at http://www.acf.hhs.gov/programs/cse/pubs/2011/reports/preliminary_report_fy2010/table_1.html
11. NATIONWIDE, REGIONAL, AND STATE BOX SCORES FY 2010, available at http://www.acf.hhs.gov/programs/cse/pubs/2011/reports/preliminary_report_fy2010/
12. U.S. Department of Health and Human Services, National Center for Health Statistics, Survey on Child Health, Washington, DC, 1993.
13. J. P. Robinson, et al., "The Rhythm of Everyday Life." Westview Press. 1988
14. "19 minutes - how long working parents give their children" By BECKY BARROW, Daily Mail, 19 July 2006, available at http://www.dailymail.co.uk/news/article-396609/19-minutes--long-working-parents-children.html#ixzz1UkH5JiYx
15. "Family Life Council says it's time to bring family back to life" Wednesday, Jun 12, 2002 By Jon Walker, available at http://www.sbcannualmeeting.net/sbc02/newsroom/newspage.asp?ID=261
16. *Id.*
17. "Why are kids leaving the church? The answer lies in parents" DUDLEY CHANCEY | for The Christian Chronicle, available at http://www.christianchronicle.org/article2158796-Why_are_kids_leaving_the_church%3F_The_answer_lies_in_parents
18. *Id.*

CHAPTER 5

THE CHURCH'S FAILURE: "IF YOUR EYE BE DARK"

While the situation surrounding us in this secular culture is predictably terrible, the prophets have long warned the church not to be at ease concerning our own situation.[1] Never before in history has the Gospel of Jesus Christ touched so many people while at the same time making so little difference on how people live. Churches are filled with people who are professing Christianity without possessing anything remotely similar to the Christian life and home described in Scripture. For centuries, the prophets have warned the people of God that if one generation fails to seek and serve God with all their hearts, the next generation will suffer the consequences of parental idolatries.

Moses warned, "Thy sons and thy daughters shall be given unto another people, and thine eyes shall look, and fail with longing for them all the day long: and there shall be no might in thine hand."[2] King David cried out, "Help, LORD; for the godly man ceaseth; for the faithful fail from among the children of men."[3] Jeremiah reported, "Seest thou not what they do in the cities of Judah and in the streets of Jerusalem? The children gather wood, and the fathers kindle the fire, and the women knead their dough, to make cakes to the queen of heaven, and to pour out drink offerings unto other gods, that they may provoke me to anger."[4] The prophet Micah mourned, "[F]rom their children have ye taken away my glory for ever."[5] The prophet Ezekiel warned Jerusalem that when God sent judgment on a nation, He would order the judgment to "begin at my sanctuary."[6] These warnings compel a much-needed sobriety in the church as we consider our great need to build godly homes.

As we turn our attention to the painfully desperate situation that the church confronts within itself in this day of compromise, we hesitate to highlight the plague of desertion that fills the ranks of the Christian church. Were it not already common knowledge, we would shy away from this painful discussion. A brief survey of statistics will reveal the sad state of American Christianity.

Any survey of church statistics presents complications. It is impossible to present statistics that apply to every reader. If we have difficulty applying these facts to our own experience with God, let us consider how the prophets dealt with that difficulty in the Scriptures. Jeremiah wrote:

> "And I said after [Israel] had done all these things, Turn thou unto me. But she returned not. And her treacherous sister Judah saw it. And I saw, when for all the causes whereby backsliding Israel committed adultery I had put her away, and given her a bill of divorce; yet her treacherous sister Judah feared not, but went and played the harlot also."[7]

Judah ignored all the warnings and judgments that God gave Israel because they thought the same condition could never happen to them. As a result, Judah repeated the same errors and suffered God's judgment. Let us not be guilty of the same mistake.

Some statistics based on Christian men reveal the source of many of the problems in the next generation:

- It is recognized among Protestant leaders that only one in ten men who enters the ministry will finish faithfully and honorably.[8]
- In one study done over a two year period, researchers discovered that on average ten pastors a month committed immorality.[9]
- Surveys reveal that 50% of evangelical Christian men believe that intimacy is not restricted to their wife.[10]
- 41% of men openly admit to using pornography.[11]
- In another survey, conservative Protestants were the worst religious group for fidelity in marriage. Only the completely ungodly ranked worse, and the Protestants barely beat them.[12]
- The divorce ratio among members of evangelical churches is virtually the same as among non-church members.[13]

The statistics on Christian parenting are equally startling.

- A national survey of 1,200 parents with children under 18 at home was conducted by LifeWay Research, the research arm of LifeWay Christian Resources of the Southern Baptist Convention. While 45% of parents indicate they watch television together each day, only 53% report they pray together at least monthly and just 31% report having religious devotionals or studies together at least monthly.[14]
- Forty-three percent of Protestant parents and 85% of Catholic parents do not receive encouragement from the Bible. As for their church, 39% of Protestant parents and 71% of Catholic parents say it is not a source of encouragement as a parent.[15]
- One study found the most common definitions of successful parenting include children having good values (25%), being happy adults (25%), finding success in life (22%), being a good person (19%), graduating from college (17%), and living independently (15%). Being godly or having faith in God was mentioned by only 9% of respondents.[16]
- Even among parents who attend religious services weekly, only 24% of them identify faith in God as a mark of parenting success.[17]
- Among born-again Christians, 29% say faith is not among the most important influences on their parenting.[18]
- Only 14% of parents say they feel they are very familiar with what the Bible has to say about parenting, even though 77% identify themselves as Christians.[19]
- Among those who attend religious services weekly, that number rises to only 36%.[20]

These statistics, among many others that we do not have time to discuss, foretell the tragic results that are occurring in the next generation.

The following statistics reveal the ultimate plague of desertion that has infected the church. Even the New York Times has reported on the "epidemic of young people leaving the church."[21] While the statistics certainly vary from one report to another, none of them report good news for the church.

- The Family Life Council reports that 88% of the children raised in evangelical homes leave church at the age of 18, never to return.[22]

- Another report states that somewhere between 70% and 88% of Christian teenagers are leaving the church by their second year in college.[23]
- Research by Ken Ham revealed that children who faithfully attend Sunday School classes in their church over the years actually are more likely to question the authority of Scripture, leave the church, believe that the Bible is less true, defend the legality of abortion and same-sex marriage, and defend premarital relationships.[24]
- Focus on the Family reports that between 64% and 94% of Christian teens leave the Church within a few years of graduating high school.[25]
- Other research shows that 64% of young people who leave church never regularly attend church again.[26]
- Over 80% of teens who do claim to be "born-again" do not believe in the existence of absolute truth.[27]
- Similar statistics caused author Josh McDowell to conclude, "I sincerely believe unless something is done now to change the spiritual state of our young people—you will become the last Christian generation."[28]

Thus, at best, the church in America is losing a majority of their children to the world. At worst, the church is quickly losing a struggle to keep even 10% of their children. This cold reality stands in clear opposition to all the promises that God made to His people concerning their children. Worse, most Christians have apparently accepted this dark reality and have fearfully concluded that the promises of God are either unattainable or not applicable to a modern culture. Fathers, we must not accept defeat in this area. We must, rather, look deeper into the heart of the problem to discover why the church is losing children at this alarming rate and why most efforts to this point have been unhelpful.

The default conclusion that these children "just didn't have a revelation" is essentially blaming God for the situation. The theory that children leave because they lack a spiritual revelation of God and His will for their lives presupposes that only God can give a revelation. Assuming that is true, such a theory pushes the blame for the mass exodus of children out of the church onto the One who sacrificed everything to save them. We will dissect this theory more later, but for now it suffices to say that the judgment of God on Israel, whether from Assyria, Babylon, or Rome, was never evidence that God refused to save the people of Israel. Rather, the destroyed condition of Jerusalem was a testimony to the people of Israel of their sin and the sin of their predecessors. The deteriorating condition of the church and the home should be the same to us.

One of the first reasons for the destruction and desertion we see in the church is that modern Christianity has abandoned the basic principles of the faith held by the Early Church and replaced them with secular entertainment, modern convenience, and so-called enlightened philosophies. As was true for Israel of old, there is a generation "which knew not the LORD, nor yet the works which he had done for Israel."[29] When children forget the mighty works of God and see their parents pursue secular goals and hobbies, they quickly grow bored with fundamental practices of the Christian faith. Indeed, many parents and church leaders are so caught up in worldly pleasures that their testimony actually compels young people to conclude that following Jesus must be a dreadfully boring use of life. As Isaiah said, "As for my people, children are their oppressors, and women rule over them. O my people, they which lead thee cause thee to err, and destroy the way of thy paths."[30]

God has a special purpose for our young people. The prophet Amos decried a similar situation in Israel when he wrote as follows:

> And I raised up of your sons for prophets, and of your young men for Nazarites. Is it not even thus, O ye children of Israel? saith the LORD. But ye gave the Nazarites wine to drink; and commanded the prophets, saying, Prophesy not. Behold, I am pressed under you, as a cart is pressed that is full of sheaves."[31]

God did not abandon our children to the world and appoint them to desert the faith. No, He formed them in the womb, designed them with a purpose, and called them to a holy calling. Yet, many times the church has silenced their gifts, compromised their holiness unto God, and pursued "more important" things. God says that such a condition is a great burden to Him. When God sees the young people that He called from the womb bored with Christianity and running to the world, it burdens and grieves Him to such a degree that He compares it to being like an overloaded cart struggling to bear the load. How God longs for a godly seed! Let us again dedicate ourselves to making that load lighter and joining with God in seeking a godly seed.

As some of the statistics cited above indicate, the modern church has produced a generation of parents that know little to nothing of the Biblical principles that are the foundation of Christian parenting. Parents have turned to virtually every other source outside of the Bible for instruction in parenting. Yet, few actually know what the Bible has to say on this all-important subject. A similar situation in early American history caused revivalist George Whitefield to conclude that the majority of Christian families avoided the reading of Scripture as if they were at risk of burning for heresy if they read it.[32] Whitefield concluded, "Brethren, this thing ought not so to be."[33]

Why do Christian parents avoid the Bible when they will turn to so many other sources for parenting advice? We avoid the Bible because it produces a crisis of decision. It demands a response. It highlights our failures and indicts us in front of our children. It forewarns us of the danger of preserving the status quo and pursuing an easy Christian life. All these things have caused the Church to turn from the Bible and instead seek parenting advice from popular culture, psychology, sociology, and even secular entertainment. The families in the Christian church must repent of this error, turn from all these idols, and return to the foundation of the Word of God.

Another major problem in the Church is the infiltration of the spirit of abortion that has permeated the Church from the society around us. The Christian church is full of the spirit of abortion, both natural and spiritual. The spirit of abortion includes the ideas that children are a bother, a hindrance, an accident, something to be prevented if at all possible, or a necessary evil naturally resulting from marriage. This idea is completely opposite of the Bible's description of childbearing, and no concept could be farther from the heart of God. Why would a Christian married couple think the same thoughts about children that ungodly fornicators think about children? Yet, our churches are full of young couples who can hardly imagine anything worse than conceiving another child. As a result, these potential parents will jump through every conceivable hoop to avoid, prevent, control, or even discontinue a pregnancy.

Brothers, this is the direct opposite of God's will and His promises. God is seeking a godly seed, and His people are running from it while using every chemical, pill, process, and procedure imaginable. God promised that our children would be blessing to us, Him, and others. If our children are not a blessing and we cannot imagine handling another one, we probably are not following God's instruction on how to give and receive a blessing in our children. We must plead with God to turn our hearts on this vital issue.

Another key problem in the Church is that our methods often unintentionally but systematically damage the family relationships that are at the heart of passing the faith from generation to generation. Studies have shown that a lack of deep relationships is a primary cause of losing young people.[34] Too often, in our churches, there has been an unhealthy, and perhaps unknowing, collusion between parents and church leaders, with parents believing "Isn't that why we have ministers?" and ministers believing "I can do a better job of this than most parents."[35]

One of the worst methods that are undermining deep relationships in the church is the modern youth group. The peer-dominated youth activities that have flooded the church have become little more than "holding tanks with pizza" that expose young people to "a superficial form of Christianity that effectively inoculates them against authentic faith."[36] More and more, youth activities containing little real spiritual basis pull young people away from the family rather than equipping and encouraging families to raise up their children in the nurture and admonition of the Lord. Many churches need to transform their methods from those that divide and separate their families to those that develop and celebrate them.

In light of these problems, and many more, our churches are in desperate need of a real revival in the area of building godly homes. The stakes could not be higher. If we continue losing our young people at the current rates, no amount of evangelism or outreach will make up for the fact that the next generation is deserting the faith. If we truly want our Lord to find faith on the earth when He returns, we must radically change our way of pursuing godliness in the next generation.

Our situation bears a strong similarity to the situation that Ezra and Nehemiah faced during the rebuilding of Jerusalem.[37] As these two men labored to lead the people in rebuilding the kingdom of Judah, they repeatedly discovered people and places of compromise among them. Nehemiah had to cleanse the temple because the priest had let the enemy reside there. Nehemiah was grieved, and he threw the enemy and all of his possession out of the house of God. When Nehemiah later discovered that others in Jerusalem had allied with the enemies of God, he boldly contended with them, rebuked them, and even chased some of them from the city. Nehemiah realized the importance of implementing true repentance. A generation was arising in Jerusalem that spoke part Ashdod and part Hebrew. It was only a matter of time until they forgot God. We must rise up in the zeal and passion of Nehemiah and cleanse the Church of compromise. If we refuse, our children will grow up speaking part Biblical truth and part secular error, and it will be a mere matter of time before they join the multitude of young people deserting the Church.

Highlighting the failure of the people of God is never a popular or pleasant task. But it is a necessary one if we hope to continue the faith for another generation. We join with William Booth, founder of the Salvation Army, in his admonition to another generation of believers:

> The painful facts we have stated cannot be denied, and in noting some of the causes which lead to them both here and hereafter, we only wish to prevent their being charged back upon God, as though the fault lay at His door. It is our privilege to justify the ways of God to men, and in doing so we have no doubt, that though the statement that children trained in the Divine method will maintain a holy walk may painfully reflect upon the action of some parents in the past, yet we shall thereby secure some more wise and holy training in the future, leading to the desired result.[38]

There was once a time when the Church could boldly preach that righteous training would produce a faithful generation. The men of God could declare that Christian churches did not lose children from uncompromised homes. The statement remains true. But compromise is far bigger and easier than we knew. Compromise is more than a standards issue. Compromise is a self-surrender issue. It is a relational issue.

As we again humble ourselves before our Maker and repent of our compromise, let us always keep in mind the challenge our Lord gave to the church whose name became synonymous with compromise.

> And unto the angel of the church of the Laodiceans write; These things saith the Amen, the faithful and true witness, the beginning of the creation of God; I know thy works, that thou art neither cold nor hot: I would thou wert cold or hot. So then because thou art lukewarm, and neither cold nor hot, I will spue thee out of my mouth. Because thou sayest, I am rich, and increased with

goods, and have need of nothing; and knowest not that thou art wretched, and miserable, and poor, and blind, and naked: I counsel thee to buy of me gold tried in the fire, that thou mayest be rich; and white raiment, that thou mayest be clothed, and that the shame of thy nakedness do not appear; and anoint thine eyes with eyesalve, that thou mayest see. As many as I love, I rebuke and chasten: be zealous therefore, and repent."[39]

---

1. See Amos 6:1
2. Deuteronomy 28:32
3. Psalm 12:1
4. Jeremiah 7:17-18
5. Micah 2:9
6. Ezekiel 9:4-6
7. Jeremiah 3:7-8
8. Steve Farrar, Finishing Strong (1995) p. 16.
9. *Id* p. 18.
10. *Id.* p. 71.
11. *Id.* p. 72.
12. *Id.*
13. "Family Life Council says it's time to bring family back to life" Wednesday, Jun 12, 2002 By Jon Walker, available at http://www.sbcannualmeeting.net/sbc02/newsroom/newspage.asp?ID=261
14. "LifeWay Research: Parents Look Inward Not Upward for Guidance" Written by Mark Kelly, available at http://www.lifeway.com/article/168963/
15. *Id.*
16. "LifeWay Research Looks at Role of Faith in Parenting" Written by Mark Kelly, available at http://www.lifeway.com/article/168964/
17. *Id.*
18. *Id.*
19. *Id.*
20. *Id.*
21. "Evangelicals Fear the Loss of Their Teenagers" By Laurie Goodstein, October 6, 2006 available at http://www.nytimes.com/2006/10/06/us/06evangelical.html?_r=1&pagewanted=print

22. "Family Life Council says it's time to bring family back to life" Wednesday, Jun 12, 2002 By Jon Walker, available at http://www.sbcannualmeeting.net/sbc02/newsroom/newspage.asp?ID=261
23. See http://electexiles.wordpress.com/2008/07/11/whats-wrong-with-youth-ministry-some-stats-and-a-proposal/Citing (Voddie Baucham, Family Driven Faith, 10).
24. "Why are young people leaving the church?", available at http://www.wnd.com/?pageId=100324#ixzz1DNyUL1w9
25. "National Apologetics Conference Challenges Youth to Confront Today's Culture" July 30, 2009 http://www.focusonthefamily.com/about_us/news_room/news-releases/20090730-national-apologetics-conference-challenges-youth.aspx
26. "Lost In Transition, a Research Reflection" by Mark Lydecker, available at http://www.edstetzer.com/2007/08/lost_in_transition_mark_lydecker.html
27. See http://electexiles.wordpress.com/2008/07/11/whats-wrong-with-youth-ministry-some-stats-and-a-proposal/Citing (Voddie Baucham, Family Driven Faith, 11)
28. See Introduction to The Last Christian Generation by Josh McDowell
29. Judges 2:10
30. Isaiah 3:12
31. Amos 2:11-13
32. George Whitefield, "The Great Duty of Family Religion" available at http://www.ccel.org/ccel/whitefield/sermons.vi.html
33. *Id.*
34. "Dropout Study Illustrates the Great Opportunity We Have," a Research Reflection by Jim Johnston, available at http://www.edstetzer.com/2007/08/dropout_study_illustrates_the_1.html
35. "Why Young Adults Drop Out of Church and What Can Be Done to Stem the Tide," a Research Reflection from Scott Stevens, available at http://www.edstetzer.com/2007/08/why_young_adults_drop_out_of_c.html
36. "Why Young Adults Are Leaving the Faith An interview with Generation Ex:Christian author Drew Dyck," available at http://www.christianitytoday.com/biblestudies/articles/evangelism/youngadultsleavingfaith.html
37. See Nehemiah 13:4-28
38. William Booth, How to Make the Children into Saints and Soldiers of Jesus Christ, (1888) available at http://www.gospeltruth.net/children/booth_training.htm. (Unfortunately, this version of Booth's treatise on parenting does not have

page numbers. Therefore, citations to Booth throughout this book will not contain page numbers.

39. Revelation 4:14-19

CHAPTER 6

THE FATHER'S NEGLECT: "A GARDEN DESTROYED"

In the midst of the darkest time Judah had ever experienced, a young boy inherits the throne.[1] After decades of national, religious, and familial treachery and failure, the nation was almost entirely ignorant of the ways of God. King Josiah, at age twenty-six, has a heart for God's work, but knows virtually nothing about God's law. As a result of an order to audit the temple, the man of God rediscovers the Word of God. Immediately, Josiah wants to hear what God has to say. Upon hearing of impending judgment on Judah, King Josiah humbles himself, rends his clothes, confesses the sins of his fathers, and inquires of the will of the Lord. Assured that judgment is, in fact, coming, Josiah summons every man in Judah to meet together before the Lord.

Standing alone, Josiah challenges an entire nation to repent with all their hearts and make covenant with a holy God. With the people fully supporting him, Josiah embarks upon a thorough annihilation of every idol, grove, altar, and high place in all of Israel and Judah. He destroys idols that have existed since Solomon reigned over a unified kingdom. Somewhere in the crowd that stands in covenant with their king and their God are the fathers or grandfathers of the princes that history will know as Daniel, Shadrach, Meshach, and Abednego. How God needs such men in our day! Yet, the churches are often full of men and fathers too distracted and demoralized to keep covenant with the God of heaven.

We are suffering from multiple generations of absentee fathers and leaderless homes. The result of the disaster in the culture and the epidemic in the church could not have taken a larger toll on the family. Homes by the millions are either missing a father completely or are occupied by such spineless, faithless excuses for fatherhood that the next generation of young men can barely comprehend what the high calling of fatherhood really means. An unholy combination of secular ambition, cowardice, and apathy works in fathers as a catalyst propelling both the religious and secular cultures around us to a certain impending destruction. And the father's neglect is the child's undoing.

Where are the men who will stand today like the generation that stood in covenant with Josiah? Where are the modern day leaders who will stand like Josiah and Jeremiah to call a generation of fathers away from their idolatries? While the true importance of the father's neglect can feel overwhelming and unfair, we dare not hide from the truth. The stakes are far too high, and the night is already upon us.

We must be prepared to stand completely alone. Charles Finney, the great American revivalist said, "If you would train your children in the way they should go, be invincibly firm in training your own family, let other families do as they may."[2] Andrew Murray, the great devotional writer said, "If our children do not believe, let us look at ourselves for the cause."[3] Finney added, "I have seldom, if ever known a family to turn out badly, in which, when I searched out the matter, I could not trace it directly or indirectly to the manner in which they had brought the children up—to some fundamental defect in family government."[4] Thus, the idea that the father's neglect is the root of the child's faithlessness is no modern conclusion. Rather, the idea that the father is not the one responsible would have been unthinkable to the cloud of witnesses who have preceded us in this race.

Let us always be haunted by the selfish response of the compromised King Hezekiah—"Is it not good if peace and truth be in my days?"[5] It is beyond comprehension that a man faithful enough to obtain extra years from God upon his request could so flippantly dismiss the prophet's prediction that Jerusalem would be ransacked and his own descendents made eunuchs and slaves. Men, we must face the fact that we really are that selfish. That realization should propel us back to the ways of God.

The testimony of Scripture is clear concerning the price of the father's neglect. God says through the weeping Jeremiah, "How shall I pardon thee for this? thy children have forsaken me, and sworn by them that are no gods: when I had fed them to the full, they then committed adultery, and assembled themselves by troops in the harlots' houses."[6] God's question makes no sense unless the fathers were responsible for the fact that their children had forsaken God. Further, Jeremiah says concerning the stumbling blocks, "the fathers and sons together shall fall upon them."[7]

Jeremiah cries out, "Our fathers have sinned, and are not; and we have borne their iniquities."[8] Hosea adds one of the most sobering warnings in the Bible, "My people are destroyed for lack of knowledge: because thou hast rejected knowledge, I will also reject thee, that thou shalt be no priest to me: seeing thou hast forgotten the law of thy God, I will also forget thy children."[9] In a world—and often a church—that is amusing itself to death, let us be sober, brethren. If we forget God's law, He has promised not merely to forget us, but to forget our children. May God have mercy on us all.

The Tale of Two Gardens

Without doubt, the weight of such warnings will cause many to refuse to accept the sound of this trumpet. Before we refuse this warning, let us consider some garden rules of parenting. In the Gospels, Jesus compares the heart conditions people have toward the Gospel to four types of soil: the way side, the rocky soil, the thorny soil, and the good soil. In our technological, industrialized mindset, often decades removed from a real agricultural influence, many rush to such a parable with a warm embrace of the doctrine of predestination. "Soil is what it is. Surely our children just come out of the womb and are destined to be one type of soil." Such a conclusion would be a shock to any farmer prepared to put "sweat equity" into his land. Modern man sees land for its difficulties and concludes that some land is unfit for the harvest. The farmer sees the potential in each type of land, and dedicates himself to a lifetime of careful development of good soil. Yet, beyond the realm of mere cultural comparisons, what say the Scriptures?

First, we need to go all the way back to the beginning responsibility of man. "And the LORD God took the man, and put him into the garden of Eden to dress it and to keep it."[10] Even in the perfect garden of God, man was responsible to dress and keep it in the proper condition. Consider in contrast to this, the garden of the slothful man.

> "I went by the field of the slothful, and by the vineyard of the man void of understanding; And, lo, it was all grown over with thorns, and nettles had covered the face thereof, and the stone wall thereof was broken down. Then I saw, and considered it well: I looked upon it, and received instruction. Yet a little sleep, a little slumber,

a little folding of the hands to sleep: So shall thy poverty come as one that travelleth; and thy want as an armed man."[11]

Are we not surrounded by homes that fit this description? At times, we all have seen the cares of life begin to crop up as the result of our own slothfulness. This man was not predestined to fail; his field was not inherently unable to produce the crop. Rather, it grew into this situation by the express and implied choices made by the father over a long period of time.

A comparison between the Gospel story and the Old Testament use of farming imagery reveals that the soil conditions are the responsibility of the gardener, not permanent situations. The parable states:

> "And when much people were gathered together, and were come to him out of every city, he spake by a parable: A sower went out to sow his seed: and as he sowed, some fell by the way side; and it was trodden down, and the fowls of the air devoured it. And some fell upon a rock; and as soon as it was sprung up, it withered away, because it lacked moisture. And some fell among thorns; and the thorns sprang up with it, and choked it. And other fell on good ground, and sprang up, and bare fruit an hundredfold. And when he had said these things, he cried, He that hath ears to hear, let him hear."[12]

Our children, then, like anyone else, can be one of four types of soil. But is good soil a mere statistical occurrence, or is it the result of something else? Clearly in nature, good soil is the result of careful stewardship. Bad soil can be irrigated, treated, plowed, fertilized, and otherwise transformed into good soil. Likewise, good soil can be wasted, ignored, or otherwise turned into useless soil. As the prophet said, "Give ye ear, and hear my voice; hearken, and hear my speech. Doth the plowman plow all day to sow? Doth he open and break the clods of his ground? [. . .] For his God doth instruct him in discretion, and doth teach him."[13]

Through teaching and discretion from God, a father can break up the hard ground of a child that seems like way side soil. Again, "Sow to yourselves in righteousness, reap in mercy; break up your fallow ground: for it is time to seek the LORD, till he come and rain righteousness upon you."[14] God uses the imagery of hardened ground repeatedly in Scripture, but He also encourages us to break up that ground. Jeremiah wrote, "For thus saith the LORD to the men of Judah and Jerusalem, Break up your fallow ground, and sow not among thorns."[15] Solomon and Isaiah speak of casting away stones, gathering stones, and gathering out the stones from the ground.[16] Proverbs states, "Thorns and snares are in the way of the forward: he that doth keep his soul shall be far from them."[17] Therefore, if we keep the souls of our children, just as Adam was told to keep the garden, thorns will be far from their soil.

Any farmer familiar with working with plants understands these principles. When a garden fails to produce, the gardener must look inward for the source of the problem rather than blaming the plants. As the field of the slothful shows, the best way to let Satan have a garden—or the next generation—is to do nothing.

Moreover, consider the garden again. If we just sow the natural seeds and leave it all to the grace of God, we will be sadly disappointed. The same is true in our homes. God in His grace has given us principles that determine the outcome in our families. The hearts of our children are like gardens. The soil must be prepared to be able to receive the seed. Proper care and attention must be given to continue the growth of that seed. We cannot just leave the responsibility to God. If the rose wilts, do you blame God, the rose, or the gardener?

One of the greatest tragedies in the calling of fatherhood is that most fathers would quickly go to the neighbor with the greenest lawn for lawn care tips, or get advice on car care, hobbies, or athletic development. Yet, few fathers will actually prioritize their children enough to seek out those who have succeeded in raising godly children and find out how they did it. We would sooner find out how to save gas mileage than how to save our relationships. We will readily take advice about how to handle every area of managing a home, except raising our children.

Worse, very few people are willing to actually pay the price for a godly home. We fathers are too busy. How can we be so busy making money, building our retirement, and chasing the American dream that we don't have time to raise a godly seed? "Stop the wheel; I want to get off."[18] Consider again the words of Charles Finney:

> Most fathers seem to be so much engaged in business, politics, or amusements, as to leave very little time for deep consideration in respect to their responsibility and influence with their children.

This is all wrong; for if there be any thing that demands the attention and time of the father, it is those things that concern the well-being of his children. If he neglect his own household, whatever else he does, he virtually "denies the faith, and is worse than an infidel."[19]

To these words of caution, we add those of George Whitefield of the Great Awakening, "For if, as the apostle argues, 'He that does not provide for his own house,' in temporal things, has denied the faith, and is worse than an infidel; to what greater degree of apostasy must he have arrived, who takes no thought to provide for the spiritual welfare of his family!"[20] Said Whitefield, "It is evident, that family prayer is a great and necessary duty; and consequently, those [. . .] that neglect it, are certainly without excuse. And it is much to be feared, if they live without family prayer, they live without God in the world."[21] Whitfield continued to say that any father who objected to family devotions in the home because it took too much time was "of the same hypocritical spirit as the traitor Judas."[22]

Lot, the Neglectful Father

As Jesus trained his followers how to handle the situations they would face, he gave them a one-sentence admonition that turned their attention to a man hundreds of years past. "Remember Lot's wife."[23] Let us heed our Lord's warning and consider, too, the tragic story of Lot. We may find Lot's story a warning to us as we often follow in his ways.

Lot is no ungodly failure of a father; rather, he is a righteous man with a fatal flaw. After years of faithfully supporting his sometimes inconsistent uncle, Abram, Lot is so blessed by God that he concludes it is time to establish his own independence. Upon learning of his nephew's impending departure, Abram offers Lot the opportunity to pick any land in Canaan as his own. Lot chooses the bountiful plain near the Jordan River, no doubt concluding that it would be a fine place to raise his family. At the outset, Lot likely had no intention to live in Sodom. Lot was a very successful travelling herdsman. City life would not even coincide with his way of life. Yet, Lot takes his first fateful step as he "pitched his tent toward Sodom."[24] At this point, Lot cannot imagine the price his decision will cost.

Like so many men and fathers throughout history, Lot's first step toward compromise is not his last. Perhaps thinking that the city would provide better financial opportunities, Lot next appears as one "who dwelt in Sodom."[25] For whatever excuse or reason, Lot leads his family from the tent pitched toward Sodom into the perversion of the city itself. When God's first judgment falls and rival kings attack the city, Lot, his family, and his possessions are captured. When Abraham and his men deliver Lot, he has the opportunity to flee the city and return with Abraham. Again, Lot stays.

Later, when God alerts Abraham of the coming destruction of Sodom and Gomorrah, Abraham pleads for mercy if only ten righteous be found there.[26] With at least four in his own family, Lot needs only six converts to save the entire city from judgment. As the angels of God walk into the city of Sodom, they find Lot sitting in the gate.[27] He now not only lives in the city, he holds a position of respect there. Lot immediately recognizes the angels and invites them into his home.

The men of Sodom press against Lot's door demanding an opportunity to work their perversion, and Lot opposes them. Then, Lot utters words he could never have imagined when he first pitched his tent toward Sodom. "Behold now, I have two daughters which have not known man; let me, I pray you, bring them out unto you, and do ye to them as is good in your eyes: only unto these men do nothing; for therefore came they under the shadow of my roof." The men of the city reply "This one fellow came in to sojourn, and he will needs be a judge." Oh, Lot! Why is it that the men of the world are more observant than the righteous who lose their way? Lot came in thinking he was a sojourner, a pilgrim. Yet, the city consumed him, until he thought he was their judge.

When the angels temporarily save Lot's life and warn him to flee, Lot runs to warn his sons-in-law. "But he seemed as one that mocked unto his sons in law." Sensing Lot's hesitation, the angels urgently compel Lot to take his family and flee the city. Stunningly, Lot lingers, hesitant to leave a city that has grown dear to him. The angels literally drag Lot, his wife, and his daughters out of the city. When the angels order Lot to flee to the mountains, Lot begs them, "Behold now, this city is near to flee unto, and it is a little one: Oh, let me escape thither, (is it not a little one?) and my soul shall live." Lot makes the same argument he has used so many times in his life. Yes, it's a sin, a compromise. But isn't it just a little one? When the angels acquiesce to Lot's latest compromise, Lot finally leaves. But his wife looks back. She dies instantly.

When Lot watches the final destruction of Sodom and Gomorrah, he belatedly realizes the need to leave the area. He goes to the mountain as the angels first directed. There, Lot hides what remains of his family in a cave and waits in fear of the now uncertain future. That night, his virgin daughters reveal how deeply their time in Sodom compromised them, and they act out unspeakable evil with their father. Moab and Ammon, the spawn of this sin, will plague the people of God for centuries. The Apostle Peter will later write that Lot "dwelling among [Sodom and Gomorrah], in seeing and hearing, vexed his righteous soul from day to day with their unlawful deeds."[28]

If Lot had known the terrible price he would pay, he never would have pitched his tent toward Sodom. His "little" compromises cost him his place with God, his wife, and his children. He paid the greatest price of all. The Scriptures abound with warnings against following Lot's example. Paul said, "they that will be rich fall into temptation and a snare, and into many foolish and hurtful lusts, [. . .] For the love of money is the root of all evil: which while some coveted after, they have erred from the faith, and pierced themselves through with many sorrows."[29] Lot certainly pierced himself with many sorrows. And, many times, so have we. Paul also warned that men would become "lovers of their own selves, covetous, boasters, proud [. . .] unthankful, unholy, without natural affection, trucebreakers, [. . .] traitors" and "lovers of pleasures more than lovers of God."[30] Things that appear to be little compromises lead us to love ourselves, betray our families, break our vows, and love pleasure more than God. In short, there are no "little" compromises.

Neglectful Fathers Offend

Remember when Jesus said that it would be better to drown in the sea than to offend a child? That is most true within the sacred calling between a father and his children. Yet, neglectful fathers always offend their children in some way. Many types of neglect cause offense. The list of things that neglectful fathers do to offend their children is too long to list in detail, but among the list are lukewarmness, anger, marital conflict, verbal abuse, and the extreme offense of molestation.

David said that he would not speak against God because, "If I say, I will speak thus; behold, I should offend against the generation of thy children."[31] We should all be so careful with our words. Likely thinking back to his father's failure, Solomon wrote that "He that troubleth his own house shall inherit the wind."[32] All the commands of Christ apply with greater responsibility in the home. For example, if one who is angry or calls another a fool is in danger of judgment, how much more judgment awaits the father who is angry and insulting to his children?

No doubt, many men who read these words were themselves offended by their own fathers. Dear brothers, if you are the son of a man who failed as a father and you let that failure limit your own fatherhood, you are only a few miles back on the same road your father travelled.[33] Solomon, again remembering his father, wrote "A righteous man falling down before the wicked is as a troubled fountain, and a corrupt spring."[34] After his grievous sins, David was a defeated father. Defeat diminishes a father's authority, discernment, steadfastness, decisiveness, and consistency.[35] David hesitated with Amnon because he had lost his authority and struggled with guilt. How could he judge Amnon for committing fornication just as he had?

Worse, Solomon was unable to escape the defeat of his father, and it was only a matter of time before Solomon committed sins far beyond his father's. As a result, Solomon failed Rehoboam. Near the end of his life, Solomon looked at his son who would reign in his stead. He wrote in despair, "Yea, I hated all my labour which I had taken under the sun: because I should leave it unto the man that shall be after me. And who knoweth whether he shall be a wise man or a fool? yet shall he have rule over all my labour."[36] How could the wisest man in the world have no faith in his son's ability, despite the fact that Solomon wrote much of the book of Proverbs to his son? Solomon had followed the same path as David before him. He failed as a father, offending his children to the uttermost.

My Father's Idols and Family Pets

Each father has some type of besetting sin. Many times the same sin will endure like a plague through generations of a family tree. These are the idols that fathers worship in front of their children. They may be sins, distractions, thought processes, or wrong priorities that are passed from one generation to another as an unholy heritage of failure. Some sins are literally a part of the family. Like some type of family pet, they hang around the family home and are welcome to do so. The family attitude seems to actually encourage the children to serve sin. This is a terrible neglect on the part of the father. Inevitably, God must dramatically intervene in the lives of the children to plead with them to destroy their father's idols and repent of their father's sins.

In the time of the judges, an angel of God visited Gideon and called him to deliver Israel from the enemy.[37] Before Gideon could answer the call, his first assignment was to tear down the altar that his father built to Baal. How many times do young people called by God first have to tear down the altars their fathers built in their lives? Another time, the parents in Israel were so backslidden that a mother dedicated eleven hundred shekels "unto the LORD from my hand for my son, to make a graven image and a molten image."[38] In turn, the son, Micah, dedicated his son as a priest to the idol. When another tribe came and took Micah's idols, he nearly started a war to retrieve them. Even now, many who dare oppose a family idol meet with great anger and resentment at such a challenge.

God used the prophets to explain the danger of family idols. Jeremiah wrote, "The sin of Judah is written with a pen of iron, and with the point of a diamond: it is graven upon the table of their heart, and upon the horns of your altars; Whilst their children remember their altars and their groves by the green trees upon the high hills."[39] Ezekiel said:

> "But I said unto their children in the wilderness, Walk ye not in the statutes of your fathers, neither observe their judgments, nor defile yourselves with their idols: I am the LORD your God; walk in my statutes, and keep my judgments, and do them; And hallow my sabbaths; and they shall be a sign between me and you, that ye may know that I am the LORD your God. Notwithstanding the children rebelled against me: [. . .] and their eyes were after their fathers' idols. Wherefore I gave them also statutes that were not good, and judgments whereby they should not live; And I polluted them in their own gifts, in that they caused to pass through the fire all that openeth the womb, that I might make them desolate, to the end that they might know that I am the LORD."[40]

The kings of Israel and Judah proved this to be true time and again. To cite just one example, "Amon sacrificed unto all the carved images which Manasseh his father had made, and served them."[41]

The danger of paternal idolatry reached its worst in the time of Christ. Jesus rebuked the men of that generation as "the children of them who killed the prophets."[42] He continued, "Fill ye up then the measures of your fathers." Then, He prophesied that judgment for all the sins of the fathers would come upon that generation. When these same people fulfilled Christ's prediction and ordered his execution, they cried out, "His blood be on us, and on our children."[43] Later, Stephen looked at many of the same faces and declared, "Ye stiffnecked and uncircumcised in heart and ears, ye do always resist the Holy Ghost: as your fathers did, so do ye."[44] Israel's denial and rejection of Christ often seems beyond our comprehension. Yet, if our children treat Jesus the way we do in our daily lives, how far will they be from denial and rejection?

The disasters occurring in the world and the church detailed in the previous chapters are the primary responsibility of neglectful fathers. Fatherhood is a holy calling. God has invited us to work as his closest allies in winning the hearts of the next generation and instilling a zealous faith in their hearts. Yet, by the millions, Christian fathers walk away from this holy calling and pursue every other priority, purpose, and position imaginable. We have neglected our duty. We have often abandoned our post and gone absent without leave of our King. We are worthy of whatever judgment God deems meet. Let us then humble ourselves before our God and plead without ceasing for His mercy and grace. We join with the Biblical king who gave this challenge:

> "Wherefore the wrath of the LORD was upon Judah and Jerusalem, and he hath delivered them to trouble, to astonishment, and to hissing, as ye see with your eyes. For, lo, our fathers have fallen by the sword, and our sons and our daughters and our wives are in captivity for this. Now it is in mine heart to make a covenant with the LORD God of Israel, that his fierce wrath may turn away from us. My sons, be not now negligent: for the LORD hath chosen you to stand before him, to serve him, and that ye should minister unto him [. . . .]"[45]

---

1. See generally 2 Kings 22-23 and 2 Chronicles 34-35
2. Charles Finney, "November 18, 1840 Letters to Parents—7" available at http://www.gospeltruth.net/children/401118_parents_7.htm.
3. Andrew Murray, Raising Your Children for Christ, (1984) p 301.

4. Charles Finney, "Family Government" December 23, 1850, At the Tabernacle, Moorfields. Available at http://www.gospeltruth.net/1849-51Penny_Pulpit/501223pp_family_govt.htm
5. 2 Kings 20:14-19
6. Jeremiah 5:7
7. Jeremiah 6:21
8. Lamentations 5:7
9. Hosea 4:6
10. Genesis 2:15
11. Proverbs 24:30-34
12. Luke 8:4-8
13. Isaiah 28:23-26
14. Hosea 10:12
15. Jeremiah 4:3
16. Ecclesiastes 3:5; Isaiah 5:2; Isaiah 62:10
17. Proverbs 22:5
18. Denny Kenaston, The Pursuit of Godly Seed, (2003) p. 111.
19. Charles Finney, "November 4, 1840 LETTERS TO PARENTS—6" available at http://www.gospeltruth.net/children/401104_parents_6.htm
20. George Whitfield, "The Great Duty of Family Religion" available at http://www.ccel.org/ccel/whitefield/sermons.vi.html
21. *Id.*
22. *Id.*
23. Luke 17:32
24. Genesis 13:11-12
25. Genesis 14:8-12
26. Genesis 18:32
27. Genesis 19:1-38
28. 2 Peter 2:6-9
29. 1 Timothy 6:9-10
30. 2 Timothy 3:1-4
31. Psalm 73:15
32. Proverbs 11:29
33. Denny Kenaston "A Home for God" available at www.charitychristianfellowship.org/sermons/listing
34. Proverbs 25:26
35. "The Defeated Father" by Emmanuel Esh available at www.charitychristianfellowship.org/sermons/listing

36. Ecclesiastes 2:18-19
37. Judges 6:1-32
38. Judges 17:1-6
39. Jeremiah 17:1-2
40. Ezekiel 20:18-26
41. 2 Chronicles 33:21-23
42. Mathew 23:29-36
43. Matthew 27:25
44. Acts 7:51-53
45. 2 Chronicles 29:8-11

Enlightening the Eyes

[The] commandment of the LORD is pure, enlightening the eyes." (Psalm 19:8)

We turn now from examining the devastation that fathers who forsake God and His ways cause in their homes, churches, and cultures. In this next section, we will leave the darker side of our study and set our sights on the high ways of a holy God and the men who follow Him with all their hearts. First, we will return to the high and holy purpose of the Christian father and search out in greater detail what that purpose really is. Then, we will focus on the father's own personal discipleship to his Master. After that, we will examine the blessed details of God's perfect methods as described in Scripture. We proceed with the sacred hope that such a deep pursuit of God's commands will bring us to a greater vision and understanding of the ways of God in our homes.

CHAPTER 7

THE FATHER'S PURPOSE: "ARROWS FOR THE LORD"

As the saying goes, a man's home is his castle. Yet, for most men, the phrase inspires a picture of a man who can sit on his easy chair and watch football uninterrupted while the rest of the family serves his every need. This image results from a lost understanding of what a castle really is. Bill Gothard explains that a castle is a place of defense for young ones and a place of training for future warriors.[1] God has given us a holy calling to build homes that provide protection from all outside enemies while we train our children in every discipline of spiritual warfare against enemies within and without. This is a high calling. Let us forsake all lesser things and set our faces like flint toward the purpose of raising arrows for God.

Let there be no mistake. Our purpose is not to raise up private armies to build our own personal empires. Rather, the allegiance we ask of our children is a life of service to the King of kings. We dare not demand where or how they will serve in God's army. We must instead do everything in our power to enlist them faithfully in his cause, and then leave their individual assignments to the Captain of the host of Israel. Meanwhile, we can pray with all our hearts that our children will be prepared to serve as valiantly as the four young men whose names endure forever as the symbol of standing for God in your youth.

Their situation is a terrible one. Jerusalem is burning and under siege.[2] With the Northern Kingdom based in Samaria already destroyed, the people of God in Judah fail to heed the warnings of the prophets, and Jeremiah prophesies that God will not deliver Jerusalem from the hand of the king of Babylon. During an early wave of attacks, the Babylonian king orders his army to find children from leading families in Jerusalem and bring them to Babylon. Stripped from the homes they love and the land they know, the boys arrive in Babylon only to discover that they will lose their manhood as well. With no hope of ever carrying on the lineage of their fathers, these four young men find themselves in the center of the promised judgment of God.

Ashpenaz, their new master, orders Daniel, Shadrach, Meshach, and Abednego to eat and drink of the king's provision. Somehow, in the midst of the complete devastation of everything they hold dear, Daniel purposes in his heart that he will not defile himself by breaking even the least of God's commands. His three friends are quick to join him, and together they determine to challenge the Babylonian empire that has already destroyed their way of life.

The four young men risk death as they refuse the king's meat and wine. Seeing their faith, the God of their fathers meets them in this early test, and with His divine help the four young men prevail and maintain their convictions. The future would bring greater tests to these men; yet, the faith that would shine in the spotlight of the fiery furnace and the lions' den did not develop in those famous moments. Instead, the results of the fiery furnace and lions' den were predetermined when four young men, full of conviction and faith despite their situation, dared to tell their conqueror that they would not even compromise their eating habits to appease him.

A Holy Purpose

We have a holy purpose in raising the children that God gives us. Bill Gothard reminds us that we must prepare them to stand alone.[3] Young men and women who will stand alone when God needs them are in great demand. Yet, this has been one of the blind spots in conservative churches. Somehow, we often conclude that we will build churches with such wonderful spiritual unity that our young people will never need to stand alone. Assuming that our children will face only positive peer pressure, we often fail to instill in our children the holy grit necessary to do right regardless of what anyone else may do, say, or think. We must forsake this "youth group" mentality and replace it with the purposeful development of young people who have their own personal relationship with Christ and who determine to do right even when no one else dares to stand with them. Let the lives of our children live out the words of the old song:

> Though none go with me, still I will follow.
> Though none go with me, still I will follow.

Though none go with me, still I will follow.
No turning back; no turning back.[4]

Such children will endure even a fiery furnace.

In each child, God gives us a special purpose of developing and shaping a soldier of God. We are charged with supervising the process that causes our children to increase "in wisdom and stature, and in favour with God and man."[5] What are the steps of this growth process? We receive a key of understanding from the Apostle Paul's description of spiritual growth in his letter to the Romans.[6]

> "Know ye not, that to whom ye yield yourselves servants to obey, his servants ye are to whom ye obey; whether of sin unto death, or of obedience unto righteousness? [. . .] I speak after the manner of men because of the infirmity of your flesh: for as ye have yielded your members servants to uncleanness and to iniquity unto iniquity; even so now yield your members servants to righteousness unto holiness. [. . .] But now being made free from sin, and become servants to God, ye have your fruit unto holiness, and the end everlasting life."[7]

Paul gives us four progressive conditions of Christian maturity. The first level is obedience. We certainly will not be able to develop any deep Christian discipleship without first learning to obey our Master. That obedience must develop into righteousness. Right attitudes, thoughts, and conduct are the marks of the real believer. Next, that righteousness must develop into holiness, a separation from the world and consecration of life unto the Lord. In the end, by the amazing grace of God, obedience, righteousness, and holiness will lead us to everlasting life with God.

This is a pattern for raising godly seed. Let us, as early as possible, secure in the minds of our young children an immediate, joyful obedience to God and His authorities on the earth. Once the will is subdued to obedience, we can train them in every area of righteous character and conduct. Then, when through God's grace they are wonderfully converted, our children can join with us and God to separate and consecrate their lives to His service. With such a foundation, they can serve God faithfully all the days of their life and receive their reward in eternity.

The inspired words of the psalmist on the purpose of children are well known. "As arrows are in the hand of a mighty man; so are children of thy youth. Happy is the man that hath his quiver full of them: they shall not be ashamed, but they shall speak with the enemies in the gate."[8] There are two great lessons in this Scripture that can be easily missed.

First, making arrows is a process. Our children are not born as arrows, but as sticks. The Christian father, as the ancient archer before him, is responsible to get the bends out of the wood so the arrow will fly straight. Just as the ancient Israeli archer patiently whittled the wood for the arrow, purposefully chose the feathers for it, and carefully assembled each arrow, so the father must carefully fashion the child according to the King's purpose.

Second, we often forget that arrows are offensive weapons. The point of a quiver full of arrows is not for the archer to stay home during the battle and admire his beautiful collection of arrows. No, the purpose of a quiver full of arrows is to send the arrows into the battle to defeat the enemies of God and deliver victory to God's people. The context of the "quiver full" picture is not the quiet security of faithful children surrounding an aging parent. The context is holy war. Monte Swan reminds us, "The quiver belongs to a warrior whose desire is to obtain as many arrows as possible to shoot into, and even behind enemy lines."[9]

A Holy Practice

If our children are to be arrows for God, we must consecrate them to God from their earliest moments. Our attitude toward each new child should be recognition of God's holy purpose for the child and agreement to work with that purpose.[10] A baby dedication will accomplish very little unless we spend the next twenty years after that moment consecrating the child to God.[11]

What does it mean to consecrate a child? Consecrate means to set apart for a special purpose, to dedicate to the service and worship of God, and to give to God.[12] This is an excellent description of our purpose as fathers. Moreover, consecration produces a complete change of attitude toward the thing consecrated; everyone involved thinks different about a consecrated person or thing.

Consider for a moment the tabernacle in the Old Testament. Prior to its consecration, the gold was just gold. The censers were just censers. The fabric was mere ordinary fabric. After the consecration, every material and piece in that tabernacle had a whole new identity. The gold that had previously belonged to the multitudes could no longer be touched by most of the people. The censers that held no special meaning before that point could now bring fire from heaven if held by the wrong person. Consecration changed everything.

The same is true for our children. If we truly consecrate them to God, everything changes. Every dirty diaper has new meaning. Every gentle embrace has higher value. Every sweet prayer brings a glimpse into eternity. This is real consecration.

If consecration is so meaningful, how do we do it?[13] First, we must recognize that consecrating our children begins with consecrating ourselves. We cannot hold our own lives back from God and expect to consecrate our children to His service. We must be the first partakers of this change in identity. More is caught than taught. Second, we must put the Word of God in their hearts. The Bible is not hesitant to declare the effect of early Bible training. The Word will prevent sin, cleanse ways, and change minds. Third, we must train with purpose. Each day, we must remember that our children belong to God alone and that we are purposing for them to be used in His kingdom. Fourth, we must pray without ceasing. Only eternity will reveal the great things that have been accomplished for God through the faithful prayers of believing parents. Fifth, we must watch over them carefully. Far too many consecrated children have been forever compromised due to unsupervised sleepovers, valueless youth fellowships, or wicked adults at school or church. Guard the children, brethren.

Many men in our churches are looking for some type of ministry in the church. Others flee from the very thought of ministry. Whichever one you are, your greatest opportunity and obligation for ministry is in a godly home. You can, and you will, change eternity through the example you set at home. Consecrate your children unto God.

The idea of consecration can be seen in different terms in one of Paul's epistles. The Apostle writes that because a parent believes in Christ, "now are your children holy."[14] The great Christian author Andrew Murray wrote, "[O]ur children belong to God. The very fact of their being born to believing parents make them His in a very special sense."[15] Dear fathers, with all our hearts, let us write upon our children, "Holiness to the Lord." It will mean more written on them than anywhere else.

God calls our children holy because living in the home of believing parents plants the seeds of holiness in the hearts of the children. This holiness is the secret heritage that the child in an unbelieving home lacks.[16] God calls our children holy. That fact should change how we think of our homes, our children, and ourselves. God has called them holy. Therefore, we must think of our homes, our children, and ourselves as separated and consecrated to the holy work of God. That holy work of God is building and restoring the kingdom of heaven by producing a godly seed and taking the gospel of the kingdom to anyone who will accept it. God has declared our children holy. We can do no less.

Consecration and holiness should be the most exciting purpose possible to a child and its parents. Yet, in its practical application, these realities can involve great discipline. How is a Christian father to convince his children to abandon secular opportunities, limit social interactions, and discipline mind and body in service of the Lord? Enthusiasm. As you may have heard, it's contagious.

Consider the sports fanatic.[17] This man invests incredible amounts of his own money on sports equipment for his son almost from the moment of conception. He somehow persuades that boy to discipline himself, sacrifice spare time, and endure sometimes ridiculous amounts of physical suffering just to be involved in some sport. Meanwhile, we Christian fathers hesitate, thinking we might damage our children if we get too serious about serving God. We must have more enthusiasm about following Christ.

It is said that William Booth was so excited about being pummeled with rotten tomatoes while he was preaching that his children could hardly contain themselves with excitement the first time they were hit with one. If we get excited about rotten tomatoes, so will our children. Our enthusiasm will show our children what really matters in life. Be enthusiastic about serving God, and they will be too.

Consecrated, holy, enthusiastic children are the key to the future of the church. When fathers possess the spiritual realities promised to them and they pass them on to their children after them, a strong church will rise from the foundation of these godly homes.[18] When these homes and churches also turn their hearts to winning souls from the world around them, we can be sure that the next generation will inherit a church that is thriving and healthy.[19] One of the greatest reasons to raise a godly family is to be better able to save souls from the world. Denny Kenaston challenges us, "Let us win our children to a whole-hearted love for Jesus Christ, and let us win a lost world to the same."[20] We must see even beyond our own children. We must train them so that they can rise up and train the ones to come.

No doubt, some will think this purpose is far too idealistic. Many will say that Christ could return before generational training can be accomplished and bear fruit. Indeed, Christ could return, but should we neglect our children and forsake multiple Scriptural commands because our Lord may soon return? Would Christ be disappointed to return and find His bride carefully and intentionally training His children to follow His ways? After all, it is Christ Himself that said the kingdom of heaven was made up of little children.

A Holy Priority

The theory all sounds so good. Yet, in the reality of application, how do we make the time for all this purposeful parenting? Our family schedules already meet our actual priorities. If our schedule doesn't include room for training our children, our priorities are wrong. We know an activity is a "number one" priority when nothing but an emergency can displace it from our schedule.[21] We must make training our children that kind of priority.

Consider again the words of William Booth, whose enthusiasm compelled his children to embrace persecution as a badge of honor. He wrote, "When the supreme concern of the entire family is to seek their own profit or pleasure or honour or something else that seems essential to their interests, how can the children be trained to a life-long supreme seeking of the things that are Jesus Christ's?"[22] Selfish priorities will predestine our children for spiritual bankruptcy. Our schedule reveals the reality of our commitment as fathers. Booth continued,

> "Parents do a great deal of sentimental talking and praying about their dear children being nurtured for the Lord, but we fear that in the hearts of very few is there any definite purpose that their sons and daughters shall be trained to follow the Lord Jesus Christ in such hardships and persecutions, self-denial, and toil, as the following of Christ really signifies."[23]

We must not represent a version of Christianity to our children that costs them so little that it has no value to them.

In all of this, we must keep sight of the purpose God has for our children. If our children do not have a vision of performing some meaningful service for God, the world will quickly provide them with some meaningless distraction to occupy their time. Booth said it this way:

> "If, then, you do not find them scope for the development of the life they have, and give them the opportunity for using their spiritual gifts, they will lose them, and either give up all profession of religion, or be content with nothing more than the form of it."[24]

God has a great work for our children to do for Him. We get the awesome privilege of helping them prepare for it.

Raising arrows for the Lord is no light purpose. It goes infinitely beyond just raising well-behaved children. Merely having a large family does not make our quiver full. Arrows are for offense. They must be straight and true. And then, they must fly. Said Booth:

> "If you wish the Lord to take possession of the soul and body of this child, so that it shall only and always do His will, you must be willing that it should spend all its life in Salvation War, wherever God may choose to send it; that it should be despised, hated, cursed, beaten, kicked, imprisoned, or killed for Christ's sake; you must let it see in you an example of what a Salvation Army Soldier ought to be, and you must teach and train it to the best of your ability, to be a faithful Soldier, giving all the time, strength, ability, and money possible to help, on the War."[25]

Our purpose is not raising nice kids. Our purpose is that our children would be mighty for God wherever he sends them on His footstool that we call Earth.[26]

One day the child is a stick that we are shaping into an arrow. Eventually, the arrow goes into the quiver. Yet, as Monte Swan describes, the day must come when "the arrow is on the string, the bow is bent, and the child is released and flying into the future toward some target beyond us. Much of the flight we will not even be around to see."[27] Our arrows may fly so high and so far that we will be thrilled and terrified at the same time.[28]

Yet, releasing an arrow is not an event. It is a process. According to Swan, target panic is what happens when an archer flinches between the moment he releases the arrow and the moment the arrow clears the bow.[29] "Target panic is responsible for up to 90 percent of misses under twenty-five yards in range[.]"[30] The remedy for target panic is faith and follow-through. Even the blink of an eye is enough to deflect the arrow as it leaves the bow.[31] Swan concludes, when all the training, discipling, shepherding, and romancing are done, releasing the arrow becomes the most important moment in that child's life. With confidence that their trajectory is guided by Christ, release them and watch them fly. There is no greater joy.[32]

---

1. Institute in Basic Youth Conflicts, Advanced Seminar Textbook, (1986) p. 21
2. Daniel 1:1-16
3. Institute in Basic Youth Conflicts, Advanced Seminar Textbook, (1986) p. 269-275
4. "I Have Decided to Follow Jesus" Public Domain.
5. Luke 2:51-52
6. The following thoughts were inspired by and developed from a sermon on Romans 6 by Bro. Paul Dyal of Jacksonville, Florida.
7. Romans 6:16-22
8. Psalm 127:4-5
9. Monte Swan, Romancing Your Child's Heart,(2002) p. 292.
10. Denny Kenaston "Raising up Godly Seed" available at www.charitychristianfellowship.org/sermons/listing
11. Denny Kenaston "Consecrating Our Children to God" by available at www.charitychristianfellowship.org/sermons/listing
12. *Id.*
13. *Id.*
14. 1 Corinthians 7:14
15. Andrew Murray, Raising Your Children for Christ, (1984) p 266.
16. *Id.* p 267.
17. Denny Kenaston, The Pursuit of Godly Seed, (2003) p. 224-225.
18. *Id.* p.46
19. *Id.*

20. *Id.* p. 47
21. Institute in Basic Youth Conflicts, Advanced Seminar Textbook, (1986) p. 23.
22. William Booth, How to Make the Children into Saints and Soldiers of Jesus Christ, (1888) available at http://www.gospeltruth.net/children/booth_training.htm.
23. *Id.*
24. *Id.*
25. *Id.*
26. Denny Kenaston, "Revival and the Home" available at www.charitychristianfellowship.org/sermons/listing
27. Monte Swan, Romancing Your Child's Heart,(2002) p. 13.
28. *Id.* p 293
29. *Id.* p 287
30. *Id.*
31. *Id.* p 288
32. *Id.* p 291

CHAPTER 8

THE FATHER'S DISCIPLESHIP: "THESE WORDS SHALL BE IN THY HEART"

To fulfill the holy calling of fatherhood, we must become disciples of our Lord. No halfhearted obedience will suffice to inspire our children to keep the faith. God repeatedly makes clear that the fathers must follow Him before they can teach the children to follow Him. Moses set forth the importance of the father's discipleship in Deuteronomy:

> "For what nation is there so great, who hath God so nigh unto them, as the LORD our God is in all things that we call upon him for? And what nation is there so great, that hath statutes and judgments so righteous as all this law, which I set before you this day? Only take heed to thyself, and keep thy soul diligently, lest thou forget the things which thine eyes have seen, and lest they depart from thy heart all the days of thy life: but teach them thy sons, and thy sons' sons; Specially the day that thou stoodest before the LORD thy God in Horeb, when the LORD said unto me, Gather me the people together, and I will make them hear my words, that they may learn to fear me all the days that they shall live upon the earth, and that they may teach their children."[1]

To be able to teach our children, we must hear the Word, fear the Lord, take heed, keep our souls, and more. Jesus calls all who believe on Him to become His disciple, but discipleship takes on a whole new level of urgency when a believer is blessed with children.

Devotion to the Word

Men who dedicate themselves to learning and applying the Word of God are always in high demand. Nowhere is the disciple's devotion to the Word of God more important than in the home. Before a father can ever be a teacher—which he must be—the father must first become a learner. God said through Moses that fathers must lay up the Word in their hearts and souls, bind them upon their hands and as frontlets between their eyes, and then teach them to the children throughout the day.[2] Children do not receive teaching well unless the heart of the teacher is passionate about the subject. If we fulfill these conditions, God promises that our days and the days of our children can be "as the days of heaven upon the earth."[3]

For many fathers throughout history, devotion to the Word of God produced the most serious of consequences. The Catholic and Anglican churches martyred untold thousands of fathers for simply reading the Scriptures in their native language. For centuries, the established churches restricted access to the Bible, and Christian fathers struggled to be disciples of a Lord whose words they could not read.

Through the grace of God and the sacrifice of men like William Tyndale, Martin Luther, and many others, fathers now have the opportunity to daily search the Scriptures. Although often taken for granted, it is impossible to overstate the importance of a father's access to the Scriptures as he develops into a disciple of Christ. Our current access to the Word of God is reminiscent of Israel, when Moses said:

> "For this commandment which I command thee this day, it is not hidden from thee, neither is it far off. It is not in heaven, that thou shouldest say, Who shall go up for us to heaven, and bring it unto us, that we may hear it, and do it? Neither is it beyond the sea, that thou shouldest say, Who shall go over the sea for us, and bring it unto us, that we may hear it, and do it? But the word is very nigh unto thee, in thy mouth, and in thy heart, that thou mayest do it."[4]

Therefore, if we do not love, study, and know the Word of God, it is by deliberate choice, and we have only ourselves to blame.

The kingdom of God is in desperate need of men with a heart like Manoah.[5] When Manoah's wife tells him of the angel's message concerning their son, Manoah is not satisfied with second-hand information. Manoah prays, begging God to send the angel again to teach him specifically what he needs to do as they raise the promised child. When the angel returns to Manoah's wife, she runs to tell her husband to come. Manaoh questions the angel, "How shall we order the child, and how shall we do unto him?"[6] Where are the men who will search the Scriptures for the answers to these types of questions? We need men who are desperate for God to instruct them how to order the children. We need men who will say, in the Spirit of Christ, that the Bible is their written commission to do the will of God in every situation. If we are going to be the type of disciples that raise a godly seed, much of that discipleship must begin with a zealous devotion for the Word of God.

Consistent Obedience

Knowing the Word is a necessary prerequisite, but real discipleship is all about consistent obedience. He who refuses to obey the Master is no disciple at all. He who obeys inconsistently is a disciple that jeopardizes his own testimony and the testimony of Christ. Moses highlighted the importance of consistent obedience when he said, "Observe and hear all these words which I command thee, that it may go well with thee, and with thy children after thee for ever, when thou doest that which is good and right in the sight of the LORD thy God."[7] The promise of God that things will go well with our children is dependent upon us actually doing that which is good and right before God. God is not blind, and He is not mocked. He is actively searching the earth for men who will obey His commands. We will reap our obedience or disobedience to God in the next generation.

Jesus Himself emphasized the fundamental importance of consistent obedience. In His famous parable, He even connected the disciple's level of obedience to the condition of his home. Jesus told the crowd assembled on the mountain:

> "And why call ye me, Lord, Lord, and do not the things which I say? Whosoever cometh to me, and heareth my sayings, and doeth them, I will shew you to whom he is like: He is like a man which built an house, and digged deep, and laid the foundation on a rock: and when the flood arose, the stream beat vehemently upon

that house, and could not shake it: for it was founded upon a rock. But he that heareth, and doeth not, is like a man that without a foundation built an house upon the earth; against which the stream did beat vehemently, and immediately it fell; and the ruin of that house was great."[8]

Many times we see consistent obedience to Christ as a mark of maturity that comes only to the older believer. Yet, Jesus says that whether or not we obey Him is actually the foundation of our house of faith. Additionally, Jesus says that our level of obedience is the factor that determines whether or not our house will stand the test of time.

Disciples have life objectives centered on eternal purposes. For this reason, the disciple cannot be consumed with temporary goals like career and possessions.[9] All temporary things must be subjected to the eternal purposes of developing a relationship with God, building His kingdom, and passing a passionate faith to the next generation. Jesus addressed the fact that a preoccupation with the insignificant can completely distort our priorities. In the parable of the Great Supper, oxen, land, and romance cause God's people to neglect His priorities and be destroyed.[10]

Consistency in our obedience is a great challenge to many fathers. Consistency flows from self-control. Self-control flows from abiding in Christ. Solomon wrote, "He that is slow to anger is better than the mighty; and he that ruleth his spirit than he that taketh a city."[11] We must get enough control over ourselves to make obedience to Christ a consistent part of our daily lives. Many men say, "If God wants me to give up this or do that, He will give me the power to do it." This is absolutely true, but also completely off point. If we have received the baptism of the Holy Spirit, God has already given us the power we need. Men do not fail for lack of divine power; we fail for lack of a submitted will.

Ultimately, fathers often avoid the consistent obedience of discipleship because we do not want to acknowledge Jesus as Lord. Why are we so hesitant?[12] First, we are painfully aware that He may ask us to do something we do not want to do. Second, we are persuaded that we know what is truly best for us. Third, we are not fully persuaded that God has our best interests at heart. All of these concerns sound similar to the unfaithful servant who failed because he thought God was too hard of a Master.

If we want our children to follow God, we must do so first. Our obedience must be consistent and without hesitation. Jesus says obedience is the foundation. How many generations do we want our foundation to hold? Our obedience to Christ will ultimately answer that question.

Is there not a cause?

Modern Christianity has often proclaimed little difference between the results of being a believer in Christ and the results of actually being His disciple. When it comes to our children, however, the results are stark contrasts with each other. The mere believer will often immunize his children from the faith by giving them just enough of Jesus to make them feel comfortable with their place in eternity. The disciple, in contrast, creates more disciples that are ready, willing, and able to serve God to the ends of the earth.

Our hypocrisy as fathers when we refuse to follow Christ completely has shipwrecked the faith of a multitude of young people. If our home-life differs from our church-life, we have cursed our children. Hypocrisy in the father is revealed by disinterest or disgust for spiritual things in the lives of his teenagers.[13] If we are praying for our children and believing that our prayers are heard—yet our own lack of self-control produces home leadership that is prone to the whims and emotions of momentary self-interest—we are building an effective barrier to the work of the grace of God in the child's life.[14] In all reality, a lack of parental self-control is a leading cause of backsliding in youth.[15]

In one of the greatest challenges to the Christian father, "good" fathering is often the worst enemy of great fathering. We must not settle for good enough. We must aim higher than raising well-behaved pagans. Don't settle for "family worship;" have instead a worshipping family.[16] Always remember, heat begets heat. Cold begets cold. Lukewarm just begets disgust.

Fathers can expect to infect only what they have caught themselves. More is caught than taught. Monte Swan states, "Our character is the hammer that drives home the truth of what we say into the minds and the hearts of our children."[17] Children are desperate for standards and guidance. We can give our children clear, loving standards and clear, loving guidance. If we hesitate to set the example and provide guidance, they will turn to their peers. In the compelling words of William Booth:

> "Everything must be in keeping with the profession made, the whole force of the example depend[s] upon its being truthful. If the children once get the idea into their little heads that the religiousness of their parents is a cloak or a pretence only, no good impression will be possible on their hearts until that idea is removed."[18]

Fathers are living epistles seen and read by their children. No amount of talking, reading, or sermon-hearing, will replace the opportunity the father has to write on his child's heart by his own day-to-day conduct. Again, Booth wrote:

> "None are quicker to find out shams and 'make-believes' than children. They can soon see what is behind the mask; and perhaps no spirit in a home is more calculated to make children hate and turn away from religion in disgust, and grow up in hatred and unbelief, than the spirit which whines and cants and professes to be what it really knows it is not. Children live too close to father and mother to be deceived by any whitewashed appearances. The theatrical performances in religion may deceive the gallery and those at a distance, outside the house, but [in the home, the performance avails] not. The father may talk in public [. . .] or he may enlarge in his prayers on love and uprightness, and self-sacrifice, and benevolence, but if the grand spirit of love, uprightness, sacrifice, and benevolence be wanting in that father's daily doings and sayings—if it be not the spirit of the house, controlling and fashioning the work, the pleasure, and the play, the children will find it out."[19]

While the father's discipleship is paramount to the process of raising children, the process of raising children is also vital to the father's discipleship. As Gary Thomas noted, "The experience of parenting comprises one of the most influential aspects of spiritual formation [. . .] ever known."[20] Unless we are spiritually frozen, the process of raising, training, and loving children will mark us indelibly and powerfully. We cannot ever be the same. We will be changed forever. Moreover, Thomas writes, "Parenting puts the spotlight on our imperfections like nothing else."[21] Parenting requires energy, understanding, and wisdom that we do not possess at a dizzying rate, 24 hours per day and 365 days a year. Therefore, parenting is an hourly reminder of our dependence on God.

In addition, the more time we spend with our children, the more open they are to God. The less time we spend with our children, the less they want to pray. If we watch carefully, we will realize that the same is true for us.[22] Parenting is an incredible force to develop spirituality in a father.

Pride is one of the worst besetting sins of humanity, and many parts of parenting are custom designed by God to eradicate pride from your life.[23] A young child has untold numbers of ways to instantly humble—and at times humiliate—the greatest or most spiritual of men. Yet, the humbling moments of early parenting are just a taste of what the incarnation was like. When we struggle to handle an exploding diaper or regurgitating infant, we are reminded that the holy Son of God subjected Himself to enduring many undignified experiences as a part of becoming human. He did that for us. The least we can do is humble down and change their diapers.

Many people first have children for myriad selfish reasons. However, when raising children ceases to be about us and starts to be about God, our view of child training will be radically transformed.[24] A proper view of parenting compels us to a deeper level of discipleship. If our parenting is based in selfishness, we will eventually run from parenting's greatest and most important challenges. But those who parent on behalf of the heavenly Father in response to His command will march into these challenges with the strength of heaven.

What we stress with our children reveals the true passion of our own hearts.[25] Do we dare to ask our children what they think we are most passionate about? Our passions will be their passions soon enough. Because each young child assumes that what we do is what they ought to do, we must become what we are praying for our children to become in God. We fathers must be what we want our children to be. If we desire honor from our children, let us honor God before the eyes of our children. Then, He will do the same to us before them.[26]

To truly be disciples of our Lord, we must let a holy love for God and His Word mingle with a tender love for our children. Our goal is to win the hearts of our beloved on earth for the sake of our Beloved in heaven. Andrew Murray writes that our relationship with God creates the spiritual atmosphere that our children breathe in our homes.[27] The father that creates an atmosphere of prayer in the home gives his children immediate access into the Holy Place. Each father can create such an opportunity for his own children. Our discipleship can bring our children closer to God, but our lack of discipleship can push them away. In our attitudes and actions, let us show our children that a life lived for the kingdom of heaven is the greatest adventure, and greatest life, they can ever have.

Brothers, if we truly recognize what the Bible says about fatherhood, obedience is not optional. There is no other definition for a Christian home. There is no other way that God can fulfill his promises to our homes. These truths must produce a desperate obedience in our hearts. Continual failure in this area cannot rightly be called Biblical Christianity. Failure is not an option, and acceptance of failure is the acceptance of rebellion against God. If obedience is not necessary for survival to us in our homes, our obedience will be inconsistent at best. A survival mentality produces consistent response. We will reap the harvest of the seed that we sow by our discipleship. We dare not hold anything back from God.

---

1. Deuteronomy 4:7-10
2. Deuteronomy 11:18-21
3. Deuteronomy 11:21
4. Deuteronomy 30:11-14
5. Judges 13:1-12
6. Judges 13:12
7. Deuteronomy 12:28
8. Luke 6:46-49
9. Walter A. Henrichsen, Disciples Are Made—Not Born, (1983) p 11.
10. Luke 14:16-24
11. Proverbs 16:32
12. Walter A. Henrichsen, Disciples Are Made—Not Born, (1983) pp. 20-22
13. Rick Leibee, "Leader and His Youth" available at www.charitychristianfellowship.org/sermons/listing
14. Andrew Murray, Raising Your Children for Christ, (1984) p. 286
15. *Id.* p 285
16. David Smith "Leader and His Home" available at www.charitychristianfellowship.org/sermons/listing
17. Monte Swan, Romancing Your Child's Heart, 2002) p. 175
18. William Booth, How to Make the Children into Saints and Soldiers of Jesus Christ, (1888) available at http://www.gospeltruth.net/children/booth_training.htm.

19. *Id.*
20. Gary Thomas, Sacred Parenting, (2004) p. 13
21. *Id.* p. 38
22. *Id.* p. 12
23. *Id.* p. 15
24. *Id.* p. 16
25. *Id.* p. 29
26. Andrew Murray, Raising Your Children for Christ, (1984) p. 84
27. *Id.* p. 93

CHAPTER 9

THE FATHER'S METHOD:
"TEACH THEM TO THY CHILDREN"

The vision is greater than the people that have it. The vision of godly seed put forth first in the pages of Scripture, and presented anew here, will only have permanent benefit if we have a plan to implement the vision. Methods matter. If we try to implement God's vision with man's methods, the results can be downright dangerous.

At one of the highest points of his reign, David inspires the people to a great vision.[1] For years, the ark of God has been dwelling in relative obscurity. The last time it was moved, the Philistines sent it back to Israel on an ox cart. David envisions bringing the ark of God to Jerusalem, and the people are thrilled to join him in an epic celebration of the ark's return. Thirty thousand of Israel's best and brightest men come to join David in the procession. From every family and tribe they come to fulfill the vision proclaimed by their godly king. After decades of idolatry and compromised leadership, the people unite with one heart and one mind to celebrate and magnify the God of Abraham, Isaac, and Jacob. Israel has not seen such a day since Joshua died.

David rises early that morning and leads the massive congregation of people to the ark's current resting place. With them, they bring a new cart, specially built by the finest craftsmen in Israel for the sole purpose of transporting the ark. The people lift the ark and carefully set it in the cart. Two brothers, Uzzah and Ahio, are among thousands of volunteers hoping to drive the cart to Jerusalem. Their father Abinadab watches proudly as David chooses Uzzah to drive the cart and Ahio to walk immediately in front of it. This is a day his family will never forget.

As Uzzah cracks the whip to begin the procession, thirty thousand people erupt in praise to God. David begins to play his harp, and the greatest musicians in Israel join him with harps, timbrels, cornets, and cymbals. Almost unnoticed at the center of the massive procession, an ox stumbles. The ark tips dangerously toward the edge of the cart. Instinctively, Uzzah reaches back to steady the ark. Over the sound of the instruments, the people hear something similar to thunder, and all eyes turn to the ark. Every system in Uzzah's body stops instantly. Ahio watches in horror as his brother's dead body falls from the cart and hits the ground. Their father, Abinadab, watches helplessly from a distance. David stands in stunned silence, shocked by the tragic end of his noble vision. Overcome with fear and clueless as to what went wrong, David looks frantically for the first place he can find to leave the ark and regroup in Jerusalem. He chooses the house of Obed-edom.

Imagine you are Obed-edom.[2] Your wife and young children gather around you in curiosity. A celebration thirty thousand strong just froze in front of your home. A young man is dead. King David wants to leave the ark of God in your home temporarily. The ark of God! You are a Gittite—a man from the Philistine city of Gath. The last time the ark was around Gittites, they sent it back to Israel as soon as possible. Plagues broke out in the city. People died. Just moments ago, God killed the son of the last man who housed the ark. Worse, God killed him specifically for using Philistine methods to transport the ark. Do you dare welcome the ark—and with it the presence of the living God of Israel—into your home?

Great vision, even godly vision, can be deadly without godly methods. Methods matter. Uzzah's story shows us how much they matter. As fathers, we stand like Obed-edom. To pursue this vision of godly seed, we must invite the presence of God into our lives and our homes in a greater way than ever before. But such an invitation carries great risk, and many families have been destroyed in this pursuit. If we are to join God in His pursuit of godly seed, we must know His methods intimately. To proceed without them means certain failure.

Teaching

The first method we must learn is the method of teaching. The process of teaching is dear to the heart of God. In the church, the teacher is one of the most esteemed gifts, and teachers are singled out for greater scrutiny because of their impact on the people. In one of the most beautiful Scriptures in the Old Testament, Moses declared:

> "Hear, O Israel: The LORD our God is one LORD: And thou shalt love the LORD thy God with all thine heart, and with all thy soul, and with all thy might. And these words, which I command thee this day, shall be in thine heart: And thou shalt teach them diligently unto thy children, and shalt talk of them when thou sittest in thine house, and when thou walkest by the way, and when thou liest down, and when thou risest up. And thou shalt bind them for a sign upon thine hand, and they shall be as frontlets between thine eyes. And thou shalt write them upon the posts of thy house, and on thy gates."[3]

Each word of the command to teach bears important meaning. "Thou" identifies who is to teach. The fathers are not to wait for Moses or the Levites to teach. Rather, they are each individually commanded to teach. "Shalt" indicates the necessity of teaching. God did not say we should, could, or would teach. He said we shalt teach. There is no alternative. "Teach" if full of meaning. The word in the Hebrew suggests the idea of sharpening something to a point and then piercing something with it. "Them" explains what we are to teach. God did not give us divine orders to teach algebra, philosophy, psychology, or physics. We are commissioned to teach the commands of God, and they must be in our hearts first before we teach them to others. "Diligently" describes how we teach. "Diligently" means to sharpen to a point. "Thy children" explains our audience. We are not all called to teach the congregation, but we are all called to teach our own children. No man in Israel was excluded from the command.

The rest of Scripture repeatedly declares the father's responsibility to teach the Word of God to his own children. Moses orders the younger generation, "Remember the days of old, consider the years of many generations: ask thy father, and he will shew thee; thy elders, and they will tell thee."[4] He tells the fathers, "Set your hearts unto all the words which I testify among you this day, which ye shall command your children to observe to do, all the words of this law. For it is not a vain thing for you; because it is your life [. . . .]"[5] The psalmist writes, "We have heard with our ears, O God, our fathers have told us, what work thou didst in their days, in the times of old."[6] Again, he writes, "One generation shall praise thy works to another, and shall declare thy mighty acts."[7] And again, "They shall speak of the glory of thy kingdom, and talk of thy power; To make known to the sons of men his mighty acts, and the glorious majesty of his kingdom."[8] Hear Solomon's recollection of living with David:

> "Hear, ye children, the instruction of a father, and attend to know understanding. For I give you good doctrine, forsake ye not my law. For I was my father's son, tender and only beloved in the sight of my mother. He taught me also, and said unto me, Let thine heart retain my words: keep my commandments, and live."[9]

Dear brothers, the truth of the Word of God cannot be avoided. We are responsible for teaching the commands of God to our children. We dare not be content to delegate such a holy calling.

Lest we conclude that avoiding the issue is the answer, Charles Finney reminds us that "your children will be educated, either by yourself or by some one else. [. . .] They will have instruction, and if you do not secure to them right instruction, they will have that which is false."[10]

No doubt, many of us severely doubt our ability to teach our children. So many fathers are now generations removed from any godly ancestors, and many have never seen a godly father teaching his children. We often don't even know what it should look and sound like. We face this calling like Moses, arguing "Lord, I am not eloquent, [. . .] but I am slow of speech, and of a slow tongue."[11] God's reply to our excuses of insecurity remains the same, "Who hath made man's mouth? or who maketh the dumb, or deaf, or the seeing, or the blind? have not I the LORD? Now therefore go, and I will be with thy mouth, and teach thee what thou shalt say."[12]

Dear brother, you are a teacher by faith. God sees things that are not as though they already were. Moreover, any man who is convinced and excited can teach.[13] Men who are barely literate can teach all types of complex information when they get excited about the subject matter. This is the one prerequisite to teaching—the Word must be in our hearts first.

Do not compare yourself critically to other teachers. You are the only father in your home. Therefore, you are the most important, most capable, most anointed teacher in your home.[14] You are the only father your children can look to for spiritual direction and edification. Give it to them before they grow bored of waiting and fill the void with meaningless thoughts. "The ability to fulfill the task is in the call."[15]

In reality, teaching is not an option anyway. You will teach your children something. You get to choose whether you will teach them obedience or disobedience to God's commands. If you aren't actively and intentionally teaching them, then you are still teaching them negative lessons. Also, if you refuse to teach, the world has many teachers that would be glad to form your child in your stead.

You do not need to know exactly how to teach to start teaching; you just need a burning desire to teach. Lift your eyes in faith and behold the promises of God concerning how you should lead your family. Dear fathers, do not let your wife do all the Biblical teaching in the home. This is not the order of God as He laid it out in Scripture. Yes, many times they have more time to prepare, but this is no excuse for abdicating the position of responsibility. If you are too busy to get the Word of God in your heart and then put it in the hearts of your children, then you are too busy, period.[16]

As we take our God-given place as the teacher in the home, let us always remember that our commission is to teach the Word of God. There are many good things that we can teach our children, but good things do not draw our children to salvation. God has promised that His Word will not return void. It will perform what it is sent to do. The preaching and teaching of the Word of God is the foundation of faith. Such teaching is also the source of vision, as David wrote, "The statutes of the LORD are right, rejoicing the heart: the commandment of the LORD is pure, enlightening the eyes."[17]

Many fathers in history risked their lives to teach the Bible to their children. Yet, all too often, we hesitate to do so even though we live in total freedom to teach our children. Like Israel of old, God has delivered His Word to us. Now, we must speak His word to our children. God has already done His part. If our children do not know God's Word, the only reason will be that fathers chose not to declare it to their children.

In teaching the Word, we must not compromise the Bible or our position as a trusted teacher by diluting the Bible or mixing truth with fiction. Imaginary stories do not mix with the truths of the Bible. Separate any discussion or reading of fairy tales from the reading of the Bible.[18] Declaring the truth of a fairy tale, which we know the children will eventually stop believing, damages our credibility on matters of faith. Spiritual truth and secular fiction have no overlap.

How does a father practically receive the Word of God, take it into his heart, sharpen it, and stick it in the hearts of his children? Isaiah explains that our teaching must be "precept upon precept, precept upon precept; line upon line, line upon line; here a little, and there a little."[19] We must be conscious of the physical and mental limitations of our younger children, even as we slowly stretch them beyond those limitations. God is not asking us to teach our children the entire doctrine of salvation in one afternoon conversation. Quite the opposite is true. To properly sharpen the Word and get it to stick, we must teach our children slowly and intentionally, one bite at a time. Yet, if we do this consistently our children will eat the whole Book through these small installations of truth.

Brothers, let us seize the teachable moments in each child's life. Our children are born prepared for us to teach them. Pastor Denny Kenaston explains that our children are born with a desire to please their parents, a desire to learn, a merciful blindness to parental faults, quick and able minds, fast memorization processes, minimal distractions, mastery of imitation, and a near gullibility in accepting what their father teaches.[20] This golden opportunity only lasts for about ten years. Thus, we cannot begin too young. No doubt many have lost their children because they did not commence teaching them the truths of the kingdom at a sufficiently early age.[21] Unfortunately, one of the greatest mistakes we often make in dealing with children, especially younger children, is to underestimate their intelligence and thereby delay the important teaching in righteousness.

While Deuteronomy encourages us to teach the Word at all times and in all situations, this constant teaching needs to be supplemented with a consistent scheduled time for family devotions or family services. In days of old, Christian families gathered together on a frequent basis for singing, prayer, and Bible teaching from the father. The practice was once so common that Andrew Murray could write without hesitation, "The practice of family worship is found in almost every Christian family. Every day a portion of God's holy Word is read together."[22] What happened to this kind of Christian home? Current trends suggest that this type of Christian home died out long ago, likely slain at the hands of the television.

We cannot be content to let church be something we do only on Sundays and Wednesday nights. Bring the Word home with you, invite the Spirit to flow freely in your home, and have church together as many days as you possibly can. As we teach, we must remember that head knowledge is never our goal. Instead, our desire is to stick the Word of God in their hearts in such a way that our teaching becomes formative instruction that actually becomes a part of who our children are.[23]

According to Tedd and Margy Tripp, formative instruction is proactive, preventative, before-the-fact instruction.[24] Timing is essential. Many times we fathers suffer under the tyranny of the urgent. As a result, we do not teach our children until the need to do so becomes obvious through blatant misconduct. Yet, corrective discipline is no substitute for formative instruction because corrective discipline happens when neither father nor child are at their respective best.[25]

The Tripps write that formative instruction has five unique goals that go far beyond the increase of knowledge or exposure to Scripture.[26] First, we help our children to see Scripture as their personal history. The characters of Scripture must become so real to our children that they see them as extended branches of their own family tree. When they see themselves as descendants in a long line of faithful saints, they will have stock in following through with this vision. Let them come to the realization that the saints of ages past are counting on them to carry the torch another mile.

Second, our goal is to teach in a way that develops godly disciplines. The old adage about teaching a man to fish is more true here than in other arenas. Praying for your child will help them through a struggle. Teaching them to pray will help them through life. Likewise, teaching them a Bible study will enlighten them on some Biblical truth. Teaching them how to study the Bible will open the door to a lifetime of communion with God.

Third, we desire to teach in a way that applies Scriptures to our daily lives. This is part of what Moses implied in the idea of teaching in all times and situations. We can do this without fear precisely because the Bible is applicable to all times and situations. Truth learned is a great potential force. Truth applied, however, is a great realized force that will transform the lives and hearts of our children forever.

Fourth, our goal is to teach our children to model spiritual life to others. Paul encouraged Timothy, his young companion, to be an example in every part of the Christian life. Our children can do the same. Even a child is known by his actions. Psychologists often advise fathers to stroke a child's ego by encouraging him to try various sports or hobbies because he is destined to find success in something. Yet, many of those same experts would shun the idea of placing spiritual responsibility on the child because they conclude he is destined for failure. Our children do not have to fail God, and the pressure of knowing that they are the light of the world will do much to encourage their faithfulness in times of testing.

Fifth, our goal in teaching is to develop our children into mature relationships with God and with us. We do not intend to raise immature adults that are eternally dependent on us for their connection to God. Our children must become Christ's followers with their own faith and convictions. One day we will no longer be present to answer their questions, but their answers will remain in the Bible where they always were. We don't want our children to be like King Saul, desperately searching for a deceased Samuel to give him direction from God. We must prepare them to go on with God without us whenever the need arises.

Cooper and Wamberg provide some practical pointers on sticking the Word in the hearts of our children.[27] We need to take control of our curriculum. If we use tools or resources outside of the Bible, we know our children better than the authors of that curriculum do. We should not be afraid to change things to make it personal for our children. Also, we can tell personal parables. When teaching the principles of Scripture, nothing will stick the point in a child's heart like a story from our own past or present experiences. Storytelling with a spiritual purpose was the most frequent teaching method of the greatest Teacher of all time.

Next, we need to "keep it concrete."[28] We should not lose a child's interest by splitting theological hairs in debates that we adults barely understand. Children can often experience truth without fully understanding it. Some fathers avoid sharing the Bible with their children because they fear that the children will not fully understand what God is saying. Fear not, adults do not understand everything God is saying in a particular passage either. Also, we need to remember to ask questions. This is another method used by the greatest Teacher. A well-designed question can teach more than a series of sermons, especially if we actually let our children talk and wrestle with the answer.

As we teach, we need to regularly check the atmosphere and our attitude.[29] In the long run, children remember more about attitude and atmosphere than individual messages. We can redeem the time by keeping a watchful lookout for high-impact opportunities to stick the Word of God into the suddenly open heart of a child. God uses the events of life to deliver supernatural opportunities for parental instruction. For this reason, we must be mentally present when our children are with us. After all, we never know what they are going to say next.

Next, we need to enter the action of teaching.[30] Children want to include us in the learning experience. Teaching from a distance is what makes public schools, and many church services, so hard for children to follow. We can jump into the moment with them and engage in learning the Word of God with our children. Fathers need not be mere spectators or professors addressing the class.[31]

God clearly understands the gripping power of a great story. The Bible is full of stories, and God uses those stories to impress eternal truths upon us. Many of the things we remember most from Scripture are not in the beautiful treatises of Paul or the songs of David, but rather in the powerful, gripping stories of the Old Testament, the Gospels, and Acts.

We can also discover new stories around the table by asking questions of anyone who happens to be sitting there. Also, the Old Testament was full of family traditions given by God specifically to help families bond together. We can create some of our own that have the same impact without illegally slaughtering the family pet.

The opportunities for teaching our children are endless. God has called each and every father to teach. The anointing is in the call. Let us pray without ceasing that God will help us master some of these practical methods and stick the Word of God deep into the hearts of our children. After all, the faith of the next generation depends on it.

Correction

It seems that no book on parenting is complete without a discussion of correction and discipline. The opinions that have been expressed, even in Christian circles, are legion. Thankfully, God has not left us subject to the whims of human philosophy, child psychology, or public conscience. His Word provides vital insights into this second essential method of raising godly seed.

Biblically speaking, correction is not a negative thing. The Bible says that, "whom the LORD loveth he correcteth; even as a father the son in whom he delighteth."[32] The writer of Hebrews explains:

> "And ye have forgotten the exhortation which speaketh unto you as unto children, My son, despise not thou the chastening of the

> Lord, nor faint when thou art rebuked of him: For whom the Lord loveth he chasteneth, and scourgeth every son whom he receiveth. If ye endure chastening, God dealeth with you as with sons; for what son is he whom the father chasteneth not? But if ye be without chastisement, whereof all are partakers, then are ye bastards, and not sons. Furthermore we have had fathers of our flesh which corrected us, and we gave them reverence: shall we not much rather be in subjection unto the Father of spirits, and live? For they verily for a few days chastened us after their own pleasure; but he for our profit, that we might be partakers of his holiness. Now no chastening for the present seemeth to be joyous, but grievous: nevertheless afterward it yieldeth the peaceable fruit of righteousness unto them which are exercised thereby."[33]

Here, we have a pattern for correcting our children. Recognizing that correction flows from love and relationship, we are to correct our children that they may be partaker's of God's holiness. Ultimately, we send our children a quiet message of love or hate depending on how we correct our children.[34] Solomon wrote, "He that spareth his rod hateth his son: but he that loveth him chasteneth him betimes."[35]

God does not hesitate to encourage the use of spanking as the primary form of correcting younger children. Indeed, God actually expresses some urgency on this subject when He says, "Chasten thy son while there is hope, and let not thy soul spare for his crying."[36] In another place, the Creator states, "Withhold not correction from the child: for if thou beatest him with the rod, he shall not die. Thou shalt beat him with the rod, and shalt deliver his soul from hell."[37] Thus, the Word of God informs us that proper correction and spanking will deliver our children from worse judgments later in life. Moreover, God says, "Correct thy son, and he shall give thee rest; yea, he shall give delight unto thy soul."[38] Thus, if our children are not a rest and a delight to us, something is wrong with our correction.

Foolishness is one key reason for spanking. God says, "Foolishness is bound in the heart of a child; but the rod of correction shall drive it far from him."[39] Because we live in a culture of men that never grow up, the idea of driving foolishness out of someone may seem like an overreaction. Yet, the Bible explains that "the thought of foolishness is sin."[40] As a result, leaving a child in foolishness is permitting strongholds of sin to develop in his life. Even small amounts of foolishness can have serious consequences.

Scripture says, "Dead flies cause the ointment of the apothecary to send forth a stinking savour: so doth a little folly him that is in reputation for wisdom and honour."[41] In addition, "The rod and reproof give wisdom: but a child left to himself bringeth his mother to shame."[42]

The purpose of spanking must be made clear. Spanking is commended and commanded in Scripture to parents as a form of correction, not as a form of punishment. The distinction between punishment and correction is important. Punishment seeks justice against the wrongdoer without mercy or concern for the wrongdoer. Punishment relies on a basis of authority rather than relationship. It has no goal or purpose of impacting the heart. If spanking is used as a form of punishment, the impact of the spanking will end at the child's posterior and cause little more than tears and temporary compliance.

In contrast, correction flows from love and relationship. The goal of correction goes beyond behavior modification. Correction is concerned not with the offense, but with the offender. Correction seeks to reconcile the wrongdoer back to God, the family, and the victim of the offense. Correction relies on a combination of a loving relationship and divine authority. It is the relational aspect of correction that generally causes real heart transformation. If spanking is consistently used as the Biblical method of correction, the impact of the spanking will bring reconciliation, a change of heart, and a lifelong development of character that will last a lifetime.

When we correct our children, we should be aware of the heart command they are fighting, not just the procedural law that they violated.[43] In teaching and correcting our children, we must address the heart issue more than any other. The Bible calls the heart the wellspring of life, and Jesus told us we speak from the heart. Every child's greatest need is a heart transformation. Yet, fathers are constantly tempted to trade the difficult pursuit of heart transformation for the easier goal of behavior modification.

Consider the common scenario of children who will not share. Asking the children who had the toy first does not deal with the heart. Instead, Tedd Tripp notes that such a methodology raises up idols of personal rights.[44] We must instead teach each child to imitate Christ, prefer others, and lay down their toys, and eventually their lives, for their friends. In this way, we can deal with the heart issue rather than the surface issue.

Tripp writes that each child's heart is revealed and formed by his relationship with God, his relationship with others, and his relationship with the "shaping influences" in his life.[45] Each child's heart has a "godward orientation."[46] God has commissioned fathers to be largely in control of whether each child's heart is turned to idols or to the God of heaven. Remember, the heart is never neutral. It is either directed to God or idols. We must watch our children and their reaction to correction to gauge where their hearts are directed.

God looks beyond outward appearances to see the heart. We must teach our children to do the same. Our children will never interpret life correctly if we teach them to focus on the outside issues rather than focusing on the heart.[47] Yet, it is so easy for fathers to lose sight of the child's heart and merely mete out punishment for outward misbehavior. Remember, the goal of parental correction, including spanking, is the restoration of the child to the father, the family, and God. The goal is always correction and restoration, not punishment.

Even with this mindset, there are a few practical admonitions that are appropriate at this point. First, we need to avoid the temptation of magnifying modern thought above the Word of God and inventing our own techniques of correction. Charles Finney noted on this point, "It seems to me, that some parents effect to be wiser than God, in taking it upon them to decide, that it is not wise to use the rod upon children."[48] Spanking can be a very uncomfortable process for many parents. Indeed, it should be. Yet, we cannot change the Word of God, nor can we just ignore the verses with which we may prefer to disagree. As fathers, we must obey God's Word in this area.

Second, we need to avoid inconsistencies and delays in correcting our children. The Bible says, "Because sentence against an evil work is not executed speedily, therefore the heart of the sons of men is fully set in them to do evil."[49] Whimsical rules and capricious enforcement will destroy the corrective process. If the father delays until he is angry, nothing good will be accomplished. Children have two lines in their mind—what we want them to do and what we will allow them to do.[50] Thus, we should warn often during training, but not during enforcement.[51] If instead we resort to multiple warnings and counting out loud, we destroy the lines of authority in the minds of our children.[52] Delaying a spanking is actually unkind to our child because it leaves the child with unresolved guilt.[53] We need to administer the correction, reconcile the relationship, and clear their conscience as soon as possible.

Third, fathers should never spank in anger. This cannot be overemphasized. Spanking in anger discredits the process and destroys the reconciliation and relationships that are at the heart of correction. To put it bluntly, spanking in anger and speaking in anger are guaranteed ways to drive away the hearts of our children. Angry fathers will not keep the hearts of the children. If we are angry, we must overcome this dangerous sin. True authority is revealed in calm, quiet commands. Shouting actually reveals a lack of authority.

Fourth, we should not spank a child in front of others. The point of the spanking is correction and reconciliation. Spanking a child in front of their siblings, peers, or other adults replaces those goals with embarrassment and humiliation. Correction should be private. Violating this principle forces the child to resist the spanking and refuse to humble the heart in an attempt to save appearances before the people who are watching.

Fifth, we cannot panic when the methods given by God take some time to work with some children. Strong-willed children are a blessing, not a curse. Just walk in faith and bring that will into subjection. Strong wills are no surprise to God. The principles of Scripture do not change just because a child has a strong will or complex temperament. Many fathers panic when they face a strong-willed child and run to the world for advice when the spanking seems unsuccessful. We can confidently stick with the Word of God. It alone has eternal guarantees.

The proper process for administering a spanking will bring restoration and reconciliation to all involved. There should first be a time of awareness about what is about to happen. Then, fathers should instruct the children in the Biblical principles that they violated. We can use this time to ask them questions about what they did wrong if they have been adequately taught prior to the incident. After that, we can administer the spanking carefully and with great self-control. Fathers should decide ahead of time how many swats the child will receive. Anything over five swats is probably excessive. After the swats, we should spend time affirming the truth of the Word of God and expressing love to the child. We should then pray with and for the child. If the child is old enough, fathers can have the child pray with and for the father. Some amazing prayers will come out of these moments. After prayer, we can exercise the process of reconciling. The child should ask God, the parent, and anyone else involved for forgiveness. We should confirm to the child both our forgiveness and the forgiveness of God. Finally, we should walk the child through the process of obeying, or sharing, or whatever they were supposed to do right in the beginning.

It is worth repeating that this whole process should be covered in prayer. Charles Finney wrote:

> "Be sure to pray much with and for them. Never punish them without praying with them. Whenever you give them serious admonition pray with them. Pray with them, when they lie down and when they rise up. And enforce the lesson by your own example, that they are never to do any thing without prayer."[54]

Fathers can enforce commands quickly and quietly. We establish true authority when we establish obedience on the first, quiet command.[55] Admittedly, each child is very different, but we have to believe that the Bible has the answer for every one of them. We must take the Word of God and go before our Father and ask Him to help us to find the principles that will help us with each individual child. God uses this to require us to stay in relationship with Him. Correction is a very important and easily distorted part of raising a godly seed. Yet, we can correct properly if the way we correct our children is an accurate representation of how God corrects us.

Training and Restraining

While we have said much, and could say much more, about the Biblical methods of teaching and correction, the next method is likely the most powerful, and most often forgotten, of all Biblical parenting methods—training and restraining. This study mandates an examination of perhaps the most confrontational verse on parenting in the entire Bible. Proverbs 22:6 says, "Train up a child in the way he should go: and when he is old, he will not depart from it."[56] The attacks on a simple belief in this Scripture are voluminous. In this chapter, we are simply going to focus on the word "train." We will save for a later point the defense of the promise that follows that word.

At the outset, we need to realize that training is not teaching, far from it. Teaching supplies knowledge to be used by a willing listener. Training seeks to influence the will itself.[57]

Teaching is about information. Training is about experience and application. Like teaching, training is not really optional. As we live, we train.

Concerning the difference between teaching and training, William Booth had much to say. He wrote, "In teaching the children we more especially influence their minds; in training them we specially deal with their wills—that is, with their hearts."[58] He also noted, "When we teach them we show them what they ought to do; when we train them we accustom them to do it."[59] And, "In teaching the children we show them how to do their duty and why it should be done, but in training we create in them the habit of doing it."[60]

Training is an absolutely necessary companion of good teaching. Without training, teaching often leads to little more than an inoculation against real Christianity. On this point, Booth writes,

> "There is nothing more common than to find children with their heads full of notions about religion, knowing Bible stories off by heart, all about the love of God, and the death of His Son, and how His servants suffered and fought and died in keeping His commands in the days of old. But when you ask them about their own Salvation, they are as ignorant and feelingless as young savages."[61]

Booth went on to call reliance on teaching without proper training the most serious lack in raising Christian children and the cause of most of our failure as fathers.[62] In his view, teaching without training produced "Multitudes of children [who] are instructed in religious notions and their memories crammed with the facts of ancient religious history, whilst their hearts are left unchanged, uncultivated, and uninspired by the Holy Spirit."[63]

A brief consideration of the "potty" training process that each parent faces with their young children illustrates the most basic understanding of the word "train" and shows clearly the difference between training and teaching. Imagine trying to "teach" your toddler how to use the potty rather than the diaper. You would have daily reading from a textbook discussing all the proper procedures. You could get a whiteboard and draw out the necessary steps. You could make a craft about using the potty. Yet, none of these things would actually result in a potty-trained child. In contrast, the actual process of training your child to potty involves sitting next to them, walking them through the process repeatedly, helping them where they need help, encouraging them, and patiently assisting them as they slowly become able to potty independently. The contrast could not be clearer.

This contrast extends to the spiritual realm as well. William Booth said it this way:

> "If you want your children to walk with God and serve Him, you will have to make them do it. You will have to take them by the hand [. . .] and lead them on step by step. Just in the same way as you [train] them to walk physically, letting them find their feet at first, then showing and encouraging them to stand alone, and then to take the first step, and so on, with all patience and perseverance, until they can walk and run and leap alone. In this way you will show them how to run the way of God's commandments."[64]

Booth maintained that "early training is the God-appointed and only method which can be reckoned upon with certainty to develop children into godly men and women."[65] In practice, we need to train our children in a multitude of spiritual things in a similar way to how we train them to potty or walk. Booth said:

> "Take the children by the hand and lead them with you into the Presence of God. Show them how to converse with Him. Tell the Lord aloud, while they kneel by, all about them, and then encourage them to tell the Lord all about themselves. In this way, draw out their hearts in actual personal dealing with the Savior."[66]

Such a process will have a far greater impact than merely teaching them about prayer.

The word "train" in Proverbs goes beyond even the training described above. The word means "to narrow, to initiate, to discipline, to dedicate."[67] It is used to describe the dedication of the altar, Solomon's temple, Ezra's temple, Nehemiah's wall, and Nebuchadnezzar's image. This definition is of great importance. Picture the two different groups involved. On one side, we have Moses, Solomon, Ezra, Nehemiah, and their laborers. Given raw materials, these faithful men carefully narrow the destiny of each tree, mineral, metal, and stone. With great attention to detail, they prepare each piece for its place in the work of God. Every person involved is focused on the purpose and holiness of the piece upon which they are called to labor. When the preparation is done, the pieces come together seamlessly. In Solomon's case, the temple is erected without the sound of a hammer because each piece is so perfectly prepared.

On the other side of the picture, Nebuchadnezzar and his minions labor carefully. Using materials pillaged from other nations, they work with the same detailed attention as the heroes above. Yet, they labor with a totally different purpose—the glorification of man. When the time of dedication comes, they will use the threat of sword and fire to force admiration of their work. Three young men, specially prepared by God, will be compelled to challenge the idolatry and risk their lives for their faith.

Remember, brothers, God gave us this picture in connection to our children. What kind of fathers do we want to be? Will we raise up for God an altar, a piece of the temple, and a piece of the wall, or will we raise to the world another useless idol? We are speaking of our children. We can narrow them, prepare them, dedicate them, train them up in the way that they should go, and when they are old, they will not depart.

When our training is successful, our children will be restrained from within. Scripture states,

> "My son, keep thy father's commandment, and forsake not the law of thy mother: Bind them continually upon thine heart, and tie them about thy neck. When thou goest, it shall lead thee; when thou sleepest, it shall keep thee; and when thou awakest, it shall talk with thee. For the commandment is a lamp; and the law is light; and reproofs of instruction are the way of life:" [68]

What a promise! Many fathers agonize about what will become of their children when the use of the rod ends due to age and size. Restraint is the plan when spanking ends. If we teach, correct, and train our children when they are young, the Word of God will be in their hearts. They will be led, kept, and directed by the commandments that are written in their hearts.

This is similar to the process that happens in the church. When our children outgrow the rod, we find out what it is like to be in the ministry.

The minister has no physical rod, but he has authority and restraint. So can fathers.[69]

If our goal is for our children to be restrained from within, we must keep our focus on the heart of the matter throughout the early years of parenting. Developing righteous character requires internalization of Biblical truth. Outward behavior is an indicator of inward conditions. We must look from fruit to roots. When it comes to children, what was once outside becomes inside very quickly.[70]

If we honestly consider the picture God painted in the definition of the word "train," we will quickly realize that training children is going to require a large amount of our time. This is no part-time calling that God gave us. Making the time we need to raise our children in this manner requires living a simpler life than the world around us lives.

We cannot accept the "quality not quantity" lie. Generations of believers who accepted this falsehood are now searching for answers as to why their children abandoned the faith. Quantity is important because children are growing nonstop and we must be involved in the process. Additionally, quantity is necessary to monitor what the child internalizes.[71] With quality and quality time, we can walk our children through the process of training. According to Dr. Henry Cloud and Dr. John Townsend, the training process often follows a cycle of introducing the reality of Scripture, observing failure, transforming failure into a learning opportunity, identifying back to Scriptural reality, and trying again.[72] Such a process mandates a substantial quantity of quality time.

Training also focuses frequently on the "do" commands rather than the "do not" commands. If a child's life is full of "do's", they will not become distraught over the "do not's." This calling is a great challenge. We must defeat many giants to succeed. Let us say with David, "Is there not a cause?"

As we train, we must be aware of the danger of training in idolatry rather than holiness. The Tripps write that modern idols include power and influence, pride and performance, possessions, pleasure and sensuality, vanity, fear of man and desire for approval, friendship, intellect, and worldly wisdom.[73] All these things are regularly trained into the hearts of our children when we lose focus.

Training and formative instruction are vital because parental interpretation is everything to our children.[74] They have no way to process stimulus other than the interpretations that we help them form. Training is also important because children sin for pleasure. They need us clearly and consistently to prove to them that righteousness brings real pleasure while sin brings lasting pain.

Unfortunately, fathers often need a big sign saying "Don't feed the idols."[75] We are often the worst culprits in encouraging our children to pursue lesser goals. We must stay focused on changing the heart and the will, not just conforming the behavior. Focusing on behavior rather than focusing on the heart at best merely manipulates our children into becoming religious sinners and at worst drives them from God with the excuse that everything good they learned was fake.[76] Merely addressing behavior ignores the real need of our children and skips the centrality of the Gospel. A child's root problem is not what he does, it is what he is, and only the Gospel can change what he is. Moreover, focusing solely on behavior often reveals the father's idols of convenience, control, public opinion, or personal desires for a child.[77]

In all training, we rely heavily on the Word of God. Unlike any other book or source, the Bible demands a response from our children. The Word of God cannot be ignored. Thankfully, the Bible provides guidance on every major issue our children will face, including pride, lust, the world, money, and selfishness.

If we want our children to be restrained, we must create a bank account of love, affection, and relationship with our children when they are young.[78] We should deposit into this account as much as possible; we will need it later. Teaching, correcting, and training will never reach where our hearts have not touched. Charles Finney said it this way:

> "If you accustom them to throw their little minds open to you, and to feel that you, in every thing sympathize with them, that they may have the most perfect confidence in you, you will naturally come to be, as you ought to be, their confident [sic] and their counselor. But if you will not give your time to this—if you turn them off and say, Oh, I cannot attend to you, or if you treat them harshly, or sarcastically—if you mortify them, and treat them with unkindness—if you manifest no sympathy with and for them, after repeated attempts to get at your heart, finding themselves baffled, they will turn sadly away, and by degrees seek sympathy and counsel from others. Thus you will lose your own influence over them, and give them over to other influences, that may ruin

them. How amazingly do parents err in these respects. Father [. . .] how sadly do you err—how grievously do you injure your children—nay, how almost certainly will you ruin them, if you drive them, by your own wickedness, or leave them, to seek for confidential companionship away from home.[79]

Our children will eventually outgrow our fences, so we must ensure that the real fences are in their hearts. There is enough of Adam born in our children to destroy them without outside influence. We have been called to lead them through the process of countering this inner Adam with the Word of God sown deep in their hearts.

Children cannot be pushed to spirituality, but they can be pulled. The difference is huge. To pull, the father must be spiritual first. Thankfully, whether in father or child, a right heart can make up for a lot of wrong moves.

Andrew Murray first penned these final thoughts.[80] Training is more than teaching. Prevention is better than cure. Example is better than precept. And love that draws is more than law that demands.

---

1. 2 Samuel 6:1-12
2. Rick Leibee, "More than Obed-edom" available at www.charitychristianfellowship.org/sermons/listing
3. Deuteronomy 6:4-9
4. Deuteronomy 32:7
5. Deuteronomy 32:46-47
6. Psalm 44:1
7. Psalm 145:4
8. Psalm 145:11-12
9. Proverbs 4:1-4
10. Charles Finney, "October 21, 1840 Letters to Parents—5" available at http://www.gospeltruth.net/children/401021_parents_5.htm
11. Exodus 4:10
12. Exodus 4:11-12
13. Denny Kenaston, "Father Is a Teacher" available at www.charitychristianfellowship.org/sermons/listing
14. *Id.*

15. Denny Kenaston, The Pursuit of Godly Seed, (2003) p. 201
16. Denny Kenaston, "Father Is a Teacher" available at www.charitychristianfellowship.org/sermons/listing
17. Psalm 19:8
18. Tedd and Margy Tripp, Instructing Your Child's Heart, (2008) p. 48
19. Isaiah 28:9-13
20. Denny Kenaston, The Pursuit of Godly Seed, (2003) pp. 204-205
21. William Booth, How to Make the Children into Saints and Soldiers of Jesus Christ, (1888) available at http://www.gospeltruth.net/children/booth_training.htm.
22. Andrew Murray, Raising Your Children for Christ, (1984) p. 294
23. Tedd and Margy Tripp, Instructing Your Child's Heart, (2008) p. 31
24. *Id.*
25. *Id.* p. 33
26. *Id.* p. 23
27. Emmett Cooper and Steve Wamberg, Making God's Word Stick, (1996) pp104-109
28. *Id.*
29. *Id.*
30. *Id.*
31. *Id.* p. 95
32. Proverbs 3:12
33. Hebrews 12:5-11
34. Denny Kenaston, The Pursuit of Godly Seed, (2003) p. 157
35. Proverbs 13:24
36. Proverbs 19:18
37. Proverbs 23:13-14
38. Proverbs 29:17
39. Proverbs 22:15
40. Proverbs 24:9
41. Ecclesiastes 10:1
42. Proverbs 29:15
43. Institute in Basic Youth Conflicts, Advanced Seminar Textbook, (1986) p. 27
44. Tedd Tripp, Shepherding Your Child's Heart (2005) p. 5
45. *Id.* p. 7
46. *Id.*
47. Tedd and Margy Tripp, Instructing Your Child's Heart, (2008) p. 53

48. Charles Finney, "October 21, 1840 Letters to Parents—5" available at http://www.gospeltruth.net/children/401021_parents_5.htm
49. Ecclesiastes 8:11
50. Denny Kenaston "Helpful Meditation" available at www.charitychristianfellowship.org/sermons/listing
51. *Id.*
52. *Id.*
53. Emmanuel Esh "The Defeated Father" available at www.charitychristianfellowship.org/sermons/listing
54. Charles Finney, "October 21, 1840 Letters to Parents—5" available at http://www.gospeltruth.net/children/401021_parents_5.htm
55. Denny Kenaston, "Helpful Meditation" available at www.charitychristianfellowship.org/sermons/listing
56. Proverbs 22:6
57. Andrew Murray, Raising Your Children for Christ, (1984) p. 279
58. William Booth, How to Make the Children into Saints and Soldiers of Jesus Christ, (1888) available at http://www.gospeltruth.net/children/booth_training.htm.
59. *Id.*
60. *Id.*
61. *Id.*
62. *Id.*
63. *Id.*
64. *Id.*
65. *Id.*
66. *Id.*
67. James Strong, The New Strong's Expanded Exhaustive Concordance of the Bible (2001) Strong's Hebrew # 2596
68. Proverbs 6:20-23
69. Denny Kenaston, "Helpful Meditation" available at www.charitychristianfellowship.org/sermons/listing
70. Henry Cloud and John Townsend, Raising Great Kids, (1999) p. 49
71. *Id.* p. 53
72. *Id.* p. 56-57
73. Tedd and Margy Tripp, Instructing Your Child's Heart, (2008) pp. 94-97
74. *Id.* pp. 105-106
75. *Id.*
76. *Id.* p. 147

77. *Id.* p. 150
78. Rick Leibee "Restraining—Beyond Just Training" available at www.charitychristianfellowship.org/sermons/listing
79. Charles Finney, "October 7, 1840 Letters to Parents—4" available at http://www.gospeltruth.net/children/401007_parents_4.htm
80. Andrew Murray, Raising Your Children for Christ, (1984) pp. 310-312

Reaping the Benefits

"As arrows are in the hand of a mighty man; so are children of the youth. Happy is the man that hath his quiver full of them: they shall not be ashamed, but they shall speak with the enemies in the gate." (Psalm 127:4,5)

While raising godly seed requires great focus, energy, and determination, it is also one of the most fulfilling callings we can ever pursue. Without doubt, this calling will demand self-disciple, self-denial, and self-sacrifice. However, the reward is beyond what words can attempt to describe. We are completely confident that those fathers who make the necessary discipline, denial, and sacrifice will never regret it. Many men from all walks of life have spent their last breath wishing they had spent more time at home. Rare indeed, however, is the man who regrets the things he sacrificed to be more intimate with his family.

In the coming pages, we rejoice to find that the godly heritage we pursue is one of the greatest treasures men have ever known. The Bible highly exalts the value of a child, and so have the great men of faith throughout all ages. Later, the Scriptures reveal that our children will be our disciples. We have the great blessing and responsibility of knowing that they will follow in our steps. After that, we focus the glory upon our heavenly Father, recognizing that we are only stewards of the children that ultimately belong to Him. Truly, the greatest blessing of fatherhood is the opportunity to offer our children back to God in thankfulness for all He has done.

CHAPTER 10

THE FATHER'S TREASURE: "THE HERITAGE OF THE LORD"

Only twenty years old, Ahaz takes his place as the king of Judah.[1] As a direct, royal descendent of David himself, Ahaz has the unchallenged right to the throne. Ahaz is king over a powerful and wealthy people, who are alternately blessed and chastened by the God of heaven. His ancestors brought peace to Israel, built Jerusalem, and erected an unparalleled temple to the Lord. More recently, his predecessors followed God, but on their own terms. As a part of the royal seed of David, Ahaz partakes of two great promises resulting from a covenant between God and that great king of Israel. First, his children are promised a continual seat on the throne of Judah. Most important, someday the Messiah is destined to come from his descendents. What a privilege! Ahaz stands in the unique place of knowing his family's past and future.

Enamored with the ways of the kings of the Northern Kingdom, King Ahaz loses sight of his place both as a descendent and an ancestor. Abandoning the old ways of David, Ahaz erects idols throughout Judah. He proceeds to worship them and offer incense unto gods of his own creation. In every hill and valley of Judah, King Ahaz defies the God of his fathers by sacrificing and burning incense unto pagan idols. Men have died for less. Yet, God is merciful and slow to judge.

One morning, King Ahaz summons his young children to accompany him for a time of idol worship. As they walk together hand in hand, the king fabricates stories of the greatness of his gods. The children listen with open hearts and wide eyes, amazed to hear of great works done by pieces of wood and stone. As they walk past the barricaded doors of Solomon's temple, they silently wonder about the power of the God who is rumored to dwell there. Vaguely, they recall the stories told to them by one of the servants about David and his covenant with that God. Suddenly, their attention goes to the steady sound of drums and ritualistic chanting from farther down in the valley. Hesitant, they look to their father's face for guidance and consolation. Their father smiles and, with a slight squeeze of the hand, guides them into the valley of Hinnom, which now has a strange orange glow.

As the royal family arrives at the center of the festivities, the chanting erupts into a frenzied scream. Frightened and confused, the young children bolt for higher ground. After only a few small steps, the king's guards seize them. Panicked, each child flails wildly until they see their father's outstretched arms. One by one, King Ahaz receives his children, embraces them, and personally throws them into the blazing inferno dedicated to the idol Molech.

King Ahaz has done the unthinkable. In killing his own children in sacrifice to a pagan god, he has broken covenant with the one true God. In that moment, he murdered his children, the descendents of David, and the potential ancestors of Jesus Christ. God will wink at his sin no longer.

Three generations later, the Babylonians are preparing to execute the judgment of God upon Judah for sins like those of Ahaz. In Judah, there is a brief moment of revival. Josiah, the eight-year-old great-grandson of the man who murdered his own children, takes the throne. As a passionate young man dedicated to the service of the true God, he leads all of Judah on a crusade against idolatry and paganism. He knows immediately where to start. Josiah descends into the valley of Hinnom and personally destroys the altar where his great-grandfather burned the children alive.[2] In honor of young Josiah's righteous zeal, God delays judgment for one more generation. In the end, King Josiah's valiant effort is too little, too late, and the sword of Babylon falls mightily on Jerusalem soon after his death.

The Bible makes clear that children are one of God's greatest blessings. They are a treasure to both God and their fathers. Yet, in every age of human history, fathers have valued other things more than their children. They have sacrificed God's treasure to many idols—sometimes literally, but more often in symbolic ways. God takes child sacrifice personally. His judgment against it is not long delayed. Throughout Scripture, the prohibition is clear, the violation intolerable, and the judgment swift.

Aware that Israel was entering a land full of pagans practicing abominations, God warned Israel to have no part in sacrificing their children. God commanded, "And thou shalt not let any of thy seed pass through the fire to Molech, neither shalt thou profane the name of thy

God: I am the LORD."³ Again He warned, "Thou shalt not do so unto the LORD thy God: for every abomination to the LORD, which he hateth, have they done unto their gods; for even their sons and their daughters they have burnt in the fire to their gods."⁴ God commanded Moses:

> "[S]ay to the children of Israel, Whosoever he be of the children of Israel, or of the strangers that sojourn in Israel, that giveth any of his seed unto Molech; [. . .] I will set my face against that man, and will cut him off from among his people; because he hath given of his seed unto Molech, to defile my sanctuary, and to profane my holy name."⁵

Thus, God made the command personal, saying that sacrificing their children would defile the sanctuary and profane His holy name.

Yet, Israel repeatedly ignored God's command. Looking back on Israel's sin, the psalmist wrote:

> "They did not destroy the nations, concerning whom the LORD commanded them: But were mingled among the heathen, and learned their works. And they served their idols: which were a snare unto them. Yea, they sacrificed their sons and their daughters unto devils, and shed innocent blood, even the blood of their sons and of their daughters, whom they sacrificed unto the idols of Canaan: and the land was polluted with blood."⁶

Here, God explains how Israel could do such unthinkable evil. First, they refused to destroy sin in the land. Then, they mingled with the heathen. As a result, they learned their works. After that, it was only a matter of time before they served their idols. Just as God had warned them, those idols became a snare. Finally, they sacrificed their own children to idols. Mingling with evil will always take us farther than we intended to go.

The prophets delivered God's final verdict on this terrible sin. Ezekiel prophesied that because Israel made their sons pass through the fire, God would no longer hear their prayers for deliverance.⁷ Jeremiah added:

> "And they built the high places of Baal, which are in the valley of the son of Hinnom, to cause their sons and their daughters to pass through the fire unto Molech; which I commanded them

not, neither came it into my mind, that they should do this abomination, to cause Judah to sin. And now therefore thus saith the LORD, the God of Israel, concerning this city, whereof ye say, It shall be delivered into the hand of the king of Babylon by the sword, and by the famine, and by the pestilence;"[8]

God makes clear that not only did He not command the sacrifice, but He cannot even imagine commanding such a thing. Ezekiel explained the heart of the issue:

"Moreover thou hast taken thy sons and thy daughters, whom thou hast borne unto me, and these hast thou sacrificed unto them to be devoured. Is this of thy whoredoms a small matter, That thou hast slain my children, and delivered them to cause them to pass through the fire for them?"[9]

God takes this sin personally because the children are born unto Him. They are, in every sense of the word, His children.

God's Children

Our children belong to God, and He is jealous over them with a godly jealousy. God orders us to carefully guard against compromising His children. God warns that the things fathers refuse to overcome will be snares, traps, scourges, and thorns that turn the children away from following God.[10]

God repeatedly declares His dealings with our children from the earliest moments. God is "He that formed thee from the womb."[11] God declares that His people are "borne by me from the belly, [and] are carried from the womb: And even to your old age I am he; and even to hoar hairs will I carry you: I have made, and I will bear; even I will carry, and will deliver you." God wants to be involved in every moment of the lives of our children. One of David's most beautiful and well-known psalms applies equally to our children:

"For thou hast possessed my reins: thou hast covered me in my mother's womb. I will praise thee; for I am fearfully and wonderfully made: marvellous are thy works; and that my soul knoweth right well. My substance was not hid from thee, when I was made in secret, and curiously wrought in the lowest parts of the earth. Thine eyes did see my substance, yet being unperfect; and in thy book all my members were written, which in continuance were fashioned, when as yet there was none of them. How precious also are thy thoughts unto me, O God! how great is the sum of them!"[12]

God is seeking a godly seed. As His people, our children belong to Him, and we must treat them accordingly. God is brooding over our children from the womb to the grave, and He is jealous over their hearts. Lest we still believe that God changed in the New Testament, Jesus repeatedly reveals God's focus on His children.

Jesus told His disciples, "Take heed that ye despise not one of these little ones; for I say unto you, That in heaven their angels do always behold the face of my Father which is in heaven."[13] The word "despise" means to think less of or esteem lightly.[14] Jesus personally compels us not to think lightly of the children He gave us. In another place, Jesus taught, "Whosoever shall receive one of such children in my name, receiveth me: and whosoever shall receive me, receiveth not me, but him that sent me."[15] The implication here is stunning for us as fathers. The way we receive our children indicates the way that we receive Jesus and the Father. Whatever we do or fail to do to the "least of these" we do or fail to do to Jesus.[16] Surely, our children are part of the least of these. Moreover, "[W]hosoever shall offend one of these little ones that believe in me, it is better for him that a millstone were hanged about his neck, and he were cast into the sea."[17] Fatherhood is no light calling. Just as with the child sacrifice in the valley of Himmon, everything we do to our children, we do to the Father who made them.

The Stewardship of Children

The Scriptures reveal that our children belong to God. They are given to us to be guarded and prepared for future work for God. He is jealous over them. Whatever we do to them, we do to Christ. The way we receive them is the way receive Christ and the Father. In sum, God has made us stewards of our children.

"Moreover it is required in stewards, that a man be found faithful."[18] Our children belong to God. What we do to them, we do to the child of God. If we offend them, we may earn a fierce and powerful enemy. Recognizing that we are stewards of God's children living temporarily in our homes, we must let that truth transform every part of our parenting. Thinking of our children as belonging to God, instead of belonging to us, raises the importance of succeeding in this calling. If we fail, we will fail a child of God. If we lose them to the world, then we lost a child of God. We must be found faithful to the call.

It is not normal to lose these precious children to the world. They are God's, and He intends to keep them in His kingdom. Yet, we are surrounded by an epidemic of departing young people. As stewards, we cannot be found faithful in such a condition. How many churches and families do we know that have successfully raised up a generation of soldiers to do battle for God? We owe it to the next generation to pay any price we must pay to leave them a holy example that they can follow as they raise their children.

Friendship with the world is the modern Nile into which the church is throwing its children.[19] In contrast, Andrew Murray explained, "The believing parent must live, act, and pray with and for his children, as one who is assured that his children are meant of God to be there in the ark with him."[20] Losing God's children must not be an option in our minds, and we must pay any price necessary to prevent such a loss.

But being a faithful steward goes far beyond just not losing God's children to the world. Consider this parable from the Lord:

> "He said therefore, A certain nobleman went into a far country to receive for himself a kingdom, and to return. And he called his ten servants, and delivered them ten pounds, and said unto them, Occupy till I come. [. . .] And it came to pass, that when he was returned, having received the kingdom, then he commanded these servants to be called unto him, to whom he had given the money, that he might know how much every man had gained by trading. [. . .] And another came, saying, Lord, behold, here is thy pound, which I have kept laid up in a napkin: For I feared thee, because thou art an austere man: thou takest up that thou layedst not down, and reapest that thou didst not sow. And he

saith unto him, Out of thine own mouth will I judge thee, thou wicked servant."[21]

Many times, the believing fathers who greatly desire to be found faithful will live a completely defensive life in fear of losing what God has entrusted to them. In the parable, the wicked servant did not do anything obviously wicked with the pound. He did not lose it, spend it, or invest it poorly. Instead, he wrapped it in a napkin and did nothing. For this alone, he was judged.

Similarly, God does not want us to be so consumed with not losing God's children that we fail to prepare them to be God's adults. In fact, God loves us and cares so much about our continued spiritual maturity that He is willing to risk placing His sons and daughters under our authority and training. Our mission is to raise godly adults, not just innocent children.

William Booth said, "Parents have no more right to train their children for the gratification of their own selfish interests and fancies than a steward has to use his master's property for his own personal advantage."[22] Rather than pursuing personal parenting goals, everything we are doing should be preparation for God to indwell our child through the baptism of the Holy Ghost. Consider the preparation involved in building Solomon's temple. Year after year and chapter after chapter, David, Solomon, and all of Israel prepared the temple. Every day of preparation was for that one glorious moment when the glory of God descended on that building. If God was so concerned about an earthly temple that He anointed the people who were building it, how much more will he anoint us to build His temple in the hearts of our children?

Consider also Christ's disciples. Each teaching, each miracle, and each conversation was preparation for the day of Pentecost. For most of the Gospels, the Lord appears to be wasting His time on these men. But in Acts chapter 2, they suddenly show the world that all the preparation had a great unseen purpose.

The same is true for our children. They desperately need a real conversion experience and the indwelling of the Holy Spirit. However, prior to conversion, we are decreasing the battles they will have to fight after conversion. By training the will, disciplining the emotions, and disciplining the body, fathers do a great service to both the child and the kingdom. When such a child is truly converted, there are no limits to what God can do with such a prepared vessel.

What kind of house do we want? What type of stewards do we want to be? What kind of spiritual inheritance do we want our children to have? Are we laying a foundation with our lives that will get us to that destination? We are talking about building the kind of homes that Jesus and John the Baptist grew up in as children.[23] Let each child know early and often that he has been given to God. If we inform them that this truth causes us to control them in certain ways, as that truth internalizes they will control themselves for the same reason.[24]

Every father ought to look upon their child as a sacred trust from Jehovah. Indeed, that is exactly what has happened. William Booth said it this way:

> "[God] has entrusted you with that boy or girl in order that you may lead it to the Savior, train it in holy living, instruct it as to the nature of the foul rebellion raging against His authority, and inspire it with undying devotion to His cause. In other words, that you may mould and shape it into a holy, loving saint, fit for the worship of God and the companionship of angels in heaven, and into a courageous, self-sacrificing, skilful warrior, able to war a good warfare on His behalf on earth. How will you deal with your trust?"[25]

The question echoes to us as fathers in this day, and the question demands an answer. How will we deal with our trust?

Esteeming the Treasure

While King Ahaz—and far too many others—devalue the blessing of having children, the Bible also includes a large group of fathers that clearly recognized the invaluable treasure of children. Consider Noah, who "prepared an ark to the saving of his house."[26] He must have realized anew how important his children were as he gathered with his sons and their wives inside the ark. Noah's three sons were, quite literally, the hope and future of humanity.

Throughout Abraham's long struggle of faith, the value he placed on children is clear. Time and again, the patriarch prays for a son. He plainly declared that all the natural blessings he received from God meant little if he died without children. Indeed, God lovingly declares of His friend,

The Calling of Fatherhood

"I know him, that he will command his children and his household after him, and they shall keep the way of the LORD."[27]

One of the greatest examples in Scripture begins in the town of Bethlehem. There, a godly man named Boaz takes faithful Ruth to be his wife. Soon thereafter, God "gave her conception, and she bare a son."[28] Young Obed matured in the love and grace of this household of faith. We know almost nothing about him, other than the fact that he, too, raised a godly young man by the name of Jesse. This amazing father, Jesse, raised a family of at least nine children. The prophet Samuel was willing to anoint any one of his eight sons as king over Israel. His youngest, David, fought giants, ruled over Israel, and wrote a substantial portion of the Bible. From his youth, David was known throughout Israel as "a son of Jesse the Bethlehemite, that is cunning in playing, and a mighty valiant man, and a man of war, and prudent in matters, and a comely person, and the LORD is with him."[29]

The rest of Jesse's children trained up faithful children after them. Jesse's daughter, Zeruiah, birthed Joab, Abishai, and Asahel, great men in David's army.[30] David's brother Shimea had a son named Jonathan that killed another giant from Gath.[31] No wonder David could write, "The lines are fallen unto me in pleasant places; yea, I have a goodly heritage."[32] Like Boaz and Ruth, we can hardly imagine the treasure that God may produce in our generations if we trust Him completely.

While church history is full of families that counted each child a blessing, one story in particular illustrates the beautiful heritage of generations of godly seed. On February 1, 1776, James Taylor rose early to tend to the animals.[33] His wedding was only hours away, and he wrestled with his conscience as he labored in the barn. The words from a sermon echoed time and again in his mind. "As for me and my house, we shall serve the Lord." James was not prepared to lay that kind of foundation. Hounded by the conviction of God, James Taylor collapsed in the hay and poured out his heart to God. He tarried there in the presence of God so long that he was late for his own wedding.

As the years passed, James Taylor became a Methodist preacher and friend of John Wesley.[34] For his service in his small English town, James would suffer persecution, including having glass shards shoved into his eyes.[35] His son, John Taylor, became a successful Christian businessman and faithful minister in the local church.[36] John's son was also named James, and he also grew up to be a godly father. Young James Taylor and his wife were deeply convicted about having children, and before their firstborn was born, they dedicated him to the Lord.[37]

Hudson Taylor was the firstborn son in this dedicated home. As a child, Hudson and his siblings gladly recalled the faithfulness of great-grandfather James Taylor.[38] The children would often play in the home, pretending to be John Wesley and his brave Methodist preachers. Every night, Hudson heard his father praying for God to send someone to China to preach the Gospel. At five years old, Hudson Taylor knelt in prayer and dedicated his life to answering his father's prayers.[39] At seventeen, Hudson fully surrendered His life to follow Christ and labor in China as a missionary.[40]

As a result, God worked mightily in Hudson's life. Hudson's work in China was one of the greatest missionary successes since the Apostle Paul. To this day, the descendents of the Taylor family are faithfully laboring in the mission field.[41] The foundation laid in that barn by James Taylor on his wedding day has now supported at least nine generations of faithful children.[42] No treasure on earth can compare to such a heritage.

The Bible repeatedly reveals the treasure of children. A wise son "maketh a glad father."[43] "Children's children are the crown of old men; and the glory of children are their fathers."[44] Solomon wrote, "My son, if thine heart be wise, my heart shall rejoice, even mine. Yea, my reins shall rejoice, when thy lips speak right things."[45] He continued, "The father of the righteous shall greatly rejoice: and he that begetteth a wise child shall have joy of him. Thy father and thy mother shall be glad, and she that bare thee shall rejoice."[46] Also, "My son, be wise, and make my heart glad, that I may answer him that reproacheth me."[47] John wrote, "I rejoiced greatly that I found of thy children walking in truth, as we have received a commandment from the Father."[48] John also said, "I have no greater joy than to hear that my children walk in truth."[49] The Bible continually celebrates the value of children.

Despite the fact that the Scriptures continually exclaim the value of our children, the church often reflects a completely different view. Many Christians find it difficult or impossible to think of children as a blessing. Foolishness is often the cause of this conflict. Proverbs declares, "He that begetteth a fool doeth it to his sorrow: and the father of a fool hath no joy."[50]

We must learn how to unbind our children from the foolishness that is bound in their hearts. Foolishness is not a stage of juvenile development.

It is a curse that will restrict our children from their potential in God. We need to unbind our children from the "terrible two's" before they follow the same patterns in the terrible twenties. If we dedicate ourselves to this cause, our relationships with our children can and should be some of the best Christian fellowship in our lives. In contrast, if we permit foolishness to fester in their hearts, our children can cause us unimaginable grief and pain. Each day, we decide anew which end we will pursue.

How much is blessing is too much?

The generational harvest resulting from godly homes is truly overwhelming. If one couple has only six children, and each generation repeats that number, the couple would have over seven thousand direct descendents in only five generations. Such a successful lineage would empower our witness to the world. Additionally, being a part of such a family is enthralling, for there is no greater joy than to spend and be spent for young people who want to serve God.

In their book, *A Full Quiver*, Rick and Jan Hess fully explain the blessing of letting God control the size of your family. In their survey of church history, the Hess family found some amazing results.[51] Jonathan Edwards was the eleventh child in his family. Charles Finney was seventh. Nate Saint was seventh of eight children. D.L. Moody was sixth of eight. Susanna Wesley was twenty-fourth. She in turn had John and Charles Wesley, her fourteenth and seventeenth children, respectively. Solomon wrote, "In the multitude of people is the king's honour: but in the want of people is the destruction of the prince."[52] As the Hess family reminds us, God has so much work to do that we can never have too many children dedicated to His cause.[53] Indeed, the work of God would have been greatly hindered if any one of the families mentioned above had stopped having children one child too soon.

Dear brothers, we must search our hearts to determine why we would hesitate to accept another blessing from God. Children are one of the greatest blessings that God can ever give. The Bible is full of faithful fathers who realized the eternal value of their children. Let us, then, fully dedicate ourselves to the pursuit of godly seed. And, if God chooses to bless us abundantly, let us gladly receive His blessing and rejoice in the treasure that only God can give.

1. 2 Chronicles 28:1-4
2. 2 Kings 23:10
3. Leviticus 18:21
4. Deuteronomy 12:31
5. Leviticus 20:2-3
6. Psalms 106:34-38
7. Ezekiel 20:30-31
8. Jeremiah 32:35-36
9. Ezekiel 16:20-21
10. Joshua 23:11-13; Deuteronomy 7:1-4
11. Isaiah 44:24
12. Psalm 139:13-17
13. Matthew 18:10
14. James Strong, The New Strong's Expanded Exhaustive Concordance of the Bible (2001) Strong's Greek #2706
15. Mark 9:36-37
16. Matthew 25:40,45
17. Mark 9:42
18. 1 Corinthians 4:2
19. Andrew Murray, Raising Your Children for Christ, (1984) p. 50
20. *Id.* p. 23
21. Luke 19:12-24
22. William Booth, How to Make the Children into Saints and Soldiers of Jesus Christ, (1888) available at http://www.gospeltruth.net/children/booth_training.htm.
23. Denny Kenaston, The Pursuit of Godly Seed, (2003) p. 104
24. Andrew Murray, Raising Your Children for Christ, (1984) p. 110
25. William Booth, How to Make the Children into Saints and Soldiers of Jesus Christ, (1888) available at http://www.gospeltruth.net/children/booth_training.htm.
26. Hebrews 11:7
27. Genesis 18:17-19
28. Ruth 4:13
29. 1 Samuel 16:18-19
30. 2 Samuel 2:18; 23:18-24
31. 1 Chronicles 20:6-7
32. Psalms 16:6

33. Howard Taylor, The Growth of a Soul, p.3
34. *Id.* p.13
35. *Id.* p. 13-14
36. *Id.* p. 21-25
37. *Id.* p. 34
38. *Id.* p. 37
39. *Id.* p. 37
40. *Id.* p. 69
41. http://www.omf.org/omf/us/about_omf_international/news/james_hudson_taylor_iii_with_christ
42. http://www.omf.org/omf/us/about_omf_international/news/james_hudson_taylor_iii_with_christ
43. Proverbs 10:1; 15:20
44. Proverbs 17:6
45. Proverbs 23:15-16
46. Proverbs 23:24-25
47. Proverbs 27:11
48. 2nd John 1:4
49. 3rd John 1:4
50. Proverbs 17:21
51. Rick and Jan Hess, A Full Quiver, (1989) p. 54
52. Proverbs 14:28; cf. Rick and Jan Hess, A Full Quiver, (1989) p. 169
53. Rick and Jan Hess, A Full Quiver, (1989) p. 169

CHAPTER 11

THE FATHER'S DISCIPLES: "THE HOUSE OF THE RECHABITES"

In the hills outside Jerusalem, a young man grieves over the sin of his beloved nation. For generations, his family has observed the people repent only to forsake the Lord later and return to idolatry. His father has often told him of the judgment that God sends upon His people for their evil ways, and now the young man cannot help but wonder when the next great judgment will come. It is certainly long overdue.

As he walks away from the city, the evil scenes he witnessed there still haunt his thoughts. How the holy city has fallen since those great days when Solomon dedicated the temple! Slowly, he turns toward Jerusalem, remembering how Solomon prayed that God would always hear the cries of His people when they turned to the temple. With his eyes fixed upon the house of God, the young man cries out aloud for guidance. "God of our fathers, how can I raise my family in a land that has forgotten you?" Slowly, the answer comes. And Jonadab, the son of Rechab, returns home with new conviction.

Several generations later, the prophet Jeremiah weeps over an idolatrous nation. Called by God to declare His judgment upon Judah, Jeremiah is tormented night and day by the visions he receives from the Lord. This night, though, the vision is different. The word of the Lord comes to Jeremiah, "Go unto the house of the Rechabites, and speak unto them, and bring them into the house of the LORD, into one of the chambers, and give them wine to drink."[1] Curious, Jeremiah summons Jaazaniah and the other Rechabites and invites them to join him at the temple.

Once the Rechabites take their seats, Jeremiah serves each of them wine and tells them to drink. With one accord, the men respond, "We will drink no wine: for Jonadab the son of Rechab our father commanded us, saying, 'Ye shall drink no wine, neither ye, nor your sons for ever: Neither

The Calling of Fatherhood

shall ye build house, nor sow seed, nor plant vineyard, nor have any: but all your days ye shall dwell in tents; that ye may live many days in the land where ye be strangers.' Thus have we obeyed the voice of Jonadab the son of Rechab our father in all that he hath charged us [. . .] we, our wives, our sons, [and] our daughters."

As Jeremiah stands in silent respect of the testimony before him, the word of the LORD comes again:

> "Thus saith the LORD of hosts, the God of Israel; Go and tell the men of Judah and the inhabitants of Jerusalem, Will ye not receive instruction to hearken to my words? saith the LORD. The words of Jonadab the son of Rechab, that he commanded his sons not to drink wine, are performed; for unto this day they drink none, but obey their father's commandment: notwithstanding I have spoken unto you, rising early and speaking; but ye hearkened not unto me. [. . .] Because the sons of Jonadab the son of Rechab have performed the commandment of their father, which he commanded them; but this people hath not hearkened unto me: Therefore thus saith the LORD God of hosts, the God of Israel; Behold, I will bring upon Judah and upon all the inhabitants of Jerusalem all the evil that I have pronounced against them."

Then, turning to the family gathered before him, Jeremiah says to the descendents of Jonadab, "Because ye have obeyed the commandment of Jonadab your father, and kept all his precepts, and done according unto all that he hath commanded you: Therefore thus saith the LORD of hosts, the God of Israel; Jonadab the son of Rechab shall not want a man to stand before me for ever." Thus, the obedience of the sons of Rechab judges a nation, and God honors their faithfulness to their father.

The story of the Rechabites is dear to many fathers who accept God's call to seek a godly seed. It should be. One father loved his family enough to give them special guidance. Despite the fact that his commands went beyond chapter and verse of Scripture, Jonadab's children and their descendents honored him with total obedience. Even the offer from the prophet Jeremiah was unable to shake their convictions. As a result, God exalted the Rechabites as an example and a judgment to an entire nation, and promised them that their descendents would forever have a place in

His kingdom. Oh, that we would be so faithful that God could say the same of our generations!

Go and Make Disciples

God commands fathers to make disciples in their home. Like the other principles we have seen, this command is not isolated in some single passage of Scripture. The discipleship of children is a continual theme of the Bible. God calls fathers to "obey his voice according to all that I command thee this day, thou and thy children, with all thine heart, and with all thy soul."[2] God desires fathers to hear, learn, fear, and observe the Word of God "that their children, which have not known any thing, may hear, and learn to fear the LORD your God, as long as ye live[.]"[3] Solomon adds that "A good man leaveth an inheritance to his children's children [. . . .]"[4] As Jonadab's story shows, the inheritance of dedication to God will long outlast homes, money, and possessions.

The command to disciple children continues in the New Testament. Paul ordered his followers to "teach the young women" to be sober, love their husbands, love their children, be discreet, be chaste, be keepers at home, be good, and be obedient to their own husbands, that the word of God be not blasphemed.[5] Paul also told his followers to teach the young men to be sober minded, to be a pattern of good works, to be uncorrupt in doctrine, to be grave, to be sincere, and to use sound speech that cannot be condemned, that the enemy would have no evil thing to say of them.[6] Without doubt, this discipleship is best accomplished within a godly home.

Accidental Disciples

Making disciples of your children requires great focus. The necessity of focus rises not from the difficulty of making disciples at home, but rather from the ease of doing so accidently. Fathers reproduce after their own kind whether we like it or not. If we refuse to focus on this responsibility and become distracted by the cares of life or ministry, we will soon have the testimony of the Samaritans. "So these nations feared the LORD, and served their graven images, both their children, and their children's children: as did their fathers, so do they unto this day."[7]

Abraham, one of the most revered fathers in the history of parenting, had two unfortunate experiences in accidental discipleship. For all his qualities—and they are many—Abraham had two flaws that he passed to his young disciple, Isaac. First, Abraham had an obvious problem with favoritism that naturally flowed from having one child of promise and several children of the flesh. Second, Abraham engaged in deception. In one famous instance, Abraham told Pharaoh that Sarah was only his sister in an attempt to save his life while surrendering his wife to unspeakable abuse.[8] Several chapters later, Abraham used the same tactics to deceive Abimelech, king of Gerar, into thinking that Sarah was Abraham's sister.[9]

Isaac learned these two lessons all too well. The favoritism that occurred between twin sons Jacob and Esau is infamous. Also, when Isaac went to Abimelech, king of Gerar, the exact same king his father Abraham deceived, Isaac told the exact same lie and claimed that Rebekah was his sister.[10] Worse, unlike his father, Isaac could not even defend his deceit with the excuse Abraham had used. Like Abraham, Isaac eventually had a young pair of eyes watching him.

Jacob learned his lessons of accidental discipleship well, and he followed them religiously. Jacob's favoritism toward Joseph is legendary. Jacob even multiplied the problem by showing favoritism among his wives. In addition, deceit was Jacob's mode of operation for most of his life. As his predecessors before him, Jacob accidently passed these traits to his own young disciples. The sons of Jacob took deceit to its deepest level, betraying their brother and then fabricating a story that nearly killed Jacob with grief. Thus, even great men of faith who lose focus can reveal the danger of accidental discipleship.

While Abraham, Isaac, and Jacob passed on some negative traits, other fathers in the Bible predestined their young disciples for total failure. In the battlefield of Mount Gilboa, the slain bodies of sons Abinadab, Malchishua, and valiant Jonathan gave testimony to their failed discipleship to King Saul.[11] In the pompous Sanhedrin, men stopped their ears as young Stephen declared with holy zeal, "Ye do always resist the Holy Ghost: as your fathers did, so do ye. Which of the prophets have not your fathers persecuted? And they have slain them which shewed before of the coming of the Just One; of whom ye have been now the betrayers and murderers."[12]

We will make disciples of our children whether we focus or not. We must choose to give this mission proper attention. What kind of disciples do we want to make? With each passing day, every father forms his children either in his own likeness or into the likeness of Christ. Like Paul, let it be said of our disciples that they follow us as we follow Christ.

The Importance of Disciples

The Bible repeatedly illustrates the importance of creating disciples. We see the heart of a young disciple in the plea of Ruth to her mother-in-law. "Intreat me not to leave thee, or to return from following after thee: for whither thou goest, I will go; and where thou lodgest, I will lodge: thy people shall be my people, and thy God my God: Where thou diest, will I die, and there will I be buried: the LORD do so to me, and more also, if ought but death part thee and me."[13] God desires that every child could say something similar to their father.

The Apostle Paul illustrates the importance of discipleship in his relationships with the young men who followed him, especially Timothy. Paul tells the church in Philippi that he will send them Timothy because he has no man so likeminded and selfless.[14] Paul adds, "[Y]e know the proof of him, that, as a son with the father, he hath served with me in the gospel."[15] Paul had such a beautiful vision of the discipleship that occurs between father and son that he used that relationship as a picture of how he related to his dearest convert.

When Timothy needed encouragement, Paul wrote "[C]ontinue thou in the things which thou hast learned and hast been assured of, knowing of whom thou hast learned them; And that from a child thou hast known the holy scriptures, which are able to make thee wise unto salvation through faith which is in Christ Jesus."[16] Paul also focused Timothy on the goal by writing, "the things that thou hast heard of me among many witnesses, the same commit thou to faithful men, who shall be able to teach others also."[17] As Paul penned some of the final words he would ever write, his great concern was that Timothy would pass the faith to others who would continue the work they both loved.

In the middle of an incredible ministry, Jesus never lost focus on His twelve disciples. The night before the crucifixion, Jesus mentioned the disciples in prayer over forty times.[18] Consider carefully what they accomplished after He was gone. Those twelve were not a waste of life. They were the very key to the lasting success of His ministry. Our children are the same for us.

If there remains any doubt about the importance of disciples, consider the fact that the word disciple appears over 260 times in the Gospels and Acts. That's more than the words salvation, love, and charity are mentioned in the entire New Testament—combined. Discipleship is at the heart of the Great Commission and is among the chief goals of Christian parenting.

In order to make disciples of our children, we must remember a few key points about disciples. First, Henrichsen explains that a disciple is different from a pupil.[19] Being a disciple is voluntary. There is no conscription in discipleship. As a result, disciples must be won, before they can ever be commanded.[20] In order to inspire a discipleship that will endure the tests of time, we fathers must win our children to a vision, not a particular person, family, or local assembly.[21]

Second, the discipler is always a link between God and the disciple.[22] Discipleship is a commitment to a person. Most importantly, discipleship is a commitment to the person of Christ.[23] This commitment to a person is what caused Paul to call his disciples "followers of us and the Lord."[24]

Third, disciples are the key to passing the faith to the next generations. Converts and believers are nice for filling a sanctuary on Sunday morning, but disciples are the pillars of the church. Disciples must be taught to recognize gifts that can be developed to help the body of Christ and opportunities that must be sacrificed to bring them closer in line with the plan of God. Discipleship requires stronger convictions and greater perspective.[25] Through God's grace, our children can go beyond even discipleship to become pacesetters and examples for the church of God.

Remember, though, that we may have to subtract before we can multiply. Even simple things often must be done slower in order to train children as disciples. Consider how long Christ belabored key points before His disciples ingrained those thoughts into their identity.

The heart of the Great Commission is discipleship, and discipleship begins at home. Even Timothy, who we discussed above as the beloved disciple of Paul the Apostle, actually began his discipleship under his faithful mother and grandmother. Be encouraged, brethren. We don't need to abandon everything for the full-time ministry to be able to fulfill the Great Commission. Each father first needs to get home to disciple his wife and children.[26] We need to make ample time for our young disciples. If Jesus would have included his disciples with Him in whatever we are doing, we should include our disciples with us too.[27]

William Booth said it this way:

"If children see before their eyes their own parents acting from godly motives and godly principles, supported by Divine power, experiencing Divine consolations, revelations, and joys, such unbelief to such children is at once and for ever made impossible. When tempted by books, atheists, and devils in after days to doubt and question the reality of supernatural and Divine things, the sainted form of such a departed parent will rise before them, and the exclamation will unconsciously rise to their lips, 'The example of my glorified father, or sainted mother, utterly forbids.'"[28]

Is this not our heart's cry, dear brothers? Let us leave such a holy example to our children that they will stand in faith and refuse all compromise because the example we leave them utterly forbids it.

---

1. Jeremiah 35:1-19
2. Deuteronomy 30:1-3
3. Deuteronomy 31:12-13
4. Proverbs 13:22
5. Titus 2:4-5
6. Titus 2:6-8
7. 2 Kings 17:41
8. Genesis 12:11-13
9. Genesis 20:1-2
10. Genesis 26:1-9
11. 1 Samuel 31:1-3
12. Acts 7:51-52
13. Ruth 1:16-17
14. Philippians 2:19-22
15. Philippians 2:22
16. 2 Timothy 3:14-15
17. 2 Timothy 2:2
18. Walter A. Henrichsen, Disciples Are Made—Not Born, (1983) p. 7
19. Walter A. Henrichsen, How to Disciple Your Children, (1981) p. 11
20. *Id.* p 13
21. Walter A. Henrichsen, Disciples Are Made—Not Born, (1983) p. 65
22. Walter A. Henrichsen, How to Disciple Your Children, (1981) p. 12
23. *Id.* p 14

24. 1Thessalonians 1:6
25. Walter A. Henrichsen, Disciples Are Made—Not Born, (1983) p. 113
26. Steve Farrar, Finishing Strong, (1995) p. 52
27. *Id.* p. 52
28. William Booth, How to Make the Children into Saints and Soldiers of Jesus Christ, (1888) available at http://www.gospeltruth.net/children/booth_training.htm.

CHAPTER 12

THE FATHER'S OFFERING: "A FAITHFUL STEWARD"

For decades, he prayed. During the day, Abram could keep himself busy with the responsibilities of life. At night, though, the stars mocked him. "Number the stars," God had said. How many times had he done that over the years? In the beginning, he would relax at the end of the day and count the stars while he imagined his descendants multiplying before his eyes. Those memories now seem so long ago. That was before he doubted God enough to lie about his wife. That was before Sarai passed the last of her childbearing years without a single pregnancy. That was before Hagar.

How he regrets that mistake! Things were simpler when Eliezer was his heir. Abram can still recall how he argued with God that night, complaining that his steward from Damascus was in line to inherit everything he owned. He can still see the fire appearing from nowhere and passing between the sacrifices. God had sworn by Himself. God had made a covenant. And then nothing happened. At his wife's urging, Abram had solved the problem himself, and literally begat a disaster in his family.

For thirteen years, God remains silent. The price for his sin is almost more than Abram can bear. God has surely abandoned him, finally disgusted with Abram's greatest display of doubt. His own body now infertile, Abram abandons all hope of another child. Then, as Abram watches the stars mock him for yet another night, the voice returns. God repeats His covenant. Abram is beyond arguing now. Instead, the ninety-nine-year-old man falls to the ground and laughs at God. Yet, as a remnant of faith flickers in his aging heart, Abraham circumcises himself, his son, and all the men in his house in obedience to the covenant of God.

One year later, the unbelievable occurs. Abraham and Sarah bring forth Isaac through a miracle of God. As Abraham dedicates his only legitimate heir to God, tears of rejoicing wash away the agony of decades of delay and doubt. Surely, the test is finally over.

Over the following years, Abraham puts into practice the principles that had long ago caused God to confidently declare that Abraham would command his children after him. Each day, Abraham thanks God for the miraculous son who is quickly growing into a young man. Isaac is proving more than capable of taking over the household whenever the need arises.

One day, the voice returns. God's command is unthinkable. To sacrifice his only son, Abraham must overcome every doubt and fear that has plagued him for so long. His fear of death twice caused him to offer his wife to a pagan king. Now, he only wishes that he could sacrifice himself in Isaac's place. His doubts concerning the promised child have caused untold hardship. Now, God demands Abraham face that test one more time. Through his obedience, God will transform Abraham from a selfish, fearful doubter into the spiritual father of all the faithful who will ever dare to follow God completely.

In a story that will be told for all eternity, Abraham awakens his son and prepares for the journey. This time, for once, there will be neither argument nor laughter in response to God's command. With each step of the three day trip, Abraham and Isaac declare their absolute surrender to and dependence upon the God of heaven. At the top of the mountain, Abraham builds the altar and lays each piece of wood in its proper place.

Isaac steps forward and accepts the bonds. With strength that can only come to the man who has touched the heart of God, Abraham lifts his son onto the altar. With a cry from his father's heart that only the heavenly Father can fully understand, Abraham raises the knife and brings it down towards his son. "Abraham, Abraham!" He freezes instantly. "Lay not thine hand upon the lad, neither do thou any thing unto him: for now I know that thou fearest God, seeing thou hast not withheld thy son, thine only son from me."[1]

The Greatest Offering

As He did with Abraham, God has a right to our children. They belong to Him. They came from Him. God alone gives life, and He gives our children life because He seeks a godly seed in the earth for His greater glory. Lest we ever think God demands too much from us, God went one step beyond even dear Abraham. We all know the Scripture. "For God so loved the world, that he gave his only begotten Son, that whosoever believeth in him should not perish, but have everlasting life. For God sent not his Son into the world to condemn the world; but that the world through him might be saved."[2] God gave us His only Son. We certainly can humbly offer Him our children in return.

Abraham was not alone in his faithful offering. Many others have joined him, and we do not have space to list them all here. We cannot proceed, however, without mentioning two more names. The first child to open a barren womb often seems to inspire exceptional levels of devotion. Hannah represents this point at its best. Her dedication of Samuel has sown seeds of faith in the hearts of parents for millennia. "For this child I prayed; and the LORD hath given me my petition which I asked of him: Therefore also I have lent him to the LORD; as long as he liveth he shall be lent to the LORD."[3] God rarely rejects the offering of a child by a dedicated parent, and God used Samuel in great and wonderful ways. He will do the same with our children if we offer them as Hannah did.

"They brought him to Jerusalem, to present him to the Lord."[4] A process that every good Jew had followed for centuries had new importance for the young couple walking toward the temple. Joseph and Mary brought no ordinary child this day. They were presenting the Messiah. No doubt their minds were full of dangerous threats, stern warnings, and overwhelming promises as they presented that infant to His Father. In many ways, the baby dedication that Joseph and Mary experienced is unique in all human history. Yet, their experience highlights an important point for all of us. When Joseph and Mary dedicated the infant Jesus, they were really dedicating themselves. When they offered Him to God, they were really offering themselves. There is no other way.

While God has called us as fathers to build godly homes and seek a godly seed, we must not be confused about this purpose. Our homes are not for us; our homes exist for God. God is not hesitant to use our homes. He is not afraid to use our young people. We cannot be afraid to let Him.

Watching our children suffer can be devastatingly painful, but Gary Thomas suggests that our hardest hurt may be their most important hurt.[5] We cannot protect them from the demands of the gospel. If we remove the cross from our child's Christianity, we leave them with merely a meaningless religion with irrelevant moral teachings. A Christianity that does not cost

The Calling of Fatherhood

anything in the way of real sacrifice is a Christianity that has no value to the next generation. Thomas writes, "God's kingdom far outweighs in significance the personal comfort of my children."[6] If God allowed His own Son to go to the cross for the sake of the kingdom, we must come to accept the fact that God is not beyond allowing our children to suffer for the kingdom as well.[7] If God would so permit, may we forbid it?

In almost every earthly profession, there are more applicants than can possibly be accepted. Yet, the kingdom of heaven is dreadfully short on laborers. Let us lay our children upon this altar and prepare them to work for the kingdom. Yes, the labor may cost them dearly. This offering may cut us to the core. Sending money and clothes to help the needy is easy. Sending a dearly beloved child to build the kingdom of heaven in their midst is something else entirely.

Our natural tendency is to protect our children. That tendency is enhanced and exercised by a conservative lifestyle that calls fathers to protect their children from the world's attacks. Yet, at some point—likely about twenty years old—the relationship changes and we welcome our children to the battlefield. To understand that part of the father's offering, consider the prayer of Jesus shortly before heading to Calvary. Only slight adaptations make His prayer applicable to this issue.

> "I have manifested thy name unto the [children] which thou gavest me [. . .]: thine they were, and thou gavest them me; and they have kept thy word. Now they have known that all things whatsoever thou hast given me are of thee. For I have given unto them the words which thou gavest me; and they have received them, [. . . .] I pray for them: I pray not for the world, but for them which thou hast given me; for they are thine. And all mine are thine [. . . .] Holy Father, keep through thine own name those whom thou hast given me, that they may be one, as we are. While I was with them in the world, I kept them in thy name: those that thou gavest me I have kept, and none of them is lost, [. . .] I have given them thy word; and the world hath hated them, because they are not of the world, even as I am not of the world. I pray not that thou shouldest take them out of the world, but that thou shouldest keep them from the evil. They are not of the world, even as I am not of the world. Sanctify them through thy truth: thy word is truth. [. . .] And for their sakes I sanctify myself, that

they also might be sanctified through the truth. Neither pray I for these alone, but for them also which shall believe [. . .] through their word."[8]

Remember, our children are our disciples, either accidentally or on purpose. Let us purpose to offer our disciples to the Father just as Jesus did.

An Offering God Honors

God does not take the paternal influence in this issue lightly. As in Isaiah's day, God is asking, "Whom shall I send, and who will go for us?"[9] Sadly, few young people are adequately prepared to volunteer the way Isaiah did. God is searching for young people who are prepared to labor, and He gives great weight to the father's role in preparing and offering the child for service to the King.

God's honor of fathers in this regard has both a negative and a positive context. God reveals the negative context in the Law. If a young woman made a vow to the Lord while she still lived in her father's house, the father had two options.[10] The father could "hold his peace" and permit the young woman to perform her vows to God. Alternatively, the father could "disallow her" from performing her vows. In such a case, God would forgive the vow and avoid forcing the young woman to choose between lying to God or dishonoring her father.[11]

On the positive side, God has honored many fathers by helping the children perform specific tasks that the father offered his children to perform. Heman was a prophet of God in Israel.[12] King David requested Heman be part of a group of musical prophets who blended the gifts of prophecy and music. God blessed Heman with seventeen children. "All these were under the hands of their father for song in the house of the LORD, with cymbals, psalteries, and harps, for the service of the house of God[.]"[13] God blessed this man with seventeen children, and then he honored him by putting all seventeen children in the ministry with him. Similarly, God permitted Solomon to build the temple that David longed to build.[14]

Preparing our children to be an offering to God certainly requires extra focus and determination. Many fathers refuse to pay the extra price. Many people say "I think that my children will turn out OK." Brethren, we must lift our eyes higher than mere survival. Our children can be leaders, missionaries, and pillars in the house of God. They are indeed the very dwelling place of the God of heaven. We need not settle for anything less than the absolute best that our children can have in God.

As we discussed, God has a right to each child's life. However, God not only has a right to each child, but the kingdom needs them. Joshua's famous declaration that he and his house would serve the Lord was a dedication to service, not just salvation. If more Christian fathers dedicated themselves, their wives, and their children to the service of God, we would not have the problems we now have with losing the next generation.[15]

Bill Gothard reminds us that one focus in preparing our children to be an offering for God is teaching our children to be able to stand alone.[16] One unusual side effect of attending a conservative church or enrolling our children in a Christian school is the false presumption that such children need not be prepared to stand alone. However, true righteousness will be unpopular even in Christian circles. Therefore, we must prepare our children to do right no matter the cost even if we barely expect them to face negative peer pressure before they are eighteen years old. Pressure to compromise exists even in the strictest churches and schools.

Encouraging our children to reach their potential is a natural part of parenting. More than any earthly potential, however, we need to help our children see the potential of conforming to the image of Christ. We must encourage them to sacrifice for God and seek His will for their lives. We are not raising godly seed so that they can sit next to us in church all their lives or own homes just down the street from ours. Self-protection is a difficult sin to catch, but it is a sin in this context. Remember, the steward who hides his talent in the napkin is harshly judged by the King.

Four Great Reasons for the Offering

William Booth notes that there are four great reasons to offer our children in the service of God.[17] Each one taken alone would justify every effort we can put forth on behalf of our children. Proper training can make sure of them all.

The first reason is the welfare of the children. While the testimonies of the prodigals can be moving examples of grace, we do not want our children to come to salvation with detours through any of the earthly hells of sin only to "land at the Saviour's feet with broken health, shattered minds, and dissipated habits, destroying every possibility of usefulness, or requiring a life-time to repair the havoc wrought."[18] Instead, we take our children by the hand in their youth, inform them often that they are dedicated to the work of God in the world, and help them to bow and submit their will to God. A child can be preserved from evil influences, relationships, and habits, and be instead "regenerated by the Holy Ghost and doubly strengthened to walk the slippery paths of youth[.]"[19] With such a foundation, our children can "face victoriously all the opposition that earth and Hell can bring against their future holy career."[20]

The second reason to offer our children early to the cause of Christ is our own interest. Booth challenges us to acknowledge that "This child, if it lives, is destined to exert a most serious influence for good or evil over my heart, and over my life, and over my home, and over all my associations[.]"[21] If our children serve God well, there is no greater joy on earth. On the contrary, if our children abandon the faith, "it will be a never-failing cause of anxiety and sorrow in this life, and very probably interfere with the fullest happiness which is possible to me in the life to come."[22]

The third reason to prepare our children for the work of the Lord is for the world's sake. Children raised in a godly home and prepared to do battle for the Lord are greater resources for the saving of souls than all the money, skill, talent, or education that men may possess. The real force for the kingdom of heaven in this world is the dedication of a heart to the Savior and the training of character and will to fulfill God's commands. If we raise children with those qualities, all mere human talents "are but as the dust before the hurricane."[23]

What do we say, fathers? Will we give our children to the Lord for the work of the kingdom of heaven? Will we not give our sons and daughters to Christ to assist Him in saving a dying world? Booth urges, "Bring them out, the best you have, all you have, and bend yourself to train them right well for the War to which you consecrate them."[24]

The whole creation is waiting for the sons of God to be revealed. This sinful world is reeling to and fro, waiting for young men and women "who are not so much concerned about what they can get from God as about what they can do for Him[.]"[25] As hard as it is to ponder, we must make our children willing to die for the cause of Christ. Few men have captured this call as succinctly as William Booth. He wrote, "The world needs Soldiers, men given up for the War, and not merely Soldiers, but veterans, men and women practiced and capable."[26] On raising warriors for God, Booth wrote:

"Our King is going to have an Army, a fighting Army, a disciplined Army, an invincible Army, a conquering Army, an Army that shall accomplish His purpose, rout His foes, and win the world to His feet. [. . .] Your boys and your girls are to be in its ranks, perchance carrying its Standards, or leading on its Battalions to victory; anyhow, see to it if you love the cause for which that Army is fighting, if you love this poor sin-bound world, and would like to have a hand in its emancipation, that you give your boys and girls to it, not as raw recruits but as capable Soldiers, and this you can only do by training and inspiring them in their childhood with the spirit and the motives of the War."[27]

Dear fathers, we are surrounded by men who serve many causes. Some of their causes are noble; many of them are not. God has personally called us to play a vital part in the most important cause on earth. Let our determination, vigilance, and perseverance be second to none.

Finally, we offer our children to God for the Lord's sake. He wants our children. They are His children more than they are ours. He is their Creator and sustainer. He redeems them to Himself. Our children should supremely love, reverence, and serve their Lord and Savior. Will we train them to do this? Again, Booth writes, "You have often wished you could do something for Him in return for all His love and sacrifice. You have now the opportunity to train and present Him with the choicest treasures you possess."[28] For all these reasons, let us offer our greatest treasures to our King.

---

1. Genesis 22:10-12
2. John 3:16-17
3. 1 Samuel 1:27-28
4. Luke 2:22-24
5. Gary Thomas, Sacred Parenting, (2004) p. 30
6. *Id.*
7. *Id.* p. 32
8. John 17:6-20
9. Isaiah 6:8
10. Numbers 30:2-5

11. Numbers 30:2-5
12. 1 Chronicles 25:5-6
13. 1 Chronicles 25:5-6
14. 2 Chronicles 6:7-10
15. Andrew Murray, Raising Your Children for Christ, (1984) pp. 94-95
16. Institute in Basic Youth Conflicts, Advanced Seminar Textbook, (1986) p. 269
17. William Booth, How to Make the Children into Saints and Soldiers of Jesus Christ, (1888) available at http://www.gospeltruth.net/children/booth_training.htm.
18. *Id.*
19. *Id.*
20. *Id.*
21. *Id.*
22. *Id.*
23. *Id.*
24. *Id.*
25. *Id.*
26. *Id.*
27. *Id.*
28. *Id.*

Building the Body

"And the things that thou hast heard of me among many witnesses, the same commit thou to faithful men, who shall be able to teach others also." (2 Timothy 2:2)

The seriousness of the calling of a Christian father often drives well-meaning fathers into isolation. While the enemies we face are powerful, God has not left us alone. While Noah and others like him have sometimes had to stand for God completely alone, the Lord has graciously provided our generation with the body of Christ and a faithful ministry to help us fulfill our calling. Additionally, our connection with other believers gives our children necessary opportunities to serve, honor, and love the people of God.

In this section, we will look first at the importance of the local assembly of believers. We will see that God's plan for the family is perfectly intertwined with His description of the church. Second, we will focus upon the three greatest human allies that God has given us. We will see again the truth first stated by Elisha, that those that are with us are greater than those that are against us. Finally, we will consider the importance of working with God's ministry and teaching our children to do the same.

CHAPTER 13

THE FATHER'S NEEDS: "IT TAKES A BODY"

Over the years, the issue of raising children has gathered much attention from many different viewpoints. Some have argued it takes a village and government assistance to raise the next generation. Others countered it takes only a strong family structure to raise children. The latter were certainly more correct, but the real truth is that it takes the body of Christ working together with the family to raise a generation of godly seed.

To be clear, God has used individual families like Noah's family and the Rechabites to represent God to the world without any supportive body of believers. If the church fails in its mission, God can do the same thing again. However, God's ultimate goal is to produce a church, not just a family. Therefore, to completely work with God, we must see beyond the borders of our own families to the needs of the body of Christ. As fathers, we need the rest of the body of Christ to work with us and support us in our calling. Similarly, the church depends on the family to produce a godly seed to carry the torch of faith in the next generation. The two units are masterfully designed by God to work together seamlessly.

While God repeatedly made covenants with specific families in the Old Testament, His goal even then was to make a covenant with an assembly of people made up of unified families. Just prior to entering the Promised Land, the people of Israel stood together to make a covenant with God. They gathered together the captains, elders, officers, men of Israel, children, wives, and strangers to enter into covenant with the LORD so that He "may establish thee today for a people unto himself, and that he may be unto thee a God, as he hath said unto thee, and as he hath sworn unto thy fathers, to Abraham, to Isaac, and to Jacob."[1]

Even in their darkest moments, the righteous fathers in Israel refused to forget the importance of the people of God as a whole. From Babylon, the psalmist wrote, "If I forget thee, O Jerusalem, let my right hand forget her cunning. If I do not remember thee, let my tongue cleave to the roof of my mouth; if I prefer not Jerusalem above my chief joy."[2] While in captivity, the fathers would tell their children about Jerusalem and plant firmly within their hearts a desire to return and restore the people of Israel.

In the New Testament, the church and family consistently appear together. Many churches actually met in the homes of the believers. There is also a beautiful example in Acts when the disciples at Tyre bring their wives and children to say goodbye to Paul, and the whole group kneels in prayer on the beach to pray for the departing apostle.[3]

The apostles clearly taught the importance of the body of Christ to the New Testament church. Paul writes:

> "But now are they many members, yet but one body. And the eye cannot say unto the hand, I have no need of thee: nor again the head to the feet, I have no need of you. Nay, much more those members of the body, which seem to be more feeble, are necessary: And those members of the body, which we think to be less honourable, upon these we bestow more abundant honour; and our uncomely parts have more abundant comeliness. For our comely parts have no need: but God hath tempered the body together, having given more abundant honour to that part which lacked: That there should be no schism in the body; but that the members should have the same care one for another. And whether one member suffer, all the members suffer with it; or one member be honoured, all the members rejoice with it. Now ye are the body of Christ, and members in particular."[4]

The language Paul uses is absolute. He does not say that we "should not" say that we do not need the other members of the body. Neither does he merely suggest against such an attitude. Rather, under the inspiration of the Holy Spirit, Paul says that we "cannot" say that we do not need the body. In contrast, we actually have the greatest need for the parts of the body that we may consider weak, feeble, dishonorable, or uncomely.

To the Ephesians, Paul writes that the church is one body, "fitly joined together and compacted by that which every joint supplieth, according to the effectual working in the measure of every part, [making] increase of the body unto the edifying of itself in love."⁵ In another place, Paul reminds us:

> "Now therefore ye are no more strangers and foreigners, but fellowcitizens with the saints, and of the household of God; And are built upon the foundation of the apostles and prophets, Jesus Christ himself being the chief corner stone; In whom all the building fitly framed together groweth unto an holy temple in the Lord: In whom ye also are builded together for an habitation of God through the Spirit."⁶

Thus, as we build our families, we must build in such a way that our families can be "fitly framed together" in the body of Christ.

The calling of fatherhood is an incredibly high calling. On the whole, the church has erred in deemphasizing the important calling of the father and the family in seeking a godly seed. However, as fathers, we must also beware any prideful tendency to withdraw or isolate our families from the body of Christ. We must build our part of the body with the intention of being fitly joined together and compacted with other believers.

In his epistles, John was clear on the importance of loving our brothers in Christ. He wrote, "We know that we have passed from death unto life, because we love the brethren. He that loveth not his brother abideth in death."⁷ John added later, "If a man say, I love God, and hateth his brother, he is a liar: for he that loveth not his brother whom he hath seen, how can he love God whom he hath not seen?"⁸ As a result, John concluded, "[W]e ought to lay down our lives for the brethren."⁹ As we labor to produce a godly seed, let us lead our children by example in the honor of laying down our lives for our brethren.

The Benefits of the Body

Beyond the clear Scriptural revelation that our families cannot serve God properly outside of the body of Christ, the relationship between the church and the family benefits our families in multiple ways. There are three great spiritual influences that work silently in our homes—the work of the Spirit of God, the power of enthusiastic, anointed examples, and prevailing intercessory prayer.¹⁰ Each of these is amplified by our relationship with the people of God.

The first spiritual influence is the working of the Spirit of God. As a part of God's church, we are partakers of the family promises in the Old Testament with the added blessing of the active working of the Holy Spirit in our lives. We can trust the Holy Spirit to give us the wisdom and direction necessary to teach, train, prepare, and counsel our children. In addition, as members of the body of Christ, we can expect God to speak to us and our children through anointed preaching, teaching, testifying, and counseling. As a result, our children can have multiple, unified channels that the Spirit can use to work in their lives.

The second spiritual influence is the power of an enthusiastic, anointed example. As mentioned previously, we need to show our children a "get to" Christianity. We "get to" pray, study, serve. and attend services. By maintaining an active part in a local assembly of believers, we can expose our children to many other enthusiastic Christians. It is important for our children to realize that not just one family or one church is seeking a godly seed. Keeping our children connected to the people of God provides greater opportunities for them to be encouraged and strengthened by the testimonies of others.

The third great spiritual influence is prevailing intercessory prayer. We must pray without ceasing for our children. In the early days, it is easy to miss the urgency of prayer. Because we know that our children cannot leave our homes and churches in their early years, we sometimes forget to watch and pray. We should wrestle in prayer like we would if our children were already lost—because until conversion, they are. After conversion, we should pray like our children are already in the mission field—because they are.[11] Here, too, a close relationship with other believers is beneficial. The body of Christ provides support and assistance to prevail in prayer. When we mourn, they mourn. When we rejoice, so do they.

It is difficult to overemphasize the importance of unity in the body of Christ. The Apostle Paul wrote repeatedly on the subject. Paul told the Corinthian believers to be "perfectly joined together."[12] He twice described the Colossian church as "knit together."[13] He taught the Corinthians that God had "tempered the body together."[14] He described the church in Ephesus as fitly joined and compacted together.[15] As fathers, working toward this kind of unity in our churches is part of our calling.

God has commissioned the family and the church to work together. The father retains the responsibility for his children, and he should beware delegating that responsibility to Sunday school teachers and peer-driven youth leaders. However, the gifts that God gives to other believers will assist us in our calling. The calling of fatherhood does not conflict with our need for the body of Christ.

---

1. Deuteronomy 29:9-13
2. Psalm 137:5-6
3. Acts 21:4-5
4. 1 Corinthians 12:20-27
5. Ephesians 4:16
6. Ephesians 2:19-22
7. 1 John 3:14
8. 1 John 4:20
9. 1 John 3:16
10. Denny Kenaston, The Pursuit of Godly Seed, (2003) pp. 248-259
11. Denny Kenaston, "Consecrating Our Children to God" available at www.charitychristianfellowship.org/sermons/listing
12. 1 Corinthians 1:10
13. Colossians 2:2, 19
14. 1 Corinthians 12:24
15. Ephesians 4:16

CHAPTER 14

THE FATHER'S ALLIES: "WHEN EVERY JOINT SUPPLIES"

As he crosses the Jordan into Judah, the young man's thoughts return to Babylon. A short time ago, he was the faithful servant of the king of Babylon. He was truly a loyal and trustworthy servant, and he rarely thought of returning to Jerusalem. Everything changed when Hanani brought word that Jerusalem remained in ruins.[1] Gripped with an unspeakable burden, the young man had begun to fast and pray. When the time was right, he begged the king's permission to return to Judah with a mission to rebuild Jerusalem. Now, Nehemiah stands in his homeland for the first time in his life. Armed only with a burden from God and letters of recommendation from the king, Nehemiah slowly proceeds to Jerusalem.

After spending three days in the city in total obscurity, Nehemiah assembles a small band of men to guide him around Jerusalem under the cover of darkness.[2] The magnitude of his task becomes clear as he surveys the broken walls and burned gates. The next morning, Nehemiah reveals his plan to the city rulers, "Ye see the distress that we are in, how Jerusalem lieth waste, and the gates thereof are burned with fire: come, and let us build up the wall of Jerusalem, that we be no more a reproach."[3] The people quickly encourage Nehemiah to begin his work and respond, "Let us rise up and build."[4] The enemies of God immediately challenge Nehemiah, but he continues without delay.

As the restoration begins, Nehemiah lays out his master plan—he assigns every family to build their own particular part of the walls. Under the watchful eye of Nehemiah, the family of the high priest builds the sheep gate.[5] In another place, the sons of Hassenaah carefully construct the fish gate.[6] Farther down, Shallum the son of Halohesh, the ruler of the half part of Jerusalem, builds his portion of the wall, while his daughters work faithfully by his side.[7] Beyond the horse gate, each priest carefully repairs

The Calling of Fatherhood

the wall that protects their homes.[8] In a short time, the wall is halfway finished, because each family had a mind to work.

Attempting to disrupt the work, Sanballat and his allies assemble against Jerusalem. In response, Nehemiah strategically locates the men to stand with "their families with their swords, their spears, and their bows" in different places on the wall.[9] As the men assume their positions, Nehemiah challenges them, "Be not ye afraid of them: remember the Lord, which is great and terrible, and fight for your brethren, your sons, and your daughters, your wives, and your houses."[10]

When the enemy retreats, the fathers return to building the wall, but now they build with a sword at their side. Realizing their vulnerability to an isolated attack, Nehemiah sends another message to the people, "The work is great and large, and we are separated upon the wall, one far from another. In what place therefore ye hear the sound of the trumpet, resort ye thither unto us: our God shall fight for us."[11]

With his plan in place, Nehemiah senses the urgency of the situation. They must complete the work before they lose the opportunity. His men do not even take the time to change their clothes. When Sanballat attempts to distract Nehemiah from the work, Nehemiah's response is quick. "I am doing a great work, so that I cannot come down: why should the work cease, whilst I leave it, and come down to you?"[12]

When the walls are built, Nehemiah appoints the fathers of Israel as watchmen and assigns every man to watch on the wall over his own house.[13] Later, when the preaching of Ezra brings great conviction to the city, the fathers separate themselves from the peoples of the land and dedicate themselves, "their wives, their sons, and their daughters, every one having knowledge, and having understanding" to follow the law of God.[14] The fathers hold fast to their brethren and make an oath together "to walk in God's law, which was given by Moses the servant of God, and to observe and do all the commandments of the LORD our Lord, and his judgments and his statutes."[15] They promise God and one another that they will not "give our daughters unto the people of the land, nor take their daughters for our sons."[16] Standing in covenant together with their families and their brethren, the men of Israel once again dedicate themselves to seek a godly seed.

Like this great group of men in Israel, God is calling our generation of fathers to seek a godly seed. At times, we may feel very alone in this calling, but we are not alone. First, the Scriptures repeatedly reveal that God is our greatest ally. Because God is on our side, we can prevail against any foe. However, God has also blessed us beyond measure with other allies in this fight. Our greatest human ally is our own spouse, who is called to labor with us and support us in this call. Also, as we successfully raise our older children, they too can join with us in pursuing the hearts of the younger children. Beyond our own homes, a band of brothers are responding to the call of God and—like the men in Nehemiah's day—holding fast to their brethren to help them in the cause. Thus, if we fight alone, we do so at our own choice and to our own peril.

Your Wife—Your Greatest Human Ally

The role of a godly mother in the pursuit of godly seed is worthy of its own book, and we cannot attempt to address it in detail here. However, above and beyond her own responsibilities, a wife is also her husband's greatest human ally in this cause. The power of a unified, godly marriage to inspire faith in the next generation is almost unrivaled. We need to carefully understand and protect this invaluable blessing that God has given us.

Recall that it was during a discussion on marriage that the prophet Malachi expressed God's burden to seek a godly seed. The relationship between a husband and wife has an immeasurable impact on the impressionable hearts of the children in their home. Fathers dare not think that they can put their marriage on the back burner while they focus on raising children for Christ.

A husband must communicate his vision to his wife to equip her to be the helpmeet God designed her to be. A huge part of a mother's calling is to help her husband, but she cannot help him to her fullest if she does not know his heart. Beware assumptions, and communicate regularly to ensure mutual clarity and understanding.

When a husband clearly communicates his vision and goals with his wife, she can apply and perform that vision during the day if the husband must be away from the home. William Booth put it this way:

> "A good family government must mean, therefore, that there is a head to whom all look up. Nominally that head is the father, but between father and mother there should be such union of spirit, aim, and will, that both shall be felt to be as one. The expressed

will of the one will then be taken as that of the other, and the children will know no difference in power and authority between the one and the other. This is the order of God, who puts both parents conjointly over their children."[17]

Booth further encouraged fathers and mothers to "agree between themselves what they want to accomplish, decide upon the methods by which to attain their end, and then act as one soul and one flesh before the children in [carrying] them out."[18] Andrew Murray challenged every father and mother to spend at least one half-hour each week in reading, conversation, and prayer regarding the training of their children.[19] If a husband fails to let his wife know what she can do to help him fulfill his vision for the family, he frustrates the very purpose God has given to his wife.

When Peter wrote to the church, he commanded husbands to dwell with their wives "according to knowledge, giving honor unto the wife, as unto the weaker vessel, and as being heirs together of the grace of life; that your prayers be not hindered."[20] Thus, despite the popular notion that husbands and wives cannot understand one another, the Bible actually compels the husband to know and understand his wife. Husbands must dedicate themselves to this mission. Many men will spend a lifetime learning how a deer, turkey, or trout thinks, what it prefers to eat, what weather it likes, and how it communicates. Yet, these same men scoff at the idea of even attempting to learn how their wife thinks and communicates. When a woman walks down the aisle and enters the covenant of marriage, she sacrifices everything to be a part of her husband's vision. Each husband must consider carefully the importance of that vision. A wife gives her life to her husband on their wedding day, and he daily spends that life on something. He must invest it well.

Paul, too, wrote on the responsibilities of husbands in marriage. In his letter to the Ephesians, Paul wrote:

> "Husbands, love your wives, even as Christ also loved the church, and gave himself for it; That he might sanctify and cleanse it with the washing of water by the word, That he might present it to himself a glorious church, not having spot, or wrinkle, or any such thing; but that it should be holy and without blemish."

This challenge cannot be overstated. To love one's wife as Christ loved the church is a call that can only be answered with supernatural help. Paul's words answer once and for all the question of who is responsible to sacrifice first. Just as Christ loved the church while they were yet sinners, the husband must love the wife regardless of her conduct toward him. He is to love first, sacrifice first, and die to self first. He is to be the example in all things.

Children should have no fear of their parents separating. Children are constantly aware of the condition of their parent's marriage. Indeed, the marriage of one generation and the faith of the next generation are intimately intertwined. As God said through Malachi:

> "[T]he LORD hath been witness between thee and the wife of thy youth, against whom thou hast dealt treacherously: yet is she thy companion, and the wife of thy covenant. And did not he make one? Yet had he the residue of the spirit. And wherefore one? That he might seek a godly seed. Therefore take heed to your spirit, and let none deal treacherously against the wife of his youth. For the LORD, the God of Israel, saith that he hateth putting away: for one covereth violence with his garment, saith the LORD of hosts: therefore take heed to your spirit, that ye deal not treacherously."[21]

God not only hates divorce, He hates the spirit of divorce. It must have no place in our homes.

Raising children from fallen infants to godly young adults is an often stressful way to spend the day, especially if your wife must do it without you. Therefore, a husband should free his wife from as many extraneous stresses as possible. If the husband will set his heart on liberating his wife from unnecessary stress, the stresses he can remove are legion.

A husband who disciplines himself can free his wife from the stress of financial mismanagement. He can also liberate his wife from stressful, unreasonable expectations concerning the chores in the home and personal appearance. Long-lasting marital strife is another stress that the husband can vanquish from the home. Many husbands cause unnecessary stress through inconsistent discipline and wandering standards. Husbands are prone to announcing rules similar to the law of the Medes and Persians—which cannot be changed and alters not—and then promptly forgetting about them by the end of the week. Naturally, this creates extra stress on the wife who seeks to enforce her husband's rules in the home. A husband can also avoid the stress of surprise decisions by including his wife early in the decision making process. Finally, the husband who helps his wife care for the home rather than making all of her household tasks more difficult can free his wife to have more time and energy for the children.

A husband's attitude toward his wife can take the young radiant bride he married and turn her into a discouraged, bitter, depressed wife and mother who perpetually feels overwhelmed with her responsibilities. This is a sin against his wife and against God. Too many women who set out to surrender the size of their family to God and pursue a godly seed later regret the decision when their husbands fail to cherish them. Wives are wounded easier than we know, and wounds produce scars over time. A husband should banish complaints and sarcasm from his conversations to and about his wife. He should also realize that it is better to offend any other woman rather than his wife.

The union between a godly man and woman in marriage is one of God's greatest tools to fashion the character of Christ in the husband, the wife, and the children. God has perfectly designed the union to compel us to sacrifice, overcome, and become more like Christ. The struggles the wife experiences are the very things that God wants to work out of the husband through helping her. Everything that happens in the marriage is an opportunity for the husband to become more like his Lord.

A wife is a beautiful gift from God. Someday each husband will give an account to God for how he treated her. A wife is truly her husband's greatest and most important human ally in the pursuit of godly seed. Solomon wrote:

> "Two are better than one; because they have a good reward for their labour. For if they fall, the one will lift up his fellow: but woe to him that is alone when he falleth; for he hath not another to help him up. Again, if two lie together, then they have heat: but how can one be warm alone? And if one prevail against him, two shall withstand him; and a threefold cord is not quickly broken."

With the blessing of a godly wife, a husband never needs to fight alone. Two really are better than one, and when the husband and wife work together in unity, they shall have good reward for their labor.

Our Children

If we raise our older children into godly young adults, we gain another invaluable ally in the fight for the hearts of our younger children. Older siblings naturally hold a special place in the hearts of younger children. For this reason, everything we invest in our older children brings a harvest in all the little ones who follow them. If we lose the hearts of our adolescents, we inherit an uphill battle for the hearts of the younger children as well. If, instead, we win our adolescents to our cause, they can work with us to ensure that the younger children follow in their steps.

We must keep the future in mind when we are tempted to compromise with our older children during their struggles. When fathers lower their standards or change their convictions in an attempt to make peace with an older child, they simultaneously lose that same ground in the hearts of the younger children. Thus, each battle is of utmost importance. All that we do now can make the next child's battle easier or harder. Which result do we want?

Because siblings naturally have great influence on one another, fathers should address this issue directly and prepare the older children to use their role well. As soon as our children can understand the concept, we should teach them that they are the examples for the younger ones that follow behind them. Ignoring the special influence between siblings will not cause it to cease. Therefore, let us embrace this influence and gain personally-trained allies. If we do not, we risk unintentionally creating an enemy within our own homes.

Our Brethren

Like the men in Nehemiah's day, we cannot build the wall around Jerusalem on our own. God commissions us to build our portion of the wall that connects to our homes, but we will be far more successful if we connect our wall to the walls built by other faithful men. God has occasionally asked men to stand completely alone; Noah is the clearest example. However, the Bible also makes clear that men fight best when they stand with faithful brethren.

When Moses stood on the hill overlooking the battle between Israel and Amalek, he lifted his rod over the people, and Israel prevailed.[22] Yet, Moses' hands soon grew heavy, and when he let down the rod to rest his arms, Amalek prevailed against Israel. Aaron and Hur realized the gravity of the situation, and they responded. Each man stationed himself to one side of Moses, and they held up his arms until Israel obtained the victory. Fathers are no different. Each of us have times when we need someone to hold up our arms and help our family win the battle. Because of this, we need to do everything in our power to be close enough to faithful brethren that they can run to our aid in the time of trouble.

The struggles we sometimes face need not take us by surprise. Like Nehemiah, because we are working on a cause that is near to the heart of God, we can expect the enemy to make both direct and covert attacks. We should, therefore, have a plan in place to deal with these events.

Joab and Abishai—brothers both by blood and by calling—knew they were facing an overpowering enemy, so they formed a plan.[23] Joab told his brother before the battle:

> "If the Syrians be too strong for me, then thou shalt help me: but if the children of Ammon be too strong for thee, then I will help thee. Be of good courage, and let us behave ourselves valiantly for our people, and for the cities of our God: and let the LORD do that which is good in his sight."

In the end, both men prevailed and won a victory for the people of God.

We need to ally with faithful men who can be trusted in the day of adversity. We need brethren who will build well, watch well, and fight well. Moses warned the people, "What man is there that is fearful and fainthearted? let him go and return unto his house, lest his brethren's heart faint as well as his heart."[24] The men and families with whom we fellowship will greatly impact the future of our families. Let us be brethren who encourage victory and never inspire defeat.

Paul instructed the believers in Galatia, "Brethren, if a man be overtaken in a fault, ye which are spiritual, restore such a one in the spirit of meekness; considering thyself, lest thou also be tempted."[25] Given the genuine risk of being "overtaken," we have a duty to make ourselves accountable to spiritual men who can restore us in the moment of temptation. Part of being a godly father is having courageous vulnerability with brethren we know we can trust.

Steve Farrar notes that finishing well requires "staying power."[26] According to Farrar, godly fathers must stay in the Word and prayer, stay close to family and brethren, stay away from obvious temptation, and stay aware to covert attacks from the enemy.[27] Isolation from our brothers in Christ will only serve to make us prone to defeat. If we refuse to be vulnerable to our brethren, we instead make ourselves vulnerable to the enemy.

Farrar challenges men to use a "circle the wagons" approach when a brother is in trouble.[28] In pioneer days, when a group of people came under attack, they would circle the wagons as a method of defense. Circling the wagons has two elements. First, we defensively gather around to protect the person or persons who are vulnerable to the enemy. Second, we offensively work together to repel the enemy and win the battle. Each of us needs dependable brethren who can orchestrate and provide this type of assistance should they see the need arise.

Our calling to raise godly seed often propels us to stand alone. As we see the chaos and compromise that surrounds us, it is easy to think, with the prophet Elijah, that we are the only ones who are faithfully serving God. But God always has a people. It is as true today as it was for Elijah—God still has His thousands that have not bowed a knee to Baal. The day may come when we must truly stand alone, but today is not that day. Today, we stand together with the allies that God has provided for us, and we know that we are greatly blessed to have them by our side.

---

1. Nehemiah 1
2. Nehemiah 2:11-15
3. Nehemiah 2:17
4. Nehemiah 2:18
5. Nehemiah 3:1
6. Nehemiah 3:4
7. Nehemiah 3:12
8. Nehemiah 3:28
9. Nehemiah 4:13
10. Nehemiah 4:14
11. Nehemiah 4:18-20
12. Nehemiah 6:3
13. Nehemiah 7:3
14. Nehemiah 10:28

15. Nehemiah 10:29
16. Nehemiah 10:30
17. William Booth, How to Make the Children into Saints and Soldiers of Jesus Christ, (1888) available at http://www.gospeltruth.net/children/booth_training.htm.
18. *Id.*
19. Andrew Murray Raising Your Children for Christ, (1984) p. 272
20. 1 Peter 3:7
21. Malachi 2:14-16
22. Exodus 17:8-12
23. 1 Chronicles 19:10-15
24. Deuteronomy 20:8
25. Galatians 6:1
26. Steve Farrar, Finishing Strong, (1995) p. 64
27. *Id.*
28. *Id.* p. 69

CHAPTER 15

THE FATHER'S OBEDIENCE: "SUBMIT YOURSELF"

Insurrection stirs within the camp.[1] The pilgrimage through the wilderness between Egypt and Canaan is taking its toll. God's provision has been nothing short of miraculous, but Israel's attitude about the journey is quickly changing from the thrill of dramatic deliverance to the repetitive drudgery of existence in an arid wasteland. Many of these men could endure the journey alone, but they grow weary of watching their families suffer and doubt. Tragically, instead of using these experiences to bring their families closer to God, a group of fathers gather together to oppose Moses and Aaron.

Korah, a Levite and relative of Moses and Aaron, leads the group. Dathan and Abiram, brothers from the tribe of Reuben, stand with him. As news spreads, 250 of the most famous, gifted men in Israel join the rebellion. Their accusation against the man of God is straightforward, though hardly original. As the group surrounds Moses and Aaron, Korah challenges Moses, saying "Ye take too much upon you, seeing all the congregation are holy, every one of them, and the LORD is among them: wherefore then lift ye up yourselves above the congregation of the LORD?"[2]

Realizing what is about to happen, Moses falls prostrate in prayer. From that position, Moses challenges the men to appear with him the next day to present their censers of incense to God. Then, looking directly at Korah, Moses rebukes the Levite with his own words:

> "[Y]e take too much upon you, ye sons of Levi. [. . .] Hear, I pray you, ye sons of Levi: Seemeth it but a small thing unto you, that the God of Israel hath separated you from the congregation of Israel, to bring you near to himself to do the service of the

> tabernacle of the LORD, and to stand before the congregation to minister unto them? And he hath brought thee near to him, and all thy brethren the sons of Levi with thee: and seek ye the priesthood also? For which cause both thou and all thy company are gathered together against the LORD: and what is Aaron, that ye murmur against him?[3]

Moses' rebuke is stern, and his words haunt Korah throughout the long night.

The next day, Moses summons the men to the tabernacle to present incense to God. Dathan and Abiram are now in full rebellion. Refusing to acknowledge the authority of Moses, they reject the command to gather at the tabernacle and encourage others to ignore Moses and Aaron. Korah, however, assembles all the congregation of Israel in front of the tabernacle.

As the people gather, the glory of the LORD appears unto the entire congregation. God tells Moses to oppose Dathan and Abiram directly. Moses leads all of Israel to the tents of the two families. Moses cries out to the gathering crowd, "Depart, I pray you, from the tents of these wicked men, and touch nothing of theirs, lest ye be consumed in all their sins."[4] Slowly, the crowd parts. Only Korah and his band of 250 men remain near the tents.

Dathan and Abiram hesitantly emerge from their tents. Their wives, sons, and young children come forward and stand next to them. The earth begins to shake. Suddenly, the ground rips apart, swallowing Dathan and Abiram, whose wives and children perish with them. Korah, too, is swallowed by the earth. As they went down alive into the pit, the earth closed upon them. Then, fire from God consumed the 250 men who stood with Korah to challenge Moses.

For their absolute rebellion, Dathan and Abiram were destroyed, and their children died with them in the pit. Although Korah, too, died in the pit, God had mercy on his children, apparently because Korah obeyed Moses' commands even while leading the rebellion. Moses later emphasized that "the children of Korah died not."[5] Later, God reveals that "the Korahites were over the work of the service, keepers of the gates of the tabernacle: and their fathers, being over the host of the LORD, were keepers of the entry."[6]

Remember Our Need

Just as Moses reminded the Levites, we, too, as fathers have been called by God to a great purpose. God has set us apart to seek a godly seed. As a result, God offers us the anointing necessary to fulfill the call, and He holds us responsible for our stewardship. However, it is possible for us to overreach our calling and thereby quench the work of God in our homes.

We stand on a narrow path between two great errors. On the one side is the error of delegation. Fathers are prone to delegate all the teaching, training, and disciplining of their children to the church and its various ministries. The promise regarding training up our children has often been misinterpreted as "Take your child to church functions, and when he is old he will not depart." This is not the case. If we are not careful, our families can be so busy with church activities that we lose the opportunity for the family to be together. This is error.

On the other side, however, is the error of isolation. Fathers who accept their responsibility are sometimes tempted to withdraw from the body of Christ and remove their children from any influence outside the home. Our families need Christian fellowship, opportunities to serve, and the influence of a faithful ministry. The calling of a father need not work in isolation. Rather, the calling is specifically designed to work in unity with the calling of the ministry in the local assembly.

As we labor to build godly homes, we must ensure that our labor is decent and in order.[7] Remember Uzzah's ill-fated attempt to save the Ark of the Covenant? David concluded, "God made a breach upon us, for that we sought him not after the due order."[8] Because God takes order seriously, we are compelled to do the same.

In Proverbs, God describes some of the key elements of building a godly home. He says, "Through wisdom is an house builded; and by understanding it is established."[9] Thus, the foundation and basic structure of our homes depend upon wisdom and understanding. The Scriptures goes on to say, "[B]y knowledge shall the chambers be filled with all precious and pleasant riches."[10] Interestingly, knowledge does not make up the structure of the home. However, knowledge fills the home with precious and pleasant things. Concerning the man leading the home, the Proverb says, "A wise man is strong; yea, a man of knowledge increaseth strength."[11] We will find real strength in wisdom, and when we have wisdom, we can increase strength through knowledge. The next verse continues, "For by wise counsel thou shalt make thy war: and in multitude of counselors there is safety."[12] A man can have great strength in wisdom and knowledge, but he makes war through the wise counsel he receives from others.

The wise man finds safety in a multitude of counselors. Thus, if we isolate ourselves from the counsel of God's ministry, we risk losing our safety and our ability to make spiritual war. Moreover, how do we obtain more wisdom, understanding, and knowledge? Certainly through prayer and study, but as a famous Ethiopian eunuch acknowledged long ago, a faithful ministry helps us better understand the Word of God.

As fathers, we also need the ministry to assist us as watchmen guarding against the enemy. Each father is responsible for watching over his own home, but sometimes we struggle to see the enemy lurking within us. Ezekiel described the ministry as watchmen who blow the trumpet as a warning of approaching danger.[13] When a minister in the church warns us of a weakness in our lives and homes, we become doubly responsible if we refuse to respond to God's warning.

In addition, God often uses the ministry to give direction on the application of Biblical principles in this present world. God told Ezekiel that the ministry was to "teach my people the difference between the holy and profane, and cause them to discern between the unclean and the clean."[14] In the everyday struggle against the temptations of the world, the help of a principled, faithful man of God is invaluable. Without spiritual admonition and guidance, fathers often tend to slide toward the condition that existed in Judges, when every man did that which he thought was right in his own eyes.[15] Such a condition has always brought trouble for the people of God.

Furthermore, the New Testament illustrates our need for the ministry to equip us to fulfill the calling that God has given us. Paul told the church at Ephesus that God gave apostles, prophets, evangelists, pastors, and teachers to the church to equip the saints to work the ministry and build the body of Christ.[16] This is God's divine order, but it has often been cast aside by all parties.

Fathers often choose not to be accountable to the local ministry. In addition, the various church ministries often circumvent the father in an attempt to raise believing children without him. God always intended the two callings to work in unity. A ministry that successfully equips fathers will never lack dynamic young people in the church. A father that makes himself accountable to the ministry will gain training, victory, and safety in the multitude of counsel.

Remember Our Example

Fathers are examples in all that they do. We cannot decide whether or not to be an example. We can only determine what kind of example we will be. As we labor to teach our children humility, submission, respect, and obedience to authority, our own relationship with the ministry is one of the greatest opportunities we have to train our children these traits by example. Hebrews challenges us to submit to those that watch for our souls.[17] Paul encouraged the Corinthians to submit themselves unto his ministry and the faithful men who helped him.[18] Paul also repeatedly challenged the saints to follow his ministry as he followed Christ.[19]

How we handle this issue is paramount. Our decisions will directly impact our children. If we slander the men of God and continually disagree with them in front of our children, we will neutralize the influence the preaching of the Word could have in their hearts. If we walk humbly and submit ourselves respectfully to God's ministry, we can set an example for our children that they will never forget.

---

1. Numbers 16:1-40
2. Numbers 16:2-3
3. Numbers 16:7-11
4. Numbers 16:26
5. Numbers 26:9-11
6. 1 Chronicles 9:19
7. 1 Corinthians 14:40
8. 1 Chronicles 15:13
9. Proverbs 24:3
10. Proverbs 24:4
11. Proverbs 24:5
12. Proverbs 24:6
13. Ezekiel 33:1-7
14. Ezekiel 44:23
15. Judges 21:25

16. Ephesians 4:11-12
17. Hebrews 13:17
18. 1 Corinthians 16:15-16
19. 1 Corinthians 4:16; 1 Corinthians 11:1; Philippians 3:17

Facing the Fire

"Watch ye, stand fast in the faith, quit you like men, be strong. Let all your things be done with charity." (1 Corinthians 16:13-14)

The allies discussed previously are desperately needed. Our enemy is determined to divide the hearts of the fathers from their children. We see the wounded and slain all around us. Those who accept the high calling of fatherhood have little time for fear, timidity, or cowardice. The war waged against the family has been long, intentional, and largely successful. With little room for error and no time for delay, we must take our stand with the saints of ages past and fight to fulfill our calling and save our homes.

In this section, we direct our attention to the fight each father will face. We must surrender our will to God, and then spend the rest of our lives helping our children do the same. Next, we focus on the enemies without and enemies within, including the enemy that lurks in our own hearts. Victory will not be easy. We will focus specifically on the issues of education and entertainment, illuminating the enemy's plan for these two often used modes of attack. After that, we will see that God has promised to help us gain the victory. We will examine what victory looks like in the hearts of the second and third generations. In the final pages of this section, we will answer many of the counterarguments frequently used by opponents of our call.

CHAPTER 16

THE FATHER'S FIGHT: "THE WAR OF THE WILL"

The high priest knows well the calling God gave him. As a direct descendant of Aaron, Eli is God's primary representative to Israel. He serves in a difficult time. There is no open vision throughout Israel, and without vision the people of Israel repeatedly cast off the restraints of the law. Everyone does what they think is right. Although God moves mightily in the lives of the judges, they are largely regional leaders with serious character flaws. With a leadership vacuum in the twelve tribes, the people look to Eli, the high priest serving in the tabernacle, to lead them.

Eli is an old man, but he still remembers the awe he had for the tabernacle as a young priest. Serving in the tabernacle is a great honor for a young Levite. Knowing that each part of the tabernacle was dedicated and used by Aaron, the family patriarch, adds special meaning for each of his descendants. As the high priest, Eli alone has access to the Ark of the Covenant. Like Moses and Aaron before him, Eli has seen the physical presence of God in the innermost part of the tabernacle.

Eli's sons, Hophni and Phinehas, do not share his reverence for the house of God. For some time, they have violated the strict code of the priesthood by taking the hallowed parts of the sacrifice that the people offered to God. Paralyzed by fear that his sons would suffer the fate of Nadab and Abihu in the wilderness, Eli turns a blind eye to his sons' transgression. He can only hope that God will do the same.

This day, however, the report from the tabernacle cannot be overlooked.[1] News comes that Hophni and Phinehas are forcefully fornicating with the women who came to offer sacrifice at the door of the tabernacle. Finally stirred to action, Eli lumbers to the tabernacle to confront his sons. He pleads, "Why do ye such things?" "[I]t is no good report that I hear: ye make the LORD'S people to transgress. If one man sin against another, the judge shall judge him: but if a man sin against the LORD, who shall intreat for him?" The young men ignore their father's pleadings "because the LORD would slay them."

God's determination to slay Hophni and Phinehas is both stunning and troubling. Why would God determine to destroy the young men who were in line to inherit the office of high priest? Why would God turn his back on the descendants of Aaron? Yet, this condition is not the result of the predestination of a sovereign God. The Bible goes on to explain the two things that forced God to this conclusion.

God sends a prophet to confront Eli about the condition of his home.[2] First, the prophet confirms God's covenant with Aaron and recounts how God had faithfully worked with Aaron's generations. The prophet then delivers God's rebuke to Eli. "Wherefore kick ye at my sacrifice and at mine offering, which I have commanded in my habitation; and honourest thy sons above me, to make yourselves fat with the chiefest of all the offerings of Israel my people?"[3] As so many other fathers like him, Eli's first great breach was the failure to control himself. Eli honored his sons above God's commandments and literally became obese from the meat his sons had confiscated in violation of the law.

God would later send a young boy named Samuel to finish the message.[4] Calling Samuel by name, the Lord informs the child that He "will judge [Eli's] house for ever for the iniquity which he knoweth; because his sons made themselves vile, and he restrained them not."[5] Samuel lies stunned until daybreak, when he approaches Eli with God's message. Eli, resigned to the impending judgment of God, replies, "It is the LORD: let him do what seemeth him good." Eli, therefore, committed the second great breach of a father by refusing to restrain his sons even when he knew they were sinning against God.

God makes Eli fully aware of his transgressions, but for Eli's home the day for restraint passed long ago. Hophni and Phinehas soon head to battle with the Philistines, and they bring the Ark of the Covenant in an attempt to force God to fight for them. Eli remains at home, sitting in near blindness, awaiting the dreadful news he knows is soon to come. The message returns from the battle, Hophni and Phinehas are dead. Worse, the Ark of the Covenant is taken by the Philistines. Eli falls dead at the news. Only young Samuel remains to lead Israel in the wake of God's judgment on an unrestrained father.

Restrain Yourself

In all areas of Christian leadership, men who hope to inspire faithful obedience in others must first overcome themselves. The calling of a Christian father is no different. If we aspire to raise godly children, we must first be godly. If we hope to impart vision to our children, we must first possess the vision. If we pray that our children will love the ways of God and fight faithfully for His kingdom, we must first stand before them, declare our allegiance solely to the King of Kings, and fight victoriously for His cause. There is no way to secure the goal in the hearts of our children without plainly proving to them that we have firmly planted and pursued the goal in our own hearts.

Charles Spurgeon warned, "Beware of no man more than yourself; we carry our worst enemies within us."[6] The Apostle Paul put it this way:

> "Know ye not that they which run in a race run all, but one receiveth the prize? So run, that ye may obtain. And every man that striveth for the mastery is temperate in all things. [. . .] I therefore so run, not as uncertainly; so fight I, not as one that beateth the air: But I keep under my body, and bring it into subjection: lest that by any means, when I have preached to others, I myself should be a castaway."[7]

The Apostle's challenge applies nowhere more than with the calling of the Christian father. We must run all if we hope to capture the hearts of our children and present them to God as an offering to Him. If we desire to preserve a godly seed in the earth, we must be temperate, self-controlled, in all things. Our first and primary focus is not controlling our children. Rather, our first focus is keeping our own body, mind, and spirit in subjection to the Father. If we fail at that, both we and our children may become casatways.

Parenting according to God's ways forces each father to confront the besetting sin or sins in his own life. Different fathers are prone to different sins. We are often more adept at discovering the sins of others than facing the foundational temptations that repeatedly shake us to our core and prevent us from successfully passing the faith to our children. Each of these sins appear harmless enough in the early stages, but they will each destroy the next generation if left unconquered in the heart of a father.

The first besetting sin faced by many fathers is laziness. The lazy or slothful father often knows to do right, but he rarely finds the energy and passion necessary to do it. This father can expound verbally on the merits of raising godly children, but he is bound by a hesitation to actually pay the price. He lives in a pattern of guilt and repentance over the failure to apply what he knows. Given time, the laziness eventually develops into apathy. The apathetic father quits caring whether he and his children do right. He is quick to suggest myriad excuses for the family's condition, but does nothing to change it. If left unchecked, the apathy develops into surrender. After failing to act and eventually failing to care, this father quits, either physically or mentally. Because life is easier if he avoids conflict, the father bound by laziness will eventually surrender his home, marriage, and children to the world if given enough time.

The second besetting sin is distraction. The distracted father is often very excited about his calling as a father. His problem stems from the fact that he is equally excited about everything else, too. Unable to say "no" to much of anything, he forgets to take the time to discern between good and evil stimulus, and has an even harder time remembering that "good" is the worst enemy of "great." Blown about by whatever wind is stirring at the moment, the distracted father breeds instability in his home. Inevitably, the distraction tends to absenteeism. The father is excessively physically or mentally absent from the home as more exciting pursuits grab his attention. Without accountability, distraction and absence produce compromise. Because the father is too busy with work, hobbies, ministries, and whatever else comes to mind, he leaves the home unguarded, and compromise quickly enters the home. Tragically, the father's distractions often lead him to actually be the agent of compromise as he abandons his convictions for the latest entertainment flavor of the day.

The third besetting sin in fathers is negativity. Sometimes paired with perfectionism, negativity is one of the fastest ways for a father to dishearten his children. Most children are inherently enthralled with life until their more experienced father informs them of the problems with life, the church, their mother, and eventually the children personally. As negativity develops into criticism, untold damage can be done to a child. If criticism turns to condemnation, the children will be deeply wounded for life. The father who looks for faults to condemn in his children will quickly produce a number of faults to condemn. On this point, Booth wrote, "Never condemn unless faithfulness to your child's highest interests demands it, and even then comply with the command of the Apostle, to be 'easy to be intreated, full of mercy and good fruits, without partiality, and without hypocrisy.'"[8]

The fourth besetting sin in fathers is anger. Untold harm has been done among generations of godly homes by angry men. The angry father erupts without warning and empties his emotions on his children while leaving painful scars that build over time. Unless this father permits God to intervene in his life and home, this anger develops into bitterness. A bitter spirit is the result of unresolved anger that is allowed to fester over time. Such a spirit gives place to the devil and defiles many. Eventually, anger and bitterness give way to abuse. Whether verbal or physical, the abusive father violates the heart of the calling of fatherhood. By betraying his children in this way, the abusive father also portrays the heavenly Father in a way that makes later salvation even harder in his children.

Brothers, when God called us to be fathers, He called us into a long and bloody war. Many men, more talented and prepared than we are, have lost the battle for the next generation. To have any hope of success, we must rely upon God's help and realize that the first enemy we must subdue dwells within our own minds. Our weapons are not carnal, but they are mighty. God will deliver us if we faithfully follow Him. These deadly strongholds of sin must be fought against, prayed against, believed against, and conquered at all costs.

If we refuse to overcome, our children have little hope. We cannot pass on the torch of faith without ourselves partaking of its flame. We cannot avoid this battle, and we dare not lose. Jesus put it this way, "Except a corn of wheat fall into the ground and die, it abideth alone: but if it die, it bringeth forth much fruit."[9] As fathers, we are partakers of one of the greatest callings of God, but the call is not an easy one. It is a call to come and die.

Then Their Will

As we fight to submit our own will to the Father, God gives us the amazing opportunity to enter the battlefield with our children and help them prepare for the same fight. Each generation must surrender to God individually. God calls each father to guide and assist his children in that process. An analogous situation faced the generation that followed Joshua and Caleb. The Bible states that God left a remnant of the Canaanite nations in Israel to prove the next generation and to teach them war.[10] In the same way, each of our children face their temptations and struggles to prove their commitment to God. We are responsible to teach them the ways of this war so that they will be ready to fully obey the Lord.

Like Eli, King David is an example of a father whose failure to control himself caused a failure to control his sons. When Adonijah starts a civil war in an attempt to claim the throne, even Joab and Abiather assist him.[11] By way of explanation, the Bible states of Adonijah, "And his father had not displeased him at any time in saying, Why hast thou done so?"[12] Because David surrendered to his own carnal desires, he failed to challenge Adonijah to submit his will to the Lord.

Causing children to submit their will to their parents is training for submitting their will to Christ. Training our children cheerful obedience will give them a huge head start on submitting to God and succeeding in every area of life. Indeed, with proper training, we can give them advanced progress against the sins and faults that plague us to this day. William Booth called the home "preparatory drill-grounds where the children are prepared for active service in the Salvation War" and noted that "one of the first necessities and principles in every effective army is unquestioning and unhesitating obedience."[13] By lovingly training such obedience at home, we prepare them to offer such obedience to the King of Kings.

The revivalist Charles Finney made similar observations. Finney instructed parents to get mastery over the child's will and then keep it.[14] Finney explained that those children who are not so trained are rarely converted and often fail to progress spiritually when converted.[15] He wrote:

> "I have had so much opportunity of making observation is this respect, that if I find a person lingering under conviction, and finding it very difficult to submit to God—if I find him grieving and quenching the Holy Spirit, and if converted, given to perpetual backsliding, I often make inquiry, and with scarcely a solitary exception, find that parental authority has never had a thorough influence over him[.]"[16]

Sussana Wesley, the beloved mother of John and Charles Wesley, agreed, stating, "I set out at an early age to conquer the will of each child. Then I continue to bring it into subjection until it is totally yielded to Christ."[17] Dear fathers, for the cause of Christ, let us subdue the wills of our children!

Jesus gives us a beautiful example of this training in His own life. As early as twelve years old, we know He wanted to be in the temple working in the ministry. Yet, throughout His youth, where would we find Him? He was growing in wisdom, stature, and favor with God and man in a sweaty carpenter's shop in tiny, disrespected Nazareth. Why? He was there to learn obedience. Christ's submission to Mary and Joseph was preparation for Gethsemane. For thirty years—even at the wedding in Cana—Jesus learned to say "Not my will, but my parent's will be done," so that in a midnight cry in Gethsemane He could pray, "Not my will but thine be done."

Contrary to popular opinion, our children can willfully and joyfully obey. This must be a firm objective and constant focus. In short, obedience is everything. It is no little issue, but not because we as fathers are that important, authoritative, or infallible. Obedience is vital because their response to the Holy Spirit's prompting is essential to conversion, and their obedience to God is the measure of their success after conversion. To put it simply, obedience is the greatest difference between Adam and Christ while they were on the earth. Which one do we want our children to emulate?

In light of the importance of obedience, we desire and pursue obedience that flows from the heart, not mere military rigidity.[18] The emphasis here is on obedience, and the language involved, especially William Booth's, can sound strict. However, even obedience should be read in conjunction with the heart to heart relationship explained earlier. A heart that loves will receive and obey. Flagrant disobedience is a sign of a wounded or wandering heart.

What type of obedience do we seek? Fathers should strive to procure in their children the same type of obedience they want their children to show to the Lord in their later years. According to Booth, "The child shall do exactly as he is told without hesitation and [. . .] this obedience shall be rendered without any consideration of punishment or reward."[19] The goal is unhesitant obedience that flows from relationship. Delayed obedience is merely disobedience by another name. Obedience that flows from threat or bribe has missed the heart of the matter. If we choose not to obtain a willing and joyful spirit of obedience in our children, all our teaching, praying, and sacrificing will likely be in vain.[20]

How do we obtain this obedience? We must accept no compromise or half-hearted attempts on this important issue. We must allow no excuse from ingenious children or idle adults to justify disobedience in our children.[21] Children can be surprisingly stubborn in their attempts at insurrection, but we must prevail, remembering that the Bible compares stubbornness and rebellion to idolatry and witchcraft. William Booth's warning against bribery merits quoting here:

> "Never practice the abominable habit of bribing your children in order to secure obedience. This folly, one would think, would need only to be named in order to be avoided, and yet how often we see it practised! Little things, just able to run, whom we should naturally expect to stand in awe of any command given by father or mother, we often see pouting and whining when asked to do some little act to which they are disinclined, and refusing to obey until they are offered sweets, or sugar, or a kiss, or some other bribe. This done, the little lords and ladies condescend to do as they are desired."[22]

We must win the battle for obedience without resorting to such compromise.

Surrendering the battle for the will of the child is but a short step away from surrendering the battle for the heart of the child. If we lose the will, we have lost the heart. If we lose the heart, we have lost the child. Permitting the child to rebel and largely do as he pleases will make it as difficult as possible for the child to submit to God and to follow the lowly Nazarene in the self-denying life He led.[23]

The end goal is not parental government. The end goal is self-government with a joyful surrender to the will of God. We must prepare each child for their own Gethsemane. Inevitably, that moment will come to each of them.

Charles Finney writes, "The great object to be attained is to teach the child to lay restraints upon himself—in other words to take upon himself the observance of God's [Word.]"[24] To do so, fathers must govern themselves and provide an example to their children. As fathers, we must be what we desire our children be. While we teach our children precept upon precept, we dare not neglect the greater power of example. Let us, then, embrace our own moment of Gethsemane and surrender our own wills to the heavenly Father. Then, let us prepare our children to do the same.

1. 1 Samuel 2:22
2. 1 Samuel 2:27-29
3. 1 Samuel 2:27-29
4. 1 Samuel 3:8-19
5. 1 Samuel 3:8-19
6. Charles Haddon Spurgeon quoted by Steve Farrar, Finishing Strong, (1995) p. 33
7. 1 Corinthians 9:24-27
8. William Booth, How to Make the Children into Saints and Soldiers of Jesus Christ, (1888) available at http://www.gospeltruth.net/children/booth_training.htm. (quoting James 3:17)
9. John 12:24
10. Judges 3:1-2
11. 1 Kings 1:5-7
12. 1 Kings 1:5-7
13. William Booth, How to Make the Children into Saints and Soldiers of Jesus Christ, (1888) available at http://www.gospeltruth.net/children/booth_training.htm.
14. Charles Finney, "September 9, 1840 Letters to Parents—3" available at http://www.gospeltruth.net/children/400909_parents_3.htm
15. Id.
16. Id.
17. Susanna Wesley quoted by Denny Kenaston, The Pursuit of Godly Seed (2003) p. 184
18. Rick Leibee, "Importance of Obedience" available at www.charitychristianfellowship.org/sermons/listing
19. William Booth, How to Make the Children into Saints and Soldiers of Jesus Christ, (1888) available at http://www.gospeltruth.net/children/booth_training.htm.
20. Id.
21. Id.
22. Id.
23. Id.
24. Charles Finney, "Family Government" December 23, 1850, At the Tabernacle, Moorfields. Available at http://www.gospeltruth.net/1849-51Penny_Pulpit/501223pp_family_govt.htm

CHAPTER 17

THE FATHER'S FOES: "BOMBARDED ON EVERY SIDE"

With a hesitant sigh, Moses musters the courage to approach the throne of Pharaoh one more time.[1] Previously, he retained hope that Pharaoh would soon relent and release the sons of Abraham from their bondage. Today is different. The word of the Lord still echoes in his ears. "I have hardened his heart, [. . .] that thou mayest tell in the ears of thy son, and of thy son's son, what things I have wrought in Egypt, and my signs which I have done among them; that ye may know how that I am the LORD." Even as Moses presents God's command to Pharaoh, he prepares for the inevitable rejection that is quick to come.

As Moses warns of an impending plague of locusts, Pharaoh's advisors recommend leniency. Pharaoh directs a new question at Moses. "Go, serve the LORD your God: but who are they that shall go?" Moses responds without hesitation, "We will go with our young and with our old, with our sons and with our daughters, with our flocks and with our herds will we go; for we must hold a feast unto the LORD." Pharaoh recoils at Moses' demand. With mock concern, he warns that evil would befall the children in the wilderness. He will only permit the men to leave. Refusing to leave the women and children in Egypt, Moses and Aaron flee the palace and return to Goshen.

Fully aware of the simmering insurrection among the tribal leaders, Moses is unsure how much longer he can maintain unity. As Pharaoh grows hard, the people of Israel grow restless for results. Moses can only relay the word of the Lord to them, assuring them that God is causing the delay to inspire faith in the hearts of the generations to come. With that confidence, Moses stretches his rod over Egypt, and the horde of locusts descends in a mass of insects greater than any before or after them.

When the locusts fail to move Pharaoh, Moses lifts his hand toward heaven, and darkness so thick it can be felt enshrouds all the land of Egypt for three days. Shaken by the defeat of Egypt's sun god, Pharoah summons Moses. "Go ye, serve the LORD; only let your flocks and your herds be stayed: let your little ones also go with you." Moses again refuses the compromise. "There shall not an hoof be left behind; for thereof must we take to serve the LORD our God; and we know not with what we must serve the LORD, until we come thither." Moses and Pharaoh will never see one another again, for the deliverance of God is nigh.

Like Moses, each father is called by God to boldly declare their mission to any who oppose God's plan. We are pilgrims and strangers on the way to the Promised Land. We are taking with us our young and our old, our sons and our daughters, and any others over whom God grants us influence. There is no compromise. No one gets left behind.

Enemies Within

As we discussed in the last chapter, the first round of opposition the father must face is within his home. Sin and compromise have many sources and innumerable allies. Moses warned the people to beware their brother, son, daughter, wife, friend, and own soul.[2] He commanded that sin could not be consented to, hearkened, pitied, spared, or concealed regardless of the affection a father may have for its source.[3] The same is true today.

As always, the father's first battle is with himself. Jesus said, "How can one enter into a strong man's house, and spoil his goods, except he first bind the strong man? and then he will spoil his house."[4] Each father is the strong man in his own home. If he is bound, the home will soon be spoiled. The enemies without come to the home to kill, steal, and destroy. Has this happened in our homes? If so, we must determine what has us bound. Fathers are often bound by hobbies, careers, dead religion, or secret sin. If we are bound, we must realize the high price it will cost our families.

Job recognized the danger of being bound as a father when he said, "I made a covenant with mine eyes; why then should I think upon a maid?"[5] We have repeatedly seen how David's failure to keep a covenant like Job's cost him everything he loved in life. In the New Testament, the Apostle Paul warned each Christian man to "possess his vessel in sanctification and honour; Not in the lust of concupiscence, even as the Gentiles which know not God:"⁶ Any enemy must bind the father before it can access the home. We must refuse to be bound.

The father's next battle is establishing authority in his home with his children. Fathers are agents of God specifically commissioned to raise up the next generation in holiness and dedication to God. Because a father's authority comes from God, He will help us behind the scenes. A father need not stomp around the house emphasizing that he is the boss. If a father feels the need to do so, he really is not in authority regardless of his shouting.⁷

Pastor Denny Kenaston states that if authority is lacking in the home, there is a proper way to develop that authority in the hearts of the children.⁸ First, the father must carry out his God-given role and responsibilities. Second, he must faithfully walk with God. Third, he must build relationships with his children instead of barking orders. Fourth, he must be consistent. Consistency is imperative to real authority. Inconsistent authority may be feared, but it is rarely loved or respected.

Because a father's authority flows directly out of a holy calling from God, this reality should erase any question the father has about his authority and radically transform the way he uses that authority.⁹ Kenaston explains that each father has four choices about how to use his authority. He can be proactive, non-active, reactive, or explosive.¹⁰

The proactive father looks ahead into the trials his children are sure to face. He plans sufficiently and trains his children before the crisis arises. He squelches fires of rebellion while they are small, and he uses the majority of his interaction with his children to build deep, loving relationships and impart positive encouragement.

In contrast, the non-active father is mentally, emotionally, and often physically absent. When the children are in his care, they are permitted to do as they will. His attention is often on "more important things"— television, movies, the computer, the internet, or video games are frequent examples. As his children turn the home into a natural disaster area, he denies his responsibilities and leaves the mother, pastor, and teachers to sort through the mess.

The reactive father is a hostage to his child's moods and actions. If the child is having a good day, fathering is a pleasure, and peace reigns in the home. If the child is having a bad day, the father ignores it as long as possible. When the child is so completely out of control that it becomes clear something must be done, the father reacts in anger and punishes the child's actions without ever dealing with the heart issues.

The explosive father is the reactive father on steroids. He tolerates the children as long as he can. However, when warnings, threats, and counting inevitably fail to produce obedience, his wrath is formidable. The devastation he leaves in his wake never solves the problem, but it does ensure that he need not deal with it for long. The hearts of his children are soon hardened, and they learn to spend time elsewhere. Often, the explosive father barely notices they are gone.

The father's next danger is unbiblical goals. Because earthly fathers are the agents of the heavenly Father entrusted with the stewardship of His children, pursuing goals that are not from God is a betrayal of the worst kind. Tedd Tripp explains that unbiblical goals include perfecting secular skills, manipulating our child through worldly psychology, pressuring our children to an early recitation of the sinner's prayer, training our children to be content with dead religious rituals, conforming their behavior without changing their heart, and submitting their actions to purposeless parental control.[11]

Like unbiblical goals, unbiblical methods are equally a betrayal of our Lord. Unbiblical methods include bribery, negotiation, contract, psychological behavior modification, emotional manipulation, guilt trips, abuse, non-corrective punishment, and erratic inconsistency.[12] If the basis of a father's authority is that he pays the bills or holds the stick, his children will not submit their hearts and will find a way to rectify the temporary inhibition as quickly as possible.[13]

As the father begins to establish Biblical authority in his home, confrontations with friends and family members often arise. Any time we change the way we parent, we can expect challenges from everyone who cares about us and about our children.[14] A father who seeks a godly seed will quickly hear multiple opinions he never sought.

Relationships with ungodly or compromised relatives can quickly become complex when a father chooses to stand for God in his home. Criticism can be both quick and cruel. If the father is not soon shaken in mind, the attention inevitably turns to the wife, as the friends and relatives attempt to dissuade the father by causing conflict in his marriage. If, by God's grace, the couple stands united in their convictions, the critics may turn their attention to the impressionable minds and hearts of the children.

Because of this danger, William Booth said, "Persons not decidedly godly should not be allowed, even if relatives, to come into close and continuous association with children."[15] Any relative who develops a close relationship with our children is likely to be a great force for either good or evil. Uncles, aunts, cousins, and grandparents exercise a far greater influence over the hearts of children than strangers because the children naturally think highly of these people. Consequently, the children are far more likely to remember and imitate the words and actions of close relatives.

As a result, it is incredibly important that such examples and influences are reinforcing the holy, useful, and good. On this point, Booth comments, "Yet we all know how common a thing it is for the parents of children to consider that there is a sort of necessity, on the ground of relationship, for them to receive into their homes, on lengthened visits, unsaved, worldly aunts, cousins, and relatives to the third and fourth generations."[16] Booth goes on to call this practice a "monstrous folly" of "indescribable" misjudgment.[17] No relative is worth losing our children to the world. If we offend them by our stand, let us do so in love and truth. The offense is their choice. If, instead, we permit them to offend our children, our Lord assures judgment for us both.

Enemies Without

Even as the father battles on multiple fronts within the camp, the enemies without the camp prepare their attack. There is indeed a great war against fathers in the western culture. As fathers are wounded and discouraged by the struggle to keep the hearts of their children, many enemies and distractions wait like snipers to finish off the kill.

Distraction is the enemy's most common and most successful strategy.[18] Untold billions of dollars are spent each year in hopes of distracting and dividing the family. Large houses, separate televisions, laptops, earphones, youth groups, Sunday Schools, and a thousand other activities and devices work together to ensure that the father and his children are anywhere but together. Technology celebrates making people more "connected" while replacing family meals, face-to-face conversation, and family devotions with texting, tweeting, and social networking. Stop the ride; it is time to get off!

Meanwhile, the world lures children primarily through unsupervised entertainment and unsupervised relationships.[19] The Bible repeatedly draws a clear contrast between our children and the world. The Psalms provide one of the clearest challenges:

> "Blessed is the man that walketh not in the counsel of the ungodly, nor standeth in the way of sinners, nor sitteth in the seat of the scornful. But his delight is in the law of the LORD; and in his law doth he meditate day and night. And he shall be like a tree planted by the rivers of water, that bringeth forth his fruit in his season; his leaf also shall not wither; and whatsoever he doeth shall prosper."[20]

We cannot expect our children to delight in the law of the Lord if we permit them to walk, stand, and sit with the world. That said, even the most diligent father will struggle to protect his children from every evil influence. However, protection is not our only method. Monte Swan reminds us that each father can out-romance any competitor the world can ever produce.[21] This is our calling.

Unsupervised relationships with peers are one of the fastest ways to lose a child's heart. Solomon warned that peers provide a new identity that draws the child away from his parents. He wrote:

> "My son, hear the instruction of thy father, and forsake not the law of thy mother: For they shall be an ornament of grace unto thy head, and chains about thy neck. My son, if sinners entice thee, consent thou not. If they say, Come with us, let us lay wait for blood, let us lurk privily for the innocent without cause: Let us swallow them up alive as the grave; and whole, as those that go down into the pit: We shall find all precious substance, we shall fill our houses with spoil: Cast in thy lot among us; let us all have one purse: My son, walk not thou in the way with them; refrain thy foot from their path:"[22]

Note carefully the use of plural pronouns in the invitation of the sinners. Peers invite children to create a new "us" that is free from the training, protection, and influence of their godly parents. Proverbs goes on to warn of a youthful generation "that curseth their father, and doth not bless their mother [. . . ,] are pure in their own eyes [. . .] whose teeth are as swords, and their jaw teeth as knives [. . . .]"[23]

Charles Finney wrote, "[W]ho can calculate the evil that may result from one hour's unrestrained and unobserved intercourse of children with each other."[24] Finney continued:

> "Many parents seem to turn their children to and fro, to wander like a wild ass' colt. If so be they are out of the way, it matters little with some parents, where or in what company they are. Now if there is any thing in the universe that deserves the severest reprehension, and I must add, the deepest damnation, it is such a reckless spirit in parents. It is tempting God. No language can describe its guilt."[25]

On the same subject, Booth challenged, "The majority of persons are positively blind—we were going to say positively insane—on this subject. They take very little note of the moral and spiritual character of the companions and playmates of their children."[26] Dear fathers, we must wake up on this issue and take a holy stand for God in constantly supervising the interaction between our children and their peers.

The deadly trap of public education is the peer problem multiplied exponentially. Things have deteriorated so much among the American church that we dare say many Christian schools are not much better. The issue of education merits its own volume, so an in-depth examination of this topic is beyond our scope here. As a result, we will not present our full argument, but rather we present the words of such giants of faith as Charles Finney, John Wesley, William Law, and William Booth on this important subject. Their words are weighty, especially considering the brighter day in which they were written. If these men lived today, they would be shocked that the argument even need be made.

Charles Finney wrote the following in 1840:

> "Be especially careful of the influences that act upon your children at common schools. It often seems to me, that parents hardly dream of the amount of corruption, filthy language, and conduct, often witnessed in common schools. Little children of the same, as well as of the opposite sexes, deeply corrupting and defiling each other. These things are often practiced, to a most shocking extent,

> without parents seeming even so much as to know of it. I would rather be at any expense, at all within my means, or even to satisfy myself with one meal a day, to enable me to educate my children at home, sooner than give them over to the influence of common schools, as they are often arranged and conducted."[27]

John Wesley, too, wrote boldly on the subject, saying "Otherwise, to send them to school (permit me to speak plainly) is little better than sending them to the devil."[28] Wesley continued:

> "By no means send them to a large boarding-school. In these seminaries too the children teach one another pride, vanity, affectation, intrigue, artifice, and, in short, everything which a Christian woman ought not to learn. Suppose a girl were well inclined, yet what would she do in a crowd of children, not one of whom has any thought of saving her soul in such company? Especially as their whole conversation points another way, and turns upon things which one would wish she would never think of. I never yet knew a pious, sensible woman that had been bred at a large boarding-school, who did not aver, one might as well send a young maid to be bred in Drury-Lane."[29]

William Law wrote that "a Christian education should have no other end, but to teach youth how to think, and judge, and act, and live, according to the strictest laws of Christianity."[30] He continued, "It is much to be lamented, that persons so naturally qualified to be great examples of piety, should, by an erroneous education, be made poor and gaudy spectacles of the greatest vanity."[31]

Stirred with righteous indignation, William Booth wrote long and passionately on the subject of education. Booth wrote:

> "Take the school question for instance. Parents know, or they might know if they would be at the trouble to enquire, what the companionship of a school usually means to children of an ordinary kind. There is no pretence to anything like practical religion. Take, for instance, twenty, fifty, or a hundred boys of the usual character in an ordinary establishment [. . .] they will be, as a rule, thorough haters of anything like real godliness, and

unceasing tormentors of any boy who might come in amongst them determined to live like Jesus Christ.³²

Booth continued, "What will those parents say for themselves in the last day, who, instead of labouring to keep their children out of temptation, for some supposed advantages deliberately lead them into it?"³³ He advised all parents to keep their children at home for their education.

Concerning the objections to home education, Booth wrote, "It is to be feared that in their attempts to get what they call 'a good education' for their children, numbers of parents undo all the good accomplished by home instruction and example."³⁴ He continued:

> "[I]if what you aim at cannot be accomplished without running the serious risk of ruining your children for time and eternity by sending them to the ordinary centers of education, and if this education cannot be obtained in any other way, you must be content with an inferior education, consoling yourself with the words of the Master:—'What shall it profit a man if he gain the whole world and lose his own soul?' We suppose you can better endure the thought of your children being imperfectly versed in languages and the higher forms of culture, and deficient in that particular polish attained by a residence in the higher scholastic institutions, than that they should prove faithless to the Master, be untrue to His interests and loose in their morals, [and] form alliances with His enemies [. . . .]"³⁵

Booth added this admonition:

> "Whether you have one or twenty children, measure all the subjects and methods of instruction that are proposed for them by this rule. With regard to every proposition, ask, 'Will this learning help my children to love God more, and to serve their generation better?' If it seems likely to do so, to qualify them more effectually for saving souls, fighting the devil, mastering sin, and following Jesus Christ, secure it for them, if possible. If it be otherwise—as you value the souls of your children, and desire to have the approbation of Jehovah in the Great Judgment Day—do nothing of the kind, whatever this seeming sacrifice may involve

either for you or them. In short, we think it will be wise to make it a rule, that, after teaching your children all that is necessary to enable them to carry on the duties of everyday life in family and business affairs, it will be safe for you to decide that they shall learn nothing that cannot really be pressed into the service of God, and used for the Salvation of souls."[36]

These great men of old leave us duly warned and challenged. Let us now pick up their mantle.

Another enemy that constantly attempts to divide children from their father is fashion. Isaiah warned against letting the daughters of Zion become haughty in their walk, adornment, perfume, figure, well set hair, and beauty.[37] William Law warned that "personal pride and affectation, a delight in beauty and fondness of finery, are tempers that must either kill all religion in the soul, or be themselves killed by it; they can no more thrive together than health and sickness."[38] He noted that if fathers permit their children to develop such attitudes, then when the children "are often seen to lose that little religion they were taught in their youth, it is no more to be wondered at than to see a little flower choked and killed amongst rank weeds."[39]

Television is public enemy number one against us winning the hearts of our children.[40] Television has the worst of two separate modes of attack on your family. First, it is one of the worst distractions known to man, and fathers seem to be especially prone to it. Second, the programming on the television is intentionally anti-family, and often simply anti-Christ. This issue, too, deserves its own volume. The cinema has slain its thousands, and the television its tens of thousands. While we must save a full assault on this enemy for another day, our families cannot afford any delay. We must rid our homes of this enemy. Better yet, let us set an example for our children by destroying it in front of them.

Fictional books can also be an enemy to your home. Booth argued:

> "Ordinary novels or love-stories should be kept from children as you would keep rank poison from them. The action of the ordinary novel upon the minds of children is pernicious in the extreme, making them dissatisfied with their present position and condition in life, and filling them with unnatural ambitions and desires. Novels make the duties of the everyday life of children and

everybody else insipid, create and develop an unnatural precocity, and altogether destroy that beautiful, simple, child-like spirit which we admire so much in children, and which we ought to make every reasonable sacrifice to preserve.[41]

Booth's point may be bold, but it rings true in many of our homes.

Let us clearly recognize that battle arrayed against us, brethren. Many may say we are too extreme or legalistic. Others will claim we are overreacting and far too serious about the matter. Yet, the Scriptures compel us to this stand. Solomon warned, "Take us the foxes, the little foxes, that spoil the vines: for our vines have tender grapes."[42] Our children are our tender grapes, and even the little foxes can raid and spoil our vine. In New Testament terms, "A little leaven leaveneth the whole lump."[43] Let us act with vigilance and tenacity. Our enemies will do no less.

---

1. Exodus 10
2. Deuteronomy 13:6-10
3. Deuteronomy 13:6-10
4. Matthew 12:29
5. Job 31:1
6. 1 Thessalonians 4:4-5
7. Denny Kenaston, The Pursuit of Godly Seed (2003) p. 239
8. *Id.* p 239-240
9. Tedd Tripp, Shepherding Your Child's Heart, (2005) p. 28
10. Denny Kenaston, The Pursuit of Godly Seed (2003) p. 242
11. Tedd Tripp, Shepherding Your Child's Heart, (2005) pp. 40-44
12. *Id.* pp. 59-65
13. Tedd and Margy Tripp, Instructing Your Child's Heart, (2008) p. 86
14. Henry Cloud and John Townsend, Raising Great Kids, (1999) p. 13
15. William Booth, How to Make the Children into Saints and Soldiers of Jesus Christ, (1888) available at http://www.gospeltruth.net/children/booth_training.htm.
16. *Id.*
17. *Id.*
18. Monte Swan, Romancing Your Child's Heart, (2002) p. 79
19. *Id.* p. 73

20. Psalm 1:1-3
21. Monte Swan, Romancing Your Child's Heart, (2002) p. 74
22. Proverbs 1:8-15
23. Proverbs 30:11-14
24. Charles Finney, "November 4, 1840 Letters to Parents—6" available at http://www.gospeltruth.net/children/401104_parents_6.htm
25. *Id.*
26. William Booth, How to Make the Children into Saints and Soldiers of Jesus Christ, (1888) available at http://www.gospeltruth.net/children/booth_training.htm.
27. Charles Finney, "October 21, 1840 Letters to Parents—5" available at http://www.gospeltruth.net/children/401021_parents_5.htm
28. John Wesley, "On Family Religion Sermon 94"
29. *Id.*
30. William Law, Serious Call to a Devout and Holy Life (1729) available at www.ccel.org/ccel/law/serious_call.i.html
31. *Id.*
32. William Booth, How to Make the Children into Saints and Soldiers of Jesus Christ, (1888) available at http://www.gospeltruth.net/children/booth_training.htm.
33. *Id.*
34. *Id.*
35. *Id.*
36. *Id.*
37. Isaiah 3:16, 24
38. William Law, Serious Call to a Devout and Holy Life (1729) available at www.ccel.org/ccel/law/serious_call.i.html
39. *Id.*
40. RCH p 125
41. William Booth, How to Make the Children into Saints and Soldiers of Jesus Christ, (1888) available at http://www.gospeltruth.net/children/booth_training.htm.
42. Song of Solomon 2:15
43. Galatians 5:9

CHAPTER 18

THE FATHER'S VICTORY: "THE BATTLE IS THE LORD'S"

The enemies of God gather together to war against Israel yet again.[1] Saul, the tormented and troubled leader of Israel, prepares his men for battle. In the valley between the two armies, Goliath of Gath, the biggest enemy this generation of Israelites has ever seen, mocks Saul, Israel, and God. The armies of Israel stand frozen in fear.

Into the trenches walks David, a young man anointed by God. As David greets his brothers who are already in the war, the shepherd first hears the giant taunt the God of Israel. Gripped with fear and shame, Eliab rebukes young David for speaking out of turn. David responds bluntly, "Is there not a cause?" Hearing the stir in the camp, Saul summons David.

David testifies to the king, "The LORD that delivered me out of the paw of the lion, and out of the paw of the bear, he will deliver me out of the hand of this Philistine." Taking a staff, five stones, a sling, and an unshakable faith in God, David descends into the valley with the giant. Cursing and threatening, Goliath approaches. David shouts, "I come to thee in the name of the LORD of hosts, the God of the armies of Israel, whom thou hast defied." As the supernatural power of faith surges through his body, David continues, "This day will the LORD deliver thee into mine hand; and I will smite thee [. . .] that all the earth may know that there is a God in Israel. And all this assembly shall know that the LORD saveth not with sword and spear: for the battle is the LORD's, and he will give you into our hands."

The time for words passes quickly, and David runs toward the giant. Before Goliath can react, the stone flies through the air. The giant crashes to the earth. The enemy scatters before the armies of God, who have found new faith from watching a young man fight a battle for God. As true now as then, when a man volunteers to fight a battle for God, the Lord fights the battle with him.

Generations earlier, another young man stands for God in the wilderness outside the Promised Land.[2] The pagan nations of Canaan had quickly learned an invaluable lesson about opposing God's people. The people of God are rarely defeated, but easily compromised. The Midianites put that plan into practice with great success. With compromise in the camp, God must judge His people instead of defending them. Plague spreads quickly through the tents of Israel.

Phinehas, the grandson of Aaron, watches in shock as an Israelite man dares to bring a Midianite mistress into the camp in blatant defiance of the commands of God. Filled with zeal, Phinehas goes after the man of Israel into the tent and thrusts both the offenders through with a javelin. Immediately, the plague stops, but twenty-four thousand people have already perished for the compromise. The Lord tells Moses that Phinehas "hath turned my wrath away from the children of Israel, while he was zealous for my sake among them, that I consumed not the children of Israel in my jealousy." For his faithfulness, God promises Phinehas a covenant of peace to his generations and the covenant of an everlasting priesthood. When a man chooses to stand for God, the Lord remembers both the man and his generations after him.

Fight for your King

The Scriptures in both the Old and New Testaments make regular use of war symbolism as it relates to the godly life. Men are repeatedly encouraged to take a stand for God. This stand has both defensive and offensive elements. The tribes of Gad, Rueben, and Manasseh illustrate both elements during the conflict to take the Promised Land.

Moses challenges these tribes not to avoid the battle, asking "Shall your brethren go to war, and shall ye sit here?"[3] The fathers in the tribes respond with a plan, "We will build [. . .] cities for our little ones: But we ourselves will go ready armed before the children of Israel[.]"[4] The children are to live in defensive cities "because of the inhabitants of the land."[5] Moses acknowledged the wisdom of the plan. He concludes, "[Y]e shall pass over armed before your brethren the children of Israel, all that are meet for the war. But your wives, and your little ones, [. . .] shall abide in your cities which I have given you."[6] The men are to follow this plan "Until the LORD have given rest unto your brethren, as well as unto you [. . .] and then shall ye return every man unto his possession, which I have given you."⁷

As fathers, we also are called into the same two-part battle. First, we must build defenses to protect our wives and our children from the enemies that inhabit the land. Second, we must be prepared to go on the offense, making disciples and gaining new spiritual ground instead of growing content with past victories.

While pursuing this plan, we can be assured that God never asks us to fight the battle alone. As Moses said, "The LORD your God which goeth before you, he shall fight for you, according to all that he did for you in Egypt before your eyes; And in the wilderness, where thou hast seen how that the LORD thy God bare thee, as a man doth bear his son, in all the way that ye went, until ye came into this place."⁸ Our vision is to become godly fathers. We can be sure that the heavenly Father will bear us as his own children while we emulate His love in our homes.

God will not abandon us in this calling. Even more, we cannot hope to succeed without His daily presence and anointing. "Except the LORD build the house, they labour in vain that build it: except the LORD keep the city, the watchman waketh but in vain."⁹ As Israel, we praise God "For He hath strengthened the bars of thy gates; He hath blessed thy children within thee."¹⁰ We take great encouragement from the words of Isaiah:

> "When the enemy shall come in like a flood, the Spirit of the LORD shall lift up a standard against him. [. . .] As for me, this is my covenant with them, saith the LORD; My spirit that is upon thee, and my words which I have put in thy mouth, shall not depart out of thy mouth, nor out of the mouth of thy seed, nor out of the mouth of thy seed's seed, saith the LORD, from henceforth and for ever."¹¹

What a promise! God promises that if His Spirit and Word are in us, they will not depart from our descendents. Why would God offer such hope? Because, dear brothers, our children are the standard that God wants to lift up against the flood of sin!

In light of such dear and precious promises, we find ourselves humbled and even somewhat fearful to recognize the extent of the calling of Christian fatherhood. We dare not think ourselves great, mighty, or capable of procuring such a promise. Yet, it is God who gave such great and mighty promises, and He cannot lie. The words of the Apostle are as true here as anywhere else:

> "For ye see your calling, brethren, how that not many wise men after the flesh, not many mighty, not many noble, are called: But God hath chosen the foolish things of the world to confound the wise; and God hath chosen the weak things of the world to confound the things which are mighty; And base things of the world, and things which are despised, hath God chosen, yea, and things which are not, to bring to nought things that are: That no flesh should glory in his presence."[12]

This is our calling. The battle is the Lord's. Let us fulfill our calling well.

Moreover, we are confident that God is equipping us for the battle. As Paul assured:

> "For though we walk in the flesh, we do not war after the flesh: (For the weapons of our warfare are not carnal, but mighty through God to the pulling down of strong holds;) Casting down imaginations, and every high thing that exalteth itself against the knowledge of God, and bringing into captivity every thought to the obedience of Christ;"[13]

God has called fathers to a high calling. The stakes could not be higher. God Himself has commissioned us to preserve and prepare the next generation of faithful citizens of the kingdom of heaven. The ability is in the call. The tools and weapons we desperately need to fulfill our mission are provided by God through Christ. God has provided His Word, Spirit, and ministry to assist us. If we follow God's ways, our victory is sure.

Our homes, then, should be full of an atmosphere of thanksgiving and victory. One of the most important parts of this vision is the climate or atmosphere that we create in our homes. Right can be done in bitterness and anger or in love, joy, and peace. If the atmosphere is wrong, we must pause the homeschooling, let the chores pass us by, and get on our faces before God as a family until love, joy, and peace is restored in the home.

Empowered by the grace and Spirit made available in the new covenant, we stand firmly upon the foundational family truths made clear in both the Old and New Testaments. Andrew Murray summarized those truths as follows: 1) God wants to be the God of our children and grandchildren; 2) God wants our children to be a chosen generation prepared for His purpose from an early age; 3) God wants parents to be ministers of the covenant to the next generation, preparing the hearts of the children to keep covenant with God.[14]

However, a godly home is not necessarily a family where people are perfectly matched together and inspire one another to live lives completely free of conflict or disagreement. Rather, a godly home is a system by which God takes individuals who are sinful and selfish and gives them a vision that is far bigger than themselves. That vision then transforms every member of the home, through years of successes and failures, into the very image of the vision that once seemed impossible.

There will inevitably be times during that process when we feel like the principles are not working. After all, if God only gave us children we already knew how to handle, we wouldn't have to grow in God to raise them. However, these inevitable moments reveal the importance of basing our roles as fathers in the bedrock of Scripture. If the principles we rely upon are of man, then they may fail us when problems arise, but if the principles we rely on are of God, we may proceed in faith regardless of temporary challenges.

God's strength is made perfect in our weakness. Fathers—even godly ones—are not God. Our mistakes, failures, and human restrictions compel us to throw ourselves at the feet of an eternal God and plead for His constant, daily intervention in our homes. None of us can parent our children so well that we obligate God to overpower their wills and save their souls. Rather, our hope is based on the very heart of God and the promises He gave us in Scripture. God is after our children. If we do our part, He will work with us daily to draw them to Himself. Nobody seeks like God seeks.

In goods day and bad days, we must not lose sight of the vision. There is far more at stake than just the momentary parenting needs of the day. Tedd and Margy Tripp challenge us, "Don't think survival—think kingdom!"[15]

The Way of Salvation in the Second Generation

We pause here to focus on what the salvation process looks like in a generation raised separate from the world. Clarification on this point is necessary because the signs that accompany faith in the next generation can be radically different from the signs in the believer who is saved out of an ungodly lifestyle. The prayers, emotions, and evidences that accompany repentance, water baptism, and receiving the Holy Spirit can be and have been faked by many young people raised in the church. When these imitators depart in later years, parents are left wondering what went wrong with the child they believed was converted before they started kindergarten. Our churches are sometimes not far from the infant baptisms that sparked a reformation centuries ago.

The process of conversion and surrender in a child raised in a godly home has several signs that differ from those for which fathers often look.[16] These signs can often be seen in examples in Scripture. Each moment in this process has the alternative potential for pitfalls or positive steps forward.

First, a youth must begin the transformation from childhood to adulthood with the recognition, "I am no longer a child." Paul talks about putting away childish things.[17] Solomon warned young people to avoid the judgment of God by recognizing that "childhood and youth are vanity."[18] Paul also noted that even an heir is treated like a servant "as long as he is a child."[19] This transformation is both natural and spiritual.

The potential positive steps forward here are numerous. The child can make his beliefs and convictions more personal. He can willfully put away foolishness. He can begin to pull his load naturally and spiritually in the home and the church. He can take responsibility for his training by seeking further instruction. His parents can include him in adult discussions at home and in the church.

The pitfalls here, however, are numerous as well. The child can seek a new identity by rebelling and doing his own thing; Fathers often respond by refusing to recognize that the child is slowly becoming an adult. If the father assumes all is well because of prior training and fails to engage in the current struggles his young person faces, the father may lose his child's heart quickly.

Second, the next generation realizes, "I have talents, potential, and opportunities in life." As a child becomes a young adult, they become more aware of the abilities they posses. As they begin to consider future education, career, and ministry goals, fathers need to guide them to the recognition that they are to be the servants of God in all that they do.

The positive steps forward involved in this realization can differ. First, God may desire to use these gifts. The young person may discover the purpose for which God added them to the kingdom. In contrast, however, this may be the young person's first real chance to sacrifice something for God. The first generation of believers often must sacrifice realities to follow Christ. They may have to clean their home of sin, separate from ungodly friends or family, or leave a career that causes them to violate God's Word. In a similar way the next generation sacrifices dreams where the prior generation sacrificed reality. Our children may naturally be able to attend the best universities, play for the greatest sports teams, or climb to the highest rungs of the corporate ladder. However, every dream, ability and opportunity our children possess should be submitted to the principles and will of God.

The pitfall in this situation is the idea that young people should pursue every opportunity with each of their abilities. God sometimes gives talents to be sacrificed rather than used. From birth, we dedicate our children to God and His kingdom. If we are not careful, we can lose our children to one of many secular idols at this juncture. Following Christ and building His kingdom may require our children to sacrifice higher ranked education, higher-paying jobs, or other opportunities. If we help them choose to follow Christ, they will not regret it.

Third, the young person realizes, "I did not personally form most of the convictions that make me who I am." This realization naturally leads to a degree of questioning in regards to beliefs and convictions. While this time may appear threatening at first, this transition is an important part of internalizing the faith in the next generation. Paul wrote repeatedly on this subject. He encouraged the Corinthians, "Brethren, be not children in understanding: [. . .] but in understanding be men."[20] He told young Timothy, "Study to shew thyself approved unto God, a workman that needeth not to be ashamed, rightly dividing the word of truth."[21] He also advised the Thessalonian believers to "stand fast, and hold the traditions which ye have been taught, whether by word, or our epistle."[22]

At this point, the great positive step forward is the opportunity to question, study, and internalize the beliefs, doctrines, and convictions foundational to our faith. Indeed, some young people emerge from this time with even stronger convictions than their parents possess. This time of searching and proving may be an opportunity for the next generation to do something better than any before them.

The pitfall to avoid is allowing our children to develop a critical, questioning spirit. Mere questioning requires no skill, energy, or study. We need to help our children learn to search for answers rather than just presenting questions. Remember, the one who asks the questions ultimately controls the conversation. Also, we should remind our children who first asked, "Yea, hath God said?" The spirit in which the questions are asked is key.

Fourth, young people need to realize, "I need a personal encounter with God." The moments when God personally introduces Himself to the next generation are some of the highlights of Scripture. Joshua lingers in the tabernacle in awe of the presence of God.[23] The child Samuel hears the voice of God for the first time.[24] Paul watches faith take root in the heart of Timothy.[25] The mantle falls to Elisha as he watches the chariot of fire.[26] Our children desperately need this kind of experience.

The positive step forward is that the children enter into a personal relationship with God. For most of their early years, the children largely know God through their parents. We must help them make the transition to a personal relationship with God, encourage them to pick up the mantle of leadership, and affirm what God is saying to them.

The pitfall is skipping this step too quickly. Some children will be compliant without a real relationship with the Lord. They may never miss a service. Yet, religion without a relationship will produce, at best, a professional benchwarmer. We should not let our children just accept our testimony. They need us to help them make their own.

Fifth, young people need to realize and appreciate, "I have received a tremendous amount from the prior generation." Each generation should appreciate the sacrifices and faithfulness of those who went before them. This starts in the home and expands exponentially from there. In addition to receiving a godly heritage from their parents, Paul says each believer is a partaker "of the inheritance of the saints in light."[27] This cloud of witnesses will compel our young people to greater sacrifice and faithfulness for God.

The positive step forward is threefold. First, young people can reward the prior generation with honor and thankfulness. Second, they can hold fast what they received. Third, they can live in awe of their responsibility to build on the testimonies of those that preceded them.

There are also two pitfalls, like ditches on both sides of a narrow path. First, young people can despise their inheritance of faith like Esau, "who for one morsel of meat sold his birthright."[28] The second ditch is more subtle. Young people often become content with what they have been given. As a result, they stop guarding, defending, and advancing the kingdom. This misplaced contentment is a seed of backsliding.

Sixth, young people must realize that there remains yet very much land to be possessed. Joshua faced this challenge with the people who followed him.[29] Young people need goals and victories to pursue. The Christian life may be accused of many things, but if our children think it is boring, we have misrepresented the call to follow Christ. We should help our children realize the spiritual mountains, ministries, and missions that are open to them. They will not have to fight many of the battles we fought. We must help them find new ones.

There are two pitfalls here. First, the older generation is often tempted to squelch the next generation's enthusiasm for new challenges. Second, the next generation sometimes uses new outreach as an excuse for compromise and sin. We must guard against both.

Next, young people should realize that their interaction with the world changes as they transition to adulthood. In the early years, fathers are responsible to help their children avoid worldly philosophy, entertainment, and influence. As the children become more experienced in their convictions and their relationship with God, a transition becomes necessary. To really do work for God, these young arrows in the quiver need to change tactics from avoiding the world to encountering and overcoming it. Young people can step forward into the offensive and defensive efforts of God's kingdom rather than resting safely inside the walls, oblivious to the spiritual battle that rages all around them.

The pitfalls here abound, and many have fallen therein. Greater exposure to worldly influences may cause weaknesses in character to rise to their surface. A young person may be drawn, for the first time, to secular acquaintances or entertainment. The next generation must understand that there are many areas of life where avoidance is always the best tactic. The paternal relationship built during their childhood and maintained through adolescence will be greatly needed as they make this transition.

The next generation also needs to be aware that real Christian discipleship is not popular anywhere, even in the most conservative churches. There is always an undercurrent in the next generation that pulls youth back toward the world. Jesus warns, "If ye were of the world, the world would love his own: but because ye are not of the world, but I have chosen you out of the world, therefore the world hateth you."[30] He continued, "Blessed are ye, when men shall hate you, and when they shall separate you from their company, and shall reproach you, and cast out your name as evil, for the Son of man's sake."[31] Again, He warned, "These things have I spoken unto you, that ye should not be offended. They shall put you out of the synagogues: yea, the time cometh, that whosoever killeth you will think that he doeth God service."[32] Jesus repeatedly prepared His disciples for the cost of following Him. We should prepare our children to pay the same price.

There are two pitfalls related to this realization. The obvious one is that young people often give up their convictions in fear of popular opinion. This failure must be preempted as early as possible. Such compromise will allow the enemy to destroy everything the prior generation builds. The second ditch is harder to detect. The young person who overcomes public ridicule may often succumb to a prideful withdrawal into a clique of trusted allies. Withdrawing from the fight is little better than losing it.

One of the hardest realizations the next generation must reach is that God may need them to serve somewhere separate from their parents and siblings. The cause of Christ demands many sacrifices, but this is one of the hardest. Many believers in the first generation are separated from family by a decision to follow Christ. Yet, these early separations—as painful as they are—generally involve separation from secular relatives who struggle to maintain deep relationships. The separation required of the next generation involves sacrificing some of the deepest and most loving relationships one can ever experience.

At times, this sacrifice can seem too hard to bear on both the parents and the young people who God calls to leave the home. Yet, the Bible and church history are full of such sacrifice. Samuel is given to the service of God at the tabernacle and rarely sees his mother. Elisha feels the mantle of Elijah and runs to say goodbye to his family. Timothy travels the world with the Apostle Paul, enduring persecution and imprisonment away from the mother and grandmother who faithfully raised him in the ways of God. Hudson Taylor watched his mother collapse in tears on the dock as he left England for China. He wrote that that he never realized what Jesus meant when he said "God so loved the world" until he watched the pain his mother endured as her son left to fulfill God's call on his life. Whatever sacrifice God asks of us, we must remember that physical separation is far preferable to spiritual separation. We would prefer that our children serve God across the globe than serve sin across the street.

All these steps build to a conclusion that will inspire more faithfulness in our children than any Sunday school prayer or childhood baptism ever could. With real conversion, a personal relationship with God, and an awareness of their place in God's plan, our children can boldly lift up a standard for God in this world. Children raised in a godly home are uniquely and specifically prepared to build the kingdom of heaven and fulfill the Great Commission. They have a life purpose that will propel them forward every day that God grants them breath. Some of the things they attempt for God will seem impossible. Indeed, God may have been waiting for centuries for a child prepared for God and ignorant of those impossibilities.

Have faith, brothers. The conversion of the next generation can look and feel far different from our own. The signs of real faith and faked religion are at times difficult to distinguish. Yet, the Spirit of God broods over our homes, seeking a godly seed in the earth. We are called to recruit our children to the ranks of the Lord's army. Let us teach them how to properly engage in the fight and help them endure as good soldiers. William Booth reminds us that with God's help, when they reach the end of this life, our children will "be able to say with [Paul], literally and truthfully, I have fought a good fight, I have finished my course, I have kept the faith. And if you do your duty properly they will be able to add to it, 'My parents taught me how to fight, and introduced me to the War.'"[33]

Confronting the Counterarguments

The arguments against the vision expressed in these pages are many. Frankly, the secular arguments do not concern us in the least. It is a waste of words to attempt to defend our way of life to someone who believes in ripping children from the womb piece by piece in the name of freedom of choice. Accusations that large families lead to overpopulation or an excessive carbon footprint miss the point to such a degree that further explanation is futile. However, a number of arguments against our vision come from within the church. These concerns deserve a response. We endeavor to begin that response here.

Counterargument #1: You cannot make your children serve God.

Opponents of our vision quickly respond that fathers cannot make their children serve God. After beginning with what first appears to be an inarguable premise, these opponents conclude that a father cannot be responsible for whether his children believe because he cannot force them to do so. While this conclusion appears reasonable at first, the entire argument rests upon two faulty assumptions.

First, many people assume that when we emphasize a father's role in the pursuit of godly seed we also expect the father to take the place of God in the process. No human father can take the place of God. Only God can produce real conviction and repentance in the heart of a child. Only God can breathe new life into their souls.

Ultimately, the relationship between a godly father and the heavenly Father is strikingly similar to the relationship between a farmer and God. A farmer is responsible to till the soil, plant the right seed, keep the garden, pull the weeds, guard against enemies, labor daily in the field, and pray without ceasing. God's responsibility is to bring life to the seed, send sunshine, provide rain, and cause the seed to grow. All of God's responsibilities are outside the control of the farmer, other than through prayer. However, all of the life, sunshine, and rain are useless without careful labor and preparation by the farmer.

The same is true of the home. There are some responsibilities that are entirely the father's responsibility. God cannot and will not do them in his stead. Some responsibilities are entirely God's, and we dare not think we can replace Him. Yet, there is one great difference between the farmer and the father—God has plainly promised to do everything in His power to save our children and preserve a godly seed in the earth. Therefore, the responsibility for the quality of the harvest remains our own.

Second, some assume that we believe fathers can take the place of the child in the process. Serving God is an individual decision made at a personal level. No father can force a conversion or end the free will of the child. To suggest the end of free will would be to claim sovereignty for a father that God does not claim for Himself.

The problem, then, is that we often fail to understand the process. Can a father prevent a minor child under proper supervision from committing suicide? Certainly, he can. In the same way, a father can prevent a minor child from committing spiritual suicide. Yet, how do you prevent a child from ending his life after he leaves the home? We simply make life so wonderful and death so terrible that the child's mind, will, and emotions cannot fathom the preparation and execution of a plan to end his life. In short, we win his heart.

The same is true in the spiritual. There is a period of time where a father can prevent a child from leaving the church or denying Christ. After that time, his greatest power is to make life with God so wonderful and life apart from God so terrible that the child cannot imagine abandoning the faith. If, instead, the father's words, attitudes, and actions show he believes serving God to be a burden and the world to be full of attractions, he sows the seeds of destruction in his children. Thus, even though a father cannot force a child to serve God, he retains the responsibility for the ultimate outcome.

Counterargument #2: Proverbs are not promises—and other attacks on the validity of Scripture.

"Proverbs are not promises" is exemplary of many ways that people attempt to discredit the Bible when they cannot reconcile what the Word of God says with what they see around them. While this example aims primarily at silencing the famous "when he is old" promise in Proverbs, attacks of this type are legion in variety. This is the first step in an approach that eventually makes the Bible irrelevant to us today.

Before we dissect this claim, consider what the Bible has to say about the Word of God. Paul told Timothy that the holy scriptures were "able to make thee wise unto salvation through faith which is in Christ Jesus."[34] He said, "All scripture is given by inspiration of God, and is profitable for doctrine, for reproof, for correction, for instruction in righteousness: That the man of God may be perfect, thoroughly furnished unto all good works."[35] Proverbs says, "Every word of God is pure."[36] Jesus prayed, "Sanctify them through thy truth: thy word is truth."[37] Jesus also said, "Search the scriptures; for [. . .] they are they which testify of me."[38] Of Moses, Jesus said, "But if ye believe not his writings, how shall ye believe my words?"[39] Referring to the law, Jesus said, "the scripture cannot be broken."[40] Jesus Himself also said, "I have spoken unto you in proverbs[. . . .]"[41]

Speaking of the Old Testament prophets, Peter wrote, "not unto themselves, but unto us they did minister[. . . .]"[42] Peter also wrote, "For the prophecy came not in old time by the will of man: but holy men of God spake as they were moved by the Holy Ghost."[43] Indeed, Peter specifically quoted the book of Proverbs, saying "But it is happened unto them according to the true proverb, The dog is turned to his own vomit again[. . . .]"[44] Peter later stirred up the Christians "That ye may be mindful of the words which were spoken before by the holy prophets[. . . .]"[45] Again, Peter said that "the word of God, [. . .] liveth and abideth for ever."[46] God told Isaiah, "So shall my word be that goeth forth out of my mouth: it shall not return unto me void, but it shall accomplish that which I please, and it shall prosper in the thing whereto I sent it."[47] Paul wrote to the church in Corinth that the Biblical account of history happened for our example and admonition.[48] The writer of Hebrews states, quoting Psalms, that Jesus said, "Lo, I come (in the volume of the book it is written of me,) to do thy will, O God."[49]

The Bible speaks for itself. The credibility of Peter, Paul, and Christ Himself depends upon the validity and reality of the Old Testament. We cannot and will not divide and conquer the Word of God to soothe our own consciences and silence the Scriptures that grieve us.

Moreover, if we did relent and relegate the book of Proverbs to some less credible type of Scripture—as if there could be such a thing—where would such a conclusion stop? If the Proverbs are "just proverbs," are not the Psalms "just" songs written by a morally compromised shepherd? Are the books of Moses "just" the ramblings of an elderly man who wandered in the desert too long? Are the Prophets "just" warnings to the natural descendents of Abraham? Are the Epistles "just" the writings of fishermen and converted Jews stuck in the cultural confines of first-century Christianity? A thousand times, no!

When we quote the Bible, whether it is Proverbs, Deuteronomy, Isaiah, or John, we quote the Word of God. The Scriptures are as alive, relevant, and powerful today as ever. Culture cannot change them. Time cannot change them. Persecution cannot change them. Papal decree, synod, creed, and convention cannot change them. And, dear brothers, we cannot change them, even when the words grieve us, judge us, and compel us to conclusions we would rather not reach.

Counterargument #3: Jesus ended the Old Testament family mindset by beginning a New Covenant.

Many Christians presume a great divide between the Old and New Testament. They argue that the Old Testament's clear focus on godly homes and generational righteousness ended with the coming of Christ. Two passages are often cited to support this notion. The first is as follows:

> "While he yet talked to the people, behold, his mother and his brethren stood without, desiring to speak with him. Then one said unto him, Behold, thy mother and thy brethren stand without, desiring to speak with thee. But he answered and said unto him that told him, Who is my mother? and who are my brethren? And he stretched forth his hand toward his disciples, and said, Behold my mother and my brethren! For whosoever shall do the will of my Father which is in heaven, the same is my brother, and sister, and mother."[50]

However, Jesus in no way minimizes the importance of family in this passage. Instead, he illustrates the importance God places on family by using it as an illustration of His relationship with His followers. To suggest that Jesus was disrespecting His mother would be contrary both to the prior situation at the wedding in Cana and the concern He showed for Mary at the cross. The Lord was revealing that all the blessings of a godly family in the Old Testament would be extended in the New Testament to include other believers. In this theme, Paul talked of serving the heavenly Father "Of whom the whole family in heaven and earth is named."[51]

The second passage people use to show that Jesus supposedly ended the Old Testament concept of family states:

> "Think not that I am come to send peace on earth: I came not to send peace, but a sword. For I am come to set a man at variance against his father, and the daughter against her mother, and the daughter in law against her mother in law. And a man's foes shall be they of his own household. He that loveth father or mother more than me is not worthy of me: and he that loveth son or daughter more than me is not worthy of me."[52]

No doubt many first-generation Christians know well the sting of these words. For centuries, conversion to Christianity from Judaism and a number of other religions has meant a sword in the home. Moreover, no one can disagree with the fact that we must love Christ more than we love our relatives. Yet, to use these verses to predict strife and separation in generations raised in godly homes is out of context, not only in this passage, but also in the rest of Scripture. As we noted earlier, the purpose of marriage is to produce a godly seed. The Lord never confronts the Old Testament Scriptures on family the way He deals with adultery or the Sabbath. In addition, the record of family life in the New Testament is void of an assumption that children will be lost to the world. Instead, there are multiple stories of whole households that are saved and serving God together. A godly home was one of Paul's necessary qualifications for new ministers. Therefore, this passage is a warning to first-generation believers, not a radical paradigm shift in how God views the family.

Counterargument #4: You will give up when you see enough righteous men fail.

This counterpoint, whether expressed or implied, is often the most troubling problem for men who truly desire to raise godly seed. How can we accept this call and this responsibility when so many great Christian men, some of whom we know and love, have lost their children to the world? Do we dare to think for a moment that we can be better fathers than those who have gone before us? This problem gives us pause and humbles us before both God and our brethren who have suffered great pain in losing their children.

Revivalist Charles Finney provides the first response. He wrote as follows:

> "There is one common and grand difficulty, which has seemed to stumble Christians, in respect to their laying hold on the promises, in regard to their children, and calculating with anything like certainty upon their being converted, sanctified, and saved. It is this: Many good men have, in all ages, had abandoned and reprobate children. To this I answer:

(1.) Good men are not always perfect in judgment, and therefore may be, and sometimes doubtless have been guilty of some capital error, in training their children.

(2.) A great many good men have been so occupied with the concerns of the Church and the world, as to pay comparatively little attention to the training of their own children. Their children have been neglected and almost of course lost. At all events, when they have been neglected, they have not been trained up in the way they should go. So that the condition has not been fulfilled.

(3.) Many good men have lived in bad neighborhoods, and found it nearly or quite impossible to train up their children in the way they should go, without changing their locations. And notwithstanding they saw the daily contact of their children was calculated to ruin them, and did, as a matter of fact, prevent their training them up in the way they should go; yet they have, probably from a sense of duty, remained where they were, to the destruction of their children. In such cases, the ruin of their children may be chargeable to their neighbors, because the influence of their neighbor's children prevented their bringing them up in the way they should go. [. . .] I would sooner have the plague in my family, than to have such influences as these. I would not suffer the nearest relative I have on earth to remain in my family, unless he would refrain from corrupting my children."[53]

Finney's points are well made. No doubt many of the greatest heroes of the faith from ancient times through today have made great errors in their homes. David, for example, made one great mistake, repented quickly, and continued to follow God, but his family unraveled as a result of his sin. Without doubt, many men of God have been absent from home so much that they lost the hearts of their children. And, like Lot, many righteous men have tarried too long in Sodom to escape untouched by sin and compromise.

However, merely isolating the myriad reasons that men—even godly men—lose their children does not address the root problem with the counterargument. How can Christians ever give up on a promise of God merely because it does not appear to be fulfilled in the lives of believers around us? We believe in the promise of His coming, yet He tarries. We believe in the promises of prayer, yet we are flooded by examples of unanswered prayer. We believe that we can have the mind of Christ, yet we are surrounded by Christians who have the mind of the world. We believe that the church will triumph over sin and prepare herself as a Bride adorned for her husband, yet we see the church losing influence and lacking moral authority.

The real question here is one of the most fundamental questions of Christianity. How can we believe that the Word of God is true when our senses and our reason often compel us to reach the opposite conclusion? Simple. We walk by faith and not by sight. Dear brothers, let this be our battle cry! When Biblical methods do not seem to work, when good families lose their children, and when it seems the vision will never come to pass, we stand. We stand in unwavering faith. We stand steadfast, unmovable, always abounding in the work of the Lord.

The Word of God is the only rock in the midst of a raging sea of human opinion. We stand on that rock. To doubt the Word of God is to throw ourselves and our families into the waves, to be driven by the wind and tossed to and fro. We may question ourselves. We may question why better men than us lost their children. But we must not question the validity of God's Word.

Counterargument #5: God predestinates some of our children to believe and some to perish.

One of the more fatalistic counterarguments against our vision is the idea of absolute predestination. According to this view, God the Father, sometime in eternity past, elected to love some of our children and assure their entrance into heaven. He also elected to hate some of our children and assure their damnation. The godly father, therefore, is just an actor on a stage going through the motions while he waits powerlessly to learn the predestined fate of his sons and daughters.

At least in the parenting context, the proponents of absolute predestination often rely upon the following Scripture:

> "And not only this; but when Rebecca also had conceived by one, even by our father Isaac; (For the children being not yet born, neither having done any good or evil, that the purpose of God

> according to election might stand, not of works, but of him that calleth;) It was said unto her, The elder shall serve the younger. As it is written, Jacob have I loved, but Esau have I hated. What shall we say then? Is there unrighteousness with God? God forbid. For he saith to Moses, I will have mercy on whom I will have mercy, and I will have compassion on whom I will have compassion. So then it is not of him that willeth, nor of him that runneth, but of God that sheweth mercy."[54]

On its surface, this Scripture appears to confirm a fatalistic interpretation. However, to properly understand what Paul is saying, we must look to the two Scriptures he quoted about Esau.

The first quotation truly comes from a time when the children were not yet born. God told Rebekah, "Two nations are in thy womb, and two manner of people shall be separated from thy bowels; and the one people shall be stronger than the other people; and the elder shall serve the younger."[55] We do not contest that God elevates some children over others in this life for reasons that are His alone. However, nothing in this Scripture says anything about salvation while the children remain in the womb. The second Scripture from which Paul quotes is from the prophet Malachi:

> "I have loved you, saith the LORD. Yet ye say, Wherein hast thou loved us? Was not Esau Jacob's brother? saith the LORD: yet I loved Jacob, And I hated Esau, and laid his mountains and his heritage waste for the dragons of the wilderness. Whereas Edom saith, We are impoverished, but we will return and build the desolate places; thus saith the LORD of hosts, They shall build, but I will throw down; and they shall call them, The border of wickedness, and, The people against whom the LORD hath indignation for ever."[56]

Two important points can be drawn from this passage. First, the statement of love and hate is not made while the children struggle in the womb. Instead, it is made in the final chapters of the Old Testament, closer to Paul's writings than Esau's birth. Second, God is really addressing how He dealt with two nations long after their ancestors lived and died rather than two children that have not yet been born.

The fact that a quote from Malachi is used to argue that we have no impact on our children's salvation is astounding when you consider that Malachi goes on to declare that God implemented marriage to seek a godly seed and that God will turn the hearts of the children and fathers toward each other. Rendering a godly home of no importance could not have been farther from the prophet's mind and theme.

Moreover, if predestination determines the conduct and faith of our children, then God's praise of some fathers and condemnation of others is downright villainous. God judges Eli for failing to restrain his children. He told David that the war within his home was the result of his sin. In contrast, God praised Abraham for commanding his children to follow in the faith. If God predetermined the fates of these children, His words were a mockery of these men.

Moreover, those who promote absolute predestination do not and cannot parent consistent with the doctrine. If a father really believes that his children are either predestined to reign with Christ regardless of their lifestyle or predetermined from eternity past to be blind, naked, miserable, and without hope on earth or help in heaven, then he would live accordingly. Free from any responsibility for his children's salvation, he should eat, drink, and be merry, for tomorrow they all die, and God will sort out His own. Yet, one may argue he should continue to parent well out of love. Here, however, is the most stunning consequence of this doctrine. Surely, as Christians, we should love what God loves and hate what He hates. If the Scripture about Esau can actually be extrapolated and applied to our families, then the election of God compels us not to even attempt to save our children in conflict with the sovereignty of God. This type of parenting is not supported by Scripture and cannot be consistently lived out in practice.

It should also be noted that those who attempt to persuade us of absolute predestination defeat their own argument. If they are right, then we are eternally predestined to believe as we do, have no doubt been deceived by God Himself, and cannot be shaken from our predetermined beliefs by any human reasoning. Thus, their argument is either false or moot. Either way, we should continue in our vision.

Counterargument #6: This is legalism.

As soon as someone favorably references the Old Testament, accusations of legalism are quick to arise. Because legalism is not a Biblical term, it requires outside definition. The dictionary definition of legalism is "strict, literal, or excessive conformity to the law or to a religious or moral code."[57] In the Christian context, accusations of legalism generally equate to following the Mosaic law.

The Law of Moses certainly contains helpful direction for fathers. We do not and need not shy away from basing some parts of our vision in the first five books of the Bible. Indeed, the famous command to teach our children in Deuteronomy follows immediately after a verse that Jesus quoted as the greatest commandment in all of Scripture. In fact, if you follow the use of the conjunction "and" in Deuteronomy chapter 6, we could even argue that the command to teach our children is a part of the same sentence that Jesus quoted.

However, the accusation that our vision is based in a "strict, literal, or excessive conformity to the law" is baseless. As we have shown time and again, this vision flows from every portion of Scripture, the vision is expressed by Abraham, Noah, Moses, Joshua, the kings, the prophets, the psalmists, the proverbs, John the Baptist, the Apostles, Jesus, and God the Father. Conformity to the law has little to do with our call. If, however, the real accusation being made is that our vision is based in conformity to the Word of God, then we will gladly accept that accusation and any label incorrectly attached with it.

Counterargument #7: Large families only made sense in the agricultural society of prior centuries.

Another attempt to discredit God's Word is the suggestion that large families were a blessing because of the agrarian society of previous centuries. There are two fundamental problems with this counterargument. First, children are a blessing because God says they are and because they are souls made in the image of God. No passage of time or change in culture can alter that fact.

Second, the fundamental assumption made in this counterpoint is appalling. The basic assumption in this argument is that large families were beneficial in an agricultural society because they could work and provide financial benefit. In contrast, more children in this modern, urban society cost money and do not provide a financial benefit.

The great blessing of a godly home described in the Word of God is not subject to utilitarian cost-benefit analysis. godly children have inherent value. To even suggest that the value of another child depends on how much money he will add to or take from the family coffers is appalling.

Counterargument #8: As a father, I need personal time, and I have Christian liberty to have hobbies and other pursuits.

When men begin to realize that the calling of a Christian father requires a change in priorities and the investment of large amounts of time, the claim to a right of personal time quickly arises. Many times, we desire to have children while living like we have none. While claiming a right to personal time, men pursue a variety of hobbies and distractions while often leaving their wives alone with the children.

The definition of a hobby reveals much. A hobby is "an activity or interest pursued for pleasure or relaxation and not as a main occupation."[58] To translate, a hobby is something pursued for the purpose of pleasing oneself and is not a part of one's real purpose in life. We cannot find in the Scriptures a description of the Christian man that leaves any substantial amount of time for the private pursuit of fleshly pleasures.

Where do we even get the idea of "free" time? It is undeniable in Scripture that believers are the servants—or slaves—of Jesus Christ. He is our King and our Lord. Paul explained it way:

> "Wherefore we labour, that, whether present or absent, we may be accepted of him. For we must all appear before the judgment seat of Christ; that every one may receive the things done in his body, according to that he hath done, whether it be good or bad. Knowing therefore the terror of the Lord, we persuade men; but we are made manifest unto God; and I trust also are made manifest in your consciences."[59]

To the Colossians, Paul wrote "And whatsoever ye do in word or deed, do all in the name of the Lord Jesus, giving thanks to God and the Father by him."[60] Do we live and think as those that will give account for every word and deed to the Lord who gave everything for us?

Jesus gave a parable that should bring great conviction to every father's heart. He told his disciples:

> "But which of you, having a servant plowing or feeding cattle, will say unto him by and by, when he is come from the field, Go and sit down to meat? And will not rather say unto him, Make ready wherewith I may sup, and gird thyself, and serve me, till I have eaten and drunken; and afterward thou shalt eat and drink? Doth he thank that servant because he did the things that were commanded him? I trow not. So likewise ye, when ye shall have done all those things which are commanded you, say, We are unprofitable servants: we have done that which was our duty to do."[61]

Fathers, how many times do we err in this regard? We labor during the day as we are commanded to do, then we return home expecting to be served, honored, and free to relax by whatever secular means we choose. Yet, how are we to serve our Lord when we return to the house? We serve him by serving the least of these. We serve him with every dirty diaper, runny nose, and soiled dish. We should not return home to relax. We should return home prepared to do our most important work.

Whatever we do or fail to do to "the least of these," we do it or fail to do it to Christ. Our children clearly qualify as the least among His brethren. Therefore, any hobby or distraction that takes us away from our children also takes us away from the service of Christ.

Permit me one personal thought among these many pages. As of this writing, my oldest son is three years old. Each night, as I tuck him into bed, we take turns praying for each other. I lay my hands on him and pray that he will sleep well, have sweet dreams, grow in faith, and obey his mother the following morning. Every night, he shuts his eyes, lays his hand on me, and prays this prayer: "Dear Jesus, please help Daddy not have to go to work tomorrow. Help him stay home and be with us so we can have a great day together. Amen." These are his unprovoked words, and they cut me to the heart. So, forgive me if I seem extreme on this point, but how can I rob my son of time together for the sake of video games, tree stands, golf, or paintball when I know he prays that prayer every night? I do not need more "me time." I need more "them time."

Honestly, can we even imagine Jesus abandoning His disciples for personal entertainment elsewhere? Granted, Jesus did leave His followers for personal time, but he did it in the middle of the night for midnight prayer. Until we define personal time the way Jesus did—an all-night prayer vigil—I find no place for private pursuits in the Scriptures.

Counterargument #9: Putting so much responsibility on fathers will produce unfair feelings of guilt when their children leave.

Our goal is to inspire fathers with vision and purpose, not to cause self-condemnation. However, the truth of Scripture is designed by God to bring conviction and godly sorrow. Indeed, God calls His Word a fire and a hammer that breaks the rocks to pieces.[62] Our convictions admittedly cause us many times of grief, repentance, and contrition.

Counterargument #10: Your vision is idealistic.

Many who genuinely appreciate this vision maintain that it is too idealistic. Accordingly, we often hear concerns that suburban life and modern expenses make it impossible for a father to spend a large quantity of quality time with his children. Trusting God to do the impossible in our lives, we plead guilty to the charge of idealism.

An ideal is a "standard of perfection, or excellence" and the "ultimate object or aim of endeavor, especially one of high or noble character."[63] An idealist is "a person who cherishes or pursues high or noble principles, purposes, goals, etc."[64] Idealism is "the cherishing or pursuit of high or noble principles, purposes, goals, etc."[65] To use such words as a derogatory label for fathers who desire to spend a large quantity of quality time with their children is to encourage fathers, instead, to disregard high or noble principles and pursue less than perfect or excellent goals. As we find ourselves surrounded by fathers and churches that accept and expect far less than excellence, this is no time to abandon our ideals.

Granted, most people use the word ideal to reference a departure from reality. However, if our vision is based in Scripture—and we are persuaded it is—then the vision founded in Scripture is the ultimate reality. We trust the Word of God over any sensory perception or logical induction. Often walking by faith and not by sight, we are compelled to pursue the reality of excellence described in Scripture.

Counterargument #11: God lost Adam, and Jesus lost Judas. No father can expect better.

In one final attempt to divert responsibility away from the father, many attempt to draw an analogy to two of the most infamous backsliders in the Bible, Adam and Judas. Because Adam betrayed God and Judas betrayed Christ when neither God nor Jesus could possibly have failed, these examples allegedly show that free will often rebels in even the most perfect scenarios. However, both these analogies fail because of fundamental differences.

First, Adam's experience has obvious differences from the father-child relationship. Many of the problems in comparing Adam to our children result from a lack of information. How mature was Adam when created? How long did he have to build a relationship with God before the fall? How clearly did God reveal Himself? Yet, the biggest difference is also the most critical. Adam could only sin once. We do not begin to suggest that a godly father can prevent his child from ever sinning. The child will sin and fail, but unlike Adam, the child lives in an atmosphere of grace and forgiveness. Adam could never remove his transgression. In fact, despite the curse upon him, Adam raised up at least two godly children and a righteous seed line through Seth. Thus, no conclusion can be made from a comparison to Adam.

Second, the comparison to Judas is also fraught with irreconcilable differences. Judas was already an adult when he first interacted with Jesus. Untold damage had likely already been done in the betrayer's past. Jesus only had around three years to work with Judas. Also, to some degree, Jesus was not called to save Judas. To focus divine attention on converting the man that was destined to instigate His death would have been an exercise of self-preservation. Indeed, Jesus apparently permitted Judas to steal from the ministry without rebuke. These differences prohibit any meaningful comparison. Even so, why would we trade all the wonderful promises God has made about our homes for a parenting theory based upon Judas Iscariot's betrayal of the Son of God?

Counterargument #12: You should not have children because of the "present distress."

Untold hardship has resulted from a misunderstanding of Paul's admonition concerning the "present distress." Paul wrote to the Corinthians:

> "Brethren, let every man, wherein he is called, therein abide with God. Now concerning virgins I have no commandment of the Lord: yet I give my judgment, as one that hath obtained mercy of the Lord to be faithful. I suppose therefore that this is good for the present distress, I say, that it is good for a man so to be. Art thou bound unto a wife? seek not to be loosed. Art thou loosed from a wife? seek not a wife. But and if thou marry, thou hast not sinned; and if a virgin marry, she hath not sinned. Nevertheless such shall have trouble in the flesh: but I spare you. But this I say, brethren, the time is short: it remaineth, that both they that have wives be as though they had none;" [66]

Somewhere along the line, several Christian leaders became persuaded that what Paul really meant to say was that married couples should not have children because of a fear of backsliding or persecution. We will deal first with the text and then with the more general issue of why modern Christians are afraid to have more children.

The text quoted above provides no basis for the idea that Christian couples today should not have children. The counsel that Paul was giving was that unmarried virgins should consider abstaining from marriage. Indeed, Paul tells those who are married not to try to change that condition. Paul admits that marriage is not a sin, and the book of Hebrews would later call marriage holy and undefiled. Importantly, however, the sole issue Paul addressed was marriage. The apostle did not address children at all in this passage. Moreover, Paul said nothing to alter the statement in Malachi that a godly seed is the purpose of marriage. Unsurprisingly, the New Testament is permeated with approving references to godly homes, and many of those references are made by the Apostle Paul.

Admittedly, Paul does suggest that in times of great persecution the marriage relationship will not be frequently consummated. However, the saints of old would have difficulty stifling their laughter to hear us label our condition "present distress." We live in one of the most uninhibited opportunities to raise a godly seed in the history of the Church. In times past, godly fathers have raised faithful children only to watch them be eaten by lions, burned at the stake, slain by the pagan spear, or drowned in the rivers of Europe for refusing infant baptism. Will we now abandon the cause because of a faceless fear of future persecution? We cannot. If God be for us, we dare not hold back in unbelief, regardless of fear of Catholic inquisition, Islamic horde, or nuclear holocaust. God has commissioned us to raise a godly seed. A cloud of witnesses from generations past forbids us an excuse. Let us fulfill our duty well.

Despite the clear call of God upon our lives, marriages, and homes, we continually face a legion of excuses not to have more children. All around us, fathers limit the size of their families for the sake of money, career, hobbies, or ministry. This is the spirit of abortion, and we have wrestled with it more than we care to admit.[67] Yet, proclaiming personal authority to refuse more children is refusing to accept additional blessings that God says have eternal value and instead replacing those blessings with our own preferences. God never ordered any father in the Bible to stop having children for the sake of career, hobby, or ministry.[68] We need to humble ourselves before God and repent of this evil.

Christians today have all kinds of reasons not to have more children, or even not to have children at all. Among this long list of reasons and excuses are the following:

- Fear of persecution
- Overzealous government intrusion
- Economic concerns
- Acceptance of fertility problems
- Cultural norms on the "normal" number of children
- Concerns of having too many children
- Problems in the church
- Problems in the nation
- Feeling that God has not called them to have children
- Feeling that it is not the "right" time to have children
- Fear that they wouldn't have enough love for multiple kids to share

Most of us have heard some discussion of the idea of having a "quiver full," and the Bible has some very important things to say about this issue.[69] However, have you ever considered what the Bible would be like if the parents of the people who lived it and wrote it thought the way modern Christians do?

Consider Noah and his wife. They lived in a world so evil that God judged the world in a way that He promised to never do again. They were in the most extreme minority possible—no one else believed in God enough to survive the flood. If there was ever a time to refuse to have children because of the condition of the world, that would be the time. Yet, Noah had three sons, and we are eternally grateful that he did.

Amram and Jochebed lived under the reign of the brutal Egyptian pharaohs. They had very little liberty in their lives. They had every reason to fear persecution and government intrusion. Pharaoh ordered that any baby boy would be killed. They could have feared not only slavery for the children, but instantaneous execution of a male child. If they had chosen not to have children because they feared the sword of Pharaoh, Moses would never have been born. Moses later wrote the first five books of the Bible, so we would be without Genesis, Exodus, Leviticus, Numbers, and Deuteronomy.

Joshua was likely born and raised in slavery. Samuel was born during a time when Israel was under constant attack, the priesthood was defiled, and there was no open vision. Despite all these obstacles, Hannah shook heaven until God opened her womb. David was at least the ninth child born to Jesse during the reign of a demon-possessed king. If Jesse had determined to stop at eight, we would lack the Psalms and the Proverbs.

Ezra, Nehemiah, and Esther were likely born in Babylon under slavery, persecution, and judgment from God. The prophets Jeremiah, Ezekiel, Daniel, Zechariah, and Malachi were all born during a time of imminent judgment from God. Some of them suffered through the destruction of Jerusalem. Others faced the obstacles of rebuking Judah during the rebuilding.

In the New Testament, Matthew, Mark, John, and Peter were all born in a time where God had been silent for 400 years. They faced Roman occupation and the extreme danger of being murdered, beaten, or pressed into service at the whim of the Roman soldiers. If there was ever a reason not to have more children for fear of not being able to train the one you already have, Mary and Joseph would be the case. Yet, if they had refused more children due to their focus on raising Jesus, we would not have the book of James, and the early church would be without one of the greatest leaders in the church at Jerusalem.

The story of Benjamin shows just how much we must depend upon the God who sees the end from the beginning. In the pain of the immediate loss, the birth of Benjamin appeared to be a tragic mistake. Jacob already had trouble raising his dozen children, and Rachel had long struggled with infertility. Her final pregnancy would cost Jacob the wife he loved most. Later, Benjamin became one of the least among the tribes of Israel. The tribe makes Biblical history in the worst of ways. After nearly being exterminated by the other tribes, Benjamin's lone fifteen minutes of fame ended with the death of King Saul. Yet, hundreds of years after this tragic birth, a Benjamite would turn the world upside down for Jesus Christ and write the letters that would define the Christian faith for all time. Without the birth of Benjamin, there would be no Apostle Paul.

Thus, we are eternally grateful that the fathers of these children did not succumb to the pressures we often fear. If those fathers thought the way so many Christians do today, we would not have the Bible that we cherish. Let us continue the pursuit of godly seed with the same faithfulness they showed in their day. We stand with confidence because the battle is the Lord's. God will not fail us. Let us make sure we do not fail Him.

---

1. 1 Samuel 17
2. Numbers 25:6-13
3. Numbers 32:6-7
4. Numbers 32:16-17
5. Numbers 32:16-17
6. Deuteronomy 3:18-20
7. Deuteronomy 3:18-20
8. Deuteronomy 1:30-31
9. Psalm 127:1
10. Psalm 147:13
11. Isaiah 59:19-21
12. 1 Corinthians 1:26-29
13. 2 Corinthians 10:3-5
14. Andrew Murray, Raising Your Children for Christ, (1984) p. 160

15. Tedd and Margy Tripp, Instructing Your Child's Heart, (2008) p. 37
16. Much of the following material is based upon a sermon entitled "The Remnant Road 2.0" by Weston Leibee available at www.charitychristianfellowship.org/sermons/listing
17. 1 Corinthians 13:11
18. Ecclesiastes 11:9-10
19. Galatians 4:1-2
20. 1 Corinthians 14:20
21. 2 Timothy 2:15
22. 2 Thessalonians 2:15
23. Exodus 33:11
24. 1 Samuel 3:1-18
25. 2 Timothy 1:5
26. 2 Kings 2:13
27. Colossians 1:12
28. Hebrews 12:16
29. Joshua 13:1
30. John 15:19
31. Luke 6:22
32. John 16:1-2
33. William Booth, How to Make the Children into Saints and Soldiers of Jesus Christ, (1888) available at http://www.gospeltruth.net/children/booth_training.htm.
34. 2 Timothy 3:15-17
35. 2 Timothy 3:15-17
36. Proverbs 30:5
37. John 17:17
38. John 5:39
39. John 5:46-47
40. John 10:34-35
41. John 16:25
42. 1 Peter 1:12
43. 2 Peter 1:21
44. 2 Peter 2:22
45. 2 Peter 3:1-2
46. 1 Peter 1:23
47. Isaiah 55:11
48. 1 Corinthians 10:1-11

49. Hebrews 10:7
50. Matthew 12:46-50
51. Ephesians 3:15
52. Matthew 10:34-37
53. Charles Finney, "November 18, 1840 Letters to Parents—7" available at http://www.gospeltruth.net/children/401118_parents_7.html
54. Romans 9:10-16
55. Genesis 25:23
56. Malachi 1:2-4
57. See http://www.merriam-webster.com/dictionary/legalism
58. http://dictionary.reference.com/browse/hobby
59. 2 Corinthians 5:9-11
60. Colossians 3:17
61. Luke 17:7-10
62. Jeremiah 23:29
63. http://dictionary.reference.com/browse/ideal
64. http://dictionary.reference.com/browse/idealist
65. http://dictionary.reference.com/browse/idealism
66. 1 Corinthians 7:24-29
67. Denny Kenaston, The Pursuit of Godly Seed, (2003) p. 36.
68. *Id.*
69. For a more in-depth discussion of and answer to the many reasons people oppose large families, see Rick and Jan Hess, A Full Quiver (1989).

Answering the Call

"And I sought for a man among them, that should make up the hedge, and stand in the gap before me for the land, that I should not destroy it: but I found none." (Ezekiel 22:30)

The calling of a Christian father is challenging, but it is also an incredible honor. God has been so good to us to include us in His plan for our children. God's plan to ensure the continuance of faith on the earth is to call fathers "that they should make [His commandments] known to their children: That the generation to come might know them, even the children which should be born; who should arise and declare them to their children: That they might set their hope in God, and not forget the works of God, but keep his commandments:"[1] What a privilege!

In our final section, we examine three final issues. First, we prove again the father's responsibility for the spiritual condition of his children. Second, we consider the necessary sacrifices that await the father who accepts this vision. Finally, we rejoice together that God has given us the awesome, inescapable opportunity to answer the call and work with Him to seek a godly seed.

CHAPTER 19

THE FATHER'S RESPONSIBILITY: "PREPARE THE PASSOVER"

Moses steps forward to address the crowd he has quickly come to know. He recognizes the faces of the tribal leaders. For so long, they were strangers to Moses, separated by the forty years of privilege Moses enjoyed in Pharaoh's house. Now, they are his dear brothers. He has come to know the pain and suffering of their slavery, and he chooses willingly to suffer with them.

This day, this moment, will be remembered for all time. Deliverance draws near. As Moses begins to speak, he has one clear mission burning in his heart. He must equip these men to prepare their homes for the coming night. Tonight, the LORD comes, and He comes both to kill and to deliver. Moses must persuade these men to follow God's commands with exactness. It is the most important evening of their lives. Calling out to the assembled fathers of Israel, Moses begins to speak:

> "Draw out and take you a lamb according to your families, and kill the passover. And ye shall take a bunch of hyssop, and dip it in the blood that is in the bason, and strike the lintel and the two side posts with the blood that is in the bason; and none of you shall go out at the door of his house until the morning. For the LORD will pass through to smite the Egyptians; and when he seeth the blood upon the lintel, and on the two side posts, the LORD will pass over the door, and will not suffer the destroyer to come in unto your houses to smite you. And ye shall observe this thing for an ordinance to thee and to thy sons for ever. And it shall come to pass, when ye be come to the land which the LORD will give you, according as he hath promised, that ye shall keep this service. And it shall come to pass, when your children shall

say unto you, What mean ye by this service? That ye shall say, It is the sacrifice of the LORD's passover, who passed over the houses of the children of Israel in Egypt, when he smote the Egyptians, and delivered our houses."[2]

Sobered by the importance of what they heard, the men of Israel bow their heads in worship of God.

The fathers immediately return home to prepare. Each father carefully chooses a spotless lamb for the Passover. As his children watch, he kills the lamb and drains out the blood. Each father carefully relays detailed instruction to his wife on how to prepare the other parts of the meal. As twilight comes to Goshen, every father of Israel carefully spreads blood over their doors. Each father then takes a seat at the family table, and the family begins to eat. Sometime during the meal, the unmistakable sound of screaming Egyptian parents begins. As the children at the table look around in horror, the father begins to explain that the destroyer has come, but that God spared their lives because of the blood on the door.

After the meal, the family huddles together in prayer. The father tells stories of Abraham, Isaac, and Jacob in hopes of distracting his children from the terror surrounding them. The hours pass slowly. No one in Goshen can sleep. Suddenly, there is a knock at the door. Hesitant at first, the father cracks open the door. The message has come from Moses—the people of Israel are free at last!

Passover, the meal so carefully designed and celebrated that night, was intentionally and entirely a family event. Every detail of the meal brings focus to the people and relationships in the individual home. At many other times and in many other feasts, the priest would lead the ceremony, offer the sacrifice, and sprinkle the blood. Not so with Passover. At Passover, each father killed his own lamb and spread the blood over his own house. From its origin, the Passover was designed by God to give the father an unforgettable opportunity to remind his children of the faithfulness of the God of Israel.

Today, we realize that much of the Passover celebration was a picture of what Jesus Christ would do for us. We no longer need to search the fields for a spotless lamb to offer in sacrifice. Our Lamb offered Himself freely for all on an old rugged cross. Yet, some things do not change with the passing of millennia. It remains the father's unique responsibility to take the blood of the Lamb and spread it over his home. The priest cannot do it for him. The mother cannot do it for him. The blood must be spread upon the home by his own hand. When we fail to fulfill that call, a destroyer still walks in the night hours of the soul, waiting to claim any child left uncovered by the blood.

The father's responsibility for the faith of the next generation is clear in Scripture. We see our responsibility in at least three ways. First, positive commands reveal our responsibility. Second, negative warnings reinforce that responsibility. Third, analogies and references in Scripture presume paternal responsibility.

Responsibility Shown in Positive Commands

Many of the positive commands given by God to fathers have already been discussed throughout these pages. We reference a few more here to illustrate how God's Word reveals our responsibility in positive ways. Moses said that God's warnings to Israel were not directed to "your children which have not known, and which have not seen" but to the parents whose eyes had seen all that God did in Egypt and the wilderness.[3] Because of this, there must be a way to transfer faith and experience to the next generation even though they cannot know or see everything their parents experienced.

The Psalmist addresses this issue repeatedly. In one Psalm, he writes, "Walk about Zion, and go round about her: tell the towers thereof. Mark ye well her bulwarks, consider her palaces; that ye may tell it to the generation following."[4] In another place, he says, "O God, thou hast taught me from my youth: and hitherto have I declared thy wondrous works. [. . .] O God, forsake me not; until I have shewed thy strength unto this generation, and thy power to every one that is to come."[5]

Isaiah makes the responsibility more clear:

> "Behold, for peace I had great bitterness: but thou hast in love to my soul delivered it from the pit of corruption: for thou hast cast all my sins behind thy back. For the grave cannot praise thee, death cannot celebrate thee: they that go down into the pit cannot hope for thy truth. The living, the living, he shall praise thee, as I do this day: the father to the children shall make known thy truth."[6]

There are a multitude of Scriptures mentioned previously that further make this point. The Bible makes it clear over and over again from almost every writer and in every era—the father's call is to produce a godly seed in the next generation. The responsibility is in the call.

Responsibility Shown in Negative Warnings

While the positive commands and promises are more enjoyable reading, the repeated warnings to fathers in Scripture further assure our responsibility. In one of the most drastic examples, David's sin with Uriah and Bathsheba brought both immediate and future judgment. David fasted and prayed for seven days, begging God throughout the sleepless nights to heal the child conceived by adultery.[7] The child died as a result of David's sin, and that sin would lead to problems in David's family for the rest of his life. In the book of Jeremiah, God asks the parents of a rebellious generation, "How shall I pardon thee for this? thy children have forsaken me, and sworn by them that are no gods: when I had fed them to the full, they then committed adultery, and assembled themselves by troops in the harlots' houses."[8] God held the parents responsible for the fact that the children forsook Him.

The New Testament does not diminish this responsibility. Indeed, Jesus personally reinforced the responsibility. When Jesus descended from the Mount of Transfiguration, the father of a possessed child came to Jesus to seek a healing for his son.[9] As the child lay foaming on the ground, Jesus turned to the father and asked, "How long is it ago since this came unto him?" The father responded, "Of a child. And ofttimes it hath cast him into the fire, and into the waters, to destroy him: but if thou canst do any thing, have compassion on us, and help us." Looking directly at the father, Jesus said, "If thou canst believe, all things are possible to him that believeth." With the anguish that only a desperate father can know, the man says with tears, "Lord, I believe; help thou mine unbelief."

The interaction between the Lord and this desperate father reveals the intimate relationship between a father's faith and a child's spiritual condition. On the positive side, no sin is so strong and no resistance so desperate that it violates the father's power to bring his child to Christ in prayer.[10] However, Jesus also threw all the responsibility for the son's healing upon the faith of the father.[11] Andrew Murray explains that the father's cry—"Lord, help my unbelief"—flowed from the agonizing realization that failure on his part would prevent Jesus from healing his child.[12]

Thus, unbelief in a father flows out of a condition of the heart, but unbelief in a child flows out of a condition of the home. If we long to bring our children to communion with Christ, let our love for our children first bring us personally to a greater faith and relationship with Christ.[13] Dear fathers, we can see so clearly in the natural that our children are directly linked to us for good or evil. It is also true in the spiritual. As Andrew Murray wrote, God's downpour of the Spirit on our children is not a separate act from His downpour of the Spirit on us.[14] Rather, God wants to pour the Spirit on them through us.

The New Testament abounds with similar warnings. Jesus said, "It were better for him that a millstone were hanged about his neck, and he cast into the sea, than that he should offend one of these little ones."[15] Paul told the Romans to be careful; that "no man put a stumblingblock or an occasion to fall in his brother's way."[16] More than anyone else, fathers can offend their children or cause them to stumble. Paul told the fathers in the church at Ephesus, "[P]rovoke not your children to wrath: but bring them up in the nurture and admonition of the Lord."[17] To the fathers in the Colossian church, he wrote, "Fathers, provoke not your children to anger, lest they be discouraged."[18] The Apostle also told Timothy, "But if any provide not for his own, and specially for those of his own house, he hath denied the faith, and is worse than an infidel."[19] Brothers, if such an admonition is true in the natural provision, it is even more applicable in spiritual provision.

The Father and the Ministry

At times, there is an unspoken tension between paternal and ministerial authority. The tension sometimes flows from the fact that neither the father nor the pastor want responsibility for the faith of the next generation. More often in today's churches, the tension results when fathers abdicate their responsibility to the church leaders. Less common, but equally troubling, is the tension that arises when the godly father and the ministry engage in a jealous competition over the hearts and faith of the children.

A godly father's exercise of divine authority and spiritual gifts in his home should not be perceived as a threat to church order. Moses illustrates this point. When God chose to anoint a number of men to serve under

Moses, Eldad and Medad were unable to join Moses at the tabernacle.[20] While these two men were still in the camp, they began to prophesy under the anointing of the Spirit of God. A young messenger ran to Moses to warn him of the events, and Joshua quickly requested that Moses forbid the men from ministering. Moses responded, "Enviest thou for my sake? would God that all the LORD'S people were prophets, and that the LORD would put his spirit upon them!" Ministers need not be intimidated by godly fathers. Indeed, godly fathers will be the minister's greatest allies and strongest supporters.

In addition, throughout the New Testament the relationship between the ministry and the church is based upon assumptions and analogies about the relationship and responsibility in the home. Paul constantly used the responsibilities of fatherhood to explain his role in the church. To the Corinthians, Paul wrote, "[A]s my beloved sons I warn you. For though ye have ten thousand instructors in Christ, yet have ye not many fathers: for in Christ Jesus I have begotten you through the gospel. Wherefore I beseech you, be ye followers of me."[21] He expressed this parallel in detail to the Thessalonians:

> "So being affectionately desirous of you, we were willing to have imparted unto you, not the gospel of God only, but also our own souls, because ye were dear unto us. For ye remember, brethren, our labour and travail: for labouring night and day, because we would not be chargeable unto any of you, we preached unto you the gospel of God. Ye are witnesses, and God also, how holily and justly and unblameably we behaved ourselves among you that believe: As ye know how we exhorted and comforted and charged every one of you, as a father doth his children, That ye would walk worthy of God, who hath called you unto his kingdom and glory. For this cause also thank we God without ceasing, because, when ye received the word of God which ye heard of us, ye received it not as the word of men, but as it is in truth, the word of God, which effectually worketh also in you that believe."[22]

Although Paul wrote these words as an analogy of his ministry, it is also one of the most beautiful descriptions of fatherhood in all of Scripture.

Later in his ministry, Paul would make leading a godly home a prerequisite to church leadership. He told Timothy a pastor should be

"One that ruleth well his own house, having his children in subjection with all gravity; (For if a man know not how to rule his own house, how shall he take care of the church of God?)"[23] He added that deacons should "be the husbands of one wife, ruling their children and their own houses well."[24] Paul also encouraged Titus to appoint men who were "blameless, the husband of one wife, having faithful children not accused of riot or unruly."[25] Paul clearly believed and taught that the spiritual condition of the children was the responsibility of the father. Paul's use of the godly home as a prerequisite to church leadership denies any other explanation.

Accepting Responsibility

The time has come for us to accept the responsibility for the spiritual condition of our children. Brothers, beware the spirit of Barak, who refused to stand for God unless a woman led him into battle.[26] God has called each father to prepare a godly seed in his home. We may delegate some of this authority to the mothers, but ultimate responsibility cannot be delegated. Our wives cannot bail us out of our responsibility. The burden lies with men and their God.

If the garden is dry and overcome with weeds, we do not blame the garden. If the home is not in order, it is not the wife and children that are at fault. It is the father.[27] In truth, one generation of godly men could entirely change the heritage of the children in our churches.

Every father must lead his children well, whether or not he is naturally suited to leadership. The chief cause of paternal failure is the lack of self-discipline in the father.[28] This problem has caused so many failures in child training that many parents question whether the principles of Scripture hold true in all circumstances with all children. Yet, Andrew Murray challenged, "[L]et us believe that the failure was man's fault."[29] Churches and Christian schools have developed all manner of programs to try to supplement what is missing in the home, but we cannot expect other institutions to succeed at what the family was commanded to do.

From birth, each child has no interest in becoming responsible. Taking up the cross is not in their plans. Our children need to be made to realize that they must deal with reality and overcome imperfections in self, others, and the world. The child needs to realize that work is good, important, and expected. Indeed, an important part of raising adults means training our children to enjoy monotonous responsibilities. This training in joyful obedience is the responsibility of the father. That responsibility cannot be delegated.

Most personality issues are really issues of will and training. If we know a child has a flaw in a certain area, we must dedicate more preventative training to go along with correcting displays of willful disobedience. Consistent order will give our children a huge springboard into godly living, and order starts with the father.[30]

Teaching and leading a young person is one of the greatest relationships on earth. We must not concede this great relationship to a less prepared and less focused youth minister. Fathers must communicate personally with their children. Fatherhood cannot be done by proxy. There is no such thing as the strong, silent type. We must get to know our children before we can effectively help them be saved.[31]

Fathers, we are responsible for the content of our homes. Every father is a watchman over the castle of his home. We must stand vigilant guard over our homes and our hearts. The Psalmist beautifully described this call:

> "I will sing of mercy and judgment: unto thee, O LORD, will I sing. I will behave myself wisely in a perfect way. O when wilt thou come unto me? I will walk within my house with a perfect heart. I will set no wicked thing before mine eyes: I hate the work of them that turn aside; it shall not cleave to me. A froward heart shall depart from me: I will not know a wicked person. [. . .] Mine eyes shall be upon the faithful of the land, that they may dwell with me: he that walketh in a perfect way, he shall serve me. He that worketh deceit shall not dwell within my house: he that telleth lies shall not tarry in my sight."[32]

Paul claimed to be speaking as a father to his children when he encouraged the Corinthians to come out and be separate from the world, touch nothing unclean, cleanse themselves from all filthiness of the flesh and spirit, and perfect holiness in the fear of God.[33]

To properly accept our responsibility for guarding our homes, we must be able to discern between the holy and profane. We must be able to identify the world and all its attempts to infiltrate our homes. Regardless of label or publisher, anything that presents imaginations of lust, greed, or pride to our children is of the world. Television is the number one enemy of our homes, with the internet following closely behind it. Christian fathers need to stop looking for redeemable qualities in secular entertainment, label it the filth that it is, and forbid its entrance into the home.

Standards that seem extreme today were once the norm in Christian households. William Booth wrote, "It has ever been the rule with us in the training of our children, that they should never read a book with the bearing and contents of which we were not ourselves familiar."[34] Charles Finney encouraged parents, "Suffer no body to live in your families, whose sentiments, or habits, or manners, or temper may corrupt your children. Guard the domestic influence as the apple of your eye."[35] He continued, "Have no person in your house, that will tell them foolish stories, sing them foolish songs, talk to them about witches, or any thing of any name or nature, which ought not to come before their youthful minds."[36] Finney further wrote, "Avoid their reading romances, plays, and whatever may beget within them a romantic and feverish state of mind."[37]

Many men recognize the obvious truth that fathers must control what their children see and hear. However, rather than standing for righteousness, most Christian fathers merely instruct their children to wait until they are older before they view and listen to what is objectionable. This loophole leaves room for the father to watch, read, and listen to whatever he likes. Brothers, we should apply the same principles to our own entertainment that we wish our children to follow. Whatever we do, our children, to a large extent, will reflect our image and breathe our spirit.

According to author Steve Farrar, fathers in the Bible had four frequent results. They were cut off early, finished poorly, finished so-so, or finished strong.[38] We must finish strong. Anything less will fundamentally undermine everything else that we do with our children. Farrar notes three ambushes that surprised many men who thought they were destined for a strong finish. Fathers in the Bible and throughout church history have been ambushed by women, ambushed by money and power, and ambushed by a neglected family.[39]

We alone are responsible for how we finish this race. Our children are watching every step we take. Silently, they are cheering for us to succeed and finish well. Let us take the mantle of responsibility and delegate it to no other. Andrew Murray put it this way:

> "[I]f your life is still more carnal than spiritual, with more of the spirit of the world than the Spirit of God[,] do not think it is strange if your children grow up unconverted. This is only right

and natural. You are hindering the Holy Spirit. You are breathing day by day into your children the spirit of the world. [. . . .] In spite of your evil influence, the blessing may reach them, through the faith of others. However, you have no reason to expect it, except as you yield yourself to be the channel for its conveyance."[40]

Let us run well, brothers. Our children depend on it.

---

1. Psalm 78:5-7
2. Exodus 12:21-27
3. Deuteronomy 11:1-8
4. Psalms 48:12-13
5. Psalm 71:17-18
6. Isaiah 38:17-19
7. 2 Samuel 12:15-23
8. Jeremiah 5:7
9. Mark 9:17-24
10. Andrew Murray, Raising Your Children for Christ, (1984) p. 192
11. *Id.* p. 193
12. *Id.* p. 194
13. *Id.* p. 196
14. *Id.* p. 255
15. Luke 17:2
16. Romans 14:13
17. Eph 6:1-4
18. Colossians 3:21
19. 1 Timothy 5:8
20. Numbers 11:26-29
21. 1 Corinthians 4:14-16
22. 1 Thessalonians 2:8-13
23. 1 Timothy 3:4-5
24. 1 Timothy 3:12
25. Titus 1:6
26. Judges 4:8-9
27. David Smith, "Leader and His Home" available at www.charitychristianfellowship.org/sermons/listing

28. Andrew Murray, Raising Your Children for Christ, (1984) p. 114
29. *Id.* p. 131
30. Rick Leibee, "Leader and His Youth" available at www.charitychristianfellowship.org/sermons/listing
31. *Id.*
32. Psalm 101:1-7
33. 1 Corinthians 6:12-7:1
34. William Booth, How to Make the Children into Saints and Soldiers of Jesus Christ, (1888) available at http://www.gospeltruth.net/children/booth_training.htm.
35. Charles Finney, "August 12, 1840 Letters to Parents—1" available at http://www.gospeltruth.net/children/400812_parents_1.htm
36. *Id.*
37. *Id.*
38. Steve Farrar, Finishing Strong, (1995) p. 36
39. *Id.* p. 38
40. Andrew Murray, Raising Your Children for Christ, (1984) p. 256

CHAPTER 20

THE FATHER'S SACRIFICE: "NO PRICE TOO GREAT"

The faithful scribe stands speechless.[1] News has come that the people of Israel have compromised the plan of God by doing according to the abominations of the nations around them. The holy seed has mingled with the people of the land. Worse, the hand of the princes and rulers has been chief in this trespass.

Immediately overcome with grief, Ezra rends his garment and rips hair from his head and beard. He slowly sinks to the ground with a conviction so unbearable that he cannot speak. For hours, Ezra sits there in silent shock. Slowly, all the men of Israel who still tremble at the Word of God gather around him.

At the time of the evening sacrifice, Ezra lifts himself to his knees and attempts to pray. With hands raised to heaven, Ezra searches for the words. The shame he feels for his people is beyond expression. Never before has he struggled so mightily to address the God he knows and serves. Finally, the words begin to come:

> "Since the days of our fathers have we been in a great trespass unto this day; and for our iniquities have we, our kings, and our priests, been delivered into the hand of the kings of the lands, to the sword, to captivity, and to a spoil, and to confusion of face, as it is this day. And now for a little space grace hath been shewed from the LORD our God, to leave us a remnant to escape, and to give us a nail in his holy place, that our God may lighten our eyes, and give us a little reviving in our bondage. For we were bondmen; yet our God hath not forsaken us in our bondage, but hath extended mercy unto us in the sight of the kings of Persia, to give us a reviving, to set up the house of our God, and

to repair the desolations thereof, and to give us a wall in Judah and in Jerusalem. And now, O our God, what shall we say after this? for we have forsaken thy commandments, Which thou hast commanded by thy servants the prophets, saying, The land, unto which ye go to possess it, is an unclean land with the filthiness of the people of the lands, with their abominations, which have filled it from one end to another with their uncleanness. Now therefore give not your daughters unto their sons, neither take their daughters unto your sons, nor seek their peace or their wealth for ever: that ye may be strong, and eat the good of the land, and leave it for an inheritance to your children for ever. And after all that is come upon us for our evil deeds, and for our great trespass, seeing that thou our God hast punished us less than our iniquities deserve, and hast given us such deliverance as this; Should we again break thy commandments, and join in affinity with the people of these abominations? wouldest not thou be angry with us till thou hadst consumed us, so that there should be no remnant nor escaping? O LORD God of Israel, thou art righteous: for we remain yet escaped, as it is this day: behold, we are before thee in our trespasses: for we cannot stand before thee because of this."

It is one of the greatest prayers of the Old Testament. Ezra has poured out his broken heart before God.

The men who have been watching silently are greatly moved. Shechaniah steps forward and speaks to Ezra on behalf of the assembly. "We have trespassed against our God," he says. "Yet now there is hope in Israel concerning this thing. Now therefore let us make a covenant with our God [.]" He encourages Ezra, "Arise; for this matter belongeth unto thee: we also will be with thee: be of good courage, and do it."

In the next three days, every God-fearing man in Judah gathers together in Jerusalem. Despite a torrential downpour, they crowd the street in front of the temple, waiting for Ezra. Each man is visibly shaken by the seriousness of their situation. Ezra stands and, shouting to be heard over the storm, addresses the people. "Ye have transgressed, and have taken strange wives, to increase the trespass of Israel." "Now therefore make confession unto the LORD God of your fathers, and do his pleasure: and separate yourselves from the people of the land, and from the strange wives."

The congregation responds in unity, "As thou hast said, so must we do." The rain, now, is so heavy they cannot stand outside. The men confess to Ezra that the separation is not "a work of one day or two: for we are many that have transgressed in this thing." With trembling, humble hearts, the men leave Jerusalem to return home and cleanse their hearts, lives, and homes "until the fierce wrath of our God for this matter" be turned away from Israel.

The Call to Sacrifice

The attitudes of Ezra and the men of Israel show us how serious this matter is with God. Admittedly, God has not called us to sever marriages and homes to preserve a national identity, but He has called us to be His people in the earth today. These men were willing to make any separation necessary to obey God's call. If they could covenant with God to make such a separation, surely we can covenant with God to separate ourselves from any career, hobby, relative, or entertainment that brings compromise into the home.

The sacrifice necessary to produce a godly seed is not light. We would have it no other way. To paraphrase David, we cannot offer unto God a sacrifice that costs us nothing.[2] The calling of a Christian father is a call to sacrifice. Success in this call demands that we sacrifice our time, our treasure, and our lives.

The Sacrifice of Time

Time's importance to raising godly children cannot be overemphasized. The heart to heart relationship necessary between father and child is sometimes difficult to develop and harder to maintain. Every step in the process requires large quantities of quality time. True quality time with a child is rarely scheduled. If you schedule enough quantity, the quality will flow naturally from your relationship. In such a setting, priceless teachable moments will surface throughout the day. There are no shortcuts to a godly home.

Paul wrote to Timothy:

> "Thou therefore endure hardness, as a good soldier of Jesus Christ. No man that warreth entangleth himself with the affairs of this

life; that he may please him who hath chosen him to be a soldier. And if a man also strive for masteries, yet is he not crowned, except he strive lawfully. The husbandman that laboureth must be first partaker of the fruits."[3]

Fathers, we are soldiers in the greatest war ever waged. We fight for the King of Kings, and our mission is to win the hearts and souls of the next generation to His service. We dare not entangle ourselves with unnecessary earthly pursuits if we hope to please the Lord who commissioned us to this task. We must strive lawfully. Above all, we must be first partaker of every sacrifice our family will endure for the sake of the call.

Dear brothers, we are in desperate need of an old-fashioned dedication. We need a dedication that abandons all carnal desires to focus on pleasing God and winning the next generation for Him. We do not have time for purposeless activity. Everything we do must be focused on the goal. If we need time alone, let us spend it in midnight prayer. If we need time to relax, let us spend it building relationships with our children. We will not build heart to heart relationships while sitting with our children watching an electronic screen. Let us unplug the electronics and spend time with our children.

What is free time? Where do you get it? Gary Thomas explains that parents do not get any extra hours in their day over the person without children.[4] As a result, a father must crucify many dreams, hobbies, and activities in order to make room for this God-given calling. This is true of any form of ministry, and fatherhood is one of the greatest ministries that a man can ever have.[5]

Brothers, how often are you and your entire family home together? We must learn to spend every moment as we would have wished we had spent it when our children leave the home or we leave this world. The opportunity we have to spend substantial time with our children is temporary. They will be adults raising their own children sooner than we like to think. If we blink, we may miss one of the greatest treasures we could ever have. If we willfully close our eyes to the opportunity, only eternity will fully reveal the cost.

"I'm too busy" is just a nice way to say "I'm too selfish."[6] To truly focus on building relationships with our children, we must permit many "good" opportunities—for both fathers and children—to slowly slip away.[7] "Good" is often the worst enemy of "great." Tragically, the unbelieving father is often wiser and more consistent than the believing father.[8] When the unbeliever spends his life pursuing secular objectives, he does so believing he pursues the greater good.[9] The believer pursues the same goals knowing that he pursues the lesser good.[10]

We cannot use work for our excuse. Only God knows how many children have been lost because their father worked long hours thinking he was investing time for his children. Yet, Henrichsen reminds us that "[I]nvesting our time for our children is different than investing our time in our children."[11] Let us learn to invest time in our children before it is too late.

The time constraints of ministry deserve special note here. The great struggle that preachers experience in keeping their children in the faith is infamous. The carnality of "preacher's kids" has become a running joke in the culture. This cannot be the plan of God. Remember, Paul made godly children a prerequisite qualification to the ministry. Therefore, if the ministry drains so much time from our schedule that we begin to lose the hearts of our children, we have misunderstood God's will. God's two great callings on a father in the ministry will not defeat one another.

Granted, serving in the ministry brings additional demands and adversities. However, Steve Farrar explains that it is "better to face the adversity of serving God together as a family than to neglect one another through a distorted understanding of sacrificing for God."[12] Church history contains many tragedies of men who were regularly away from home for the sake of ministry. Their marriages often ended in divorce, and their children turned to suicide, homosexuality, and atheism as a result of their fathers' absence. What does it profit a man if he should win the whole world and lose his own family?[13] Concerning this dilemma, D.L. Moody once said, "[M]y duty is to my family first."[14] God's calls will not conflict. If we lose our children, we will be of little help to the church or the world. Brothers, we must remember our first priority.

The Sacrifice of Treasure

Raising godly children will also require a sacrifice of treasure. If God blesses us with many children, we may often have opportunity to watch God do miracles in providing for our homes. Whatever the cost, the father whose table is surrounded by godly children is richer than any man on earth.

If we fear lower incomes, older cars, and cheaper clothes, we should frequently recall the words of Christ. It was Jesus who assured us, "But seek ye first the kingdom of God, and his righteousness; and all these things shall be added unto you."[15] In considering this promise, we are encouraged that Jesus directly connected the spiritual care of children to the kingdom of heaven.[16] Thus, we can be confident that God will provide the needs of those fathers who righteously engage in the pursuit of a godly seed.

The loss of money, career, or possessions is nothing compared to the blessing of a godly seed. While many sources within and without compel us to engage in the rat race and attempt to keep up with the people around us, we will find our salvation nearer than when we first believed if we will exchange these worldly pursuits for the pursuit of godly seed. Paul gave a stark warning:

> "But they that will be rich fall into temptation and a snare, and into many foolish and hurtful lusts, which drown men in destruction and perdition. For the love of money is the root of all evil: which while some coveted after, they have erred from the faith, and pierced themselves through with many sorrows."[17]

The American dream has proven to be nightmare time and again. God has called us to pursue far better things than the temptations, snares, lusts, and sorrows of money. He has called us to pursue the hearts of our children. Please, fathers, do not trade the eternal pursuit for a temporary one.

Steve Farrar writes that this life is too short to be intimidated by "stupid expectations at our jobs."[18] Our children don't need extra things. They need us. And they need us to be home. The words penned by Charles Finney in 1840 are even truer today, "If parents would satisfy themselves with a competency of this world's goods, and abandon their fastidious and fashionable ways of living, they would, in almost all cases, have abundant time for companionship with their children."[19]

Dear brothers, our Lord informed us long ago that our treasure reveals our heart. If some secular pursuit draws us away from our children, we must rise up in strength and destroy that idol in the name of our holy God. If television, internet, sports, video games, books, boats, hunting, fishing, or pornography is robbing us of our time at home with our children, then let us burn these idols in the back yard with our children watching. Let us prove our love to them. If we refuse, then at least we can have the courtesy to tell our children openly that we love these things more than we love them. God forbid!

The Sacrifice of Self

The struggle to sacrifice time and treasure tends to reveal that we are more selfish creatures than we care to admit. The calling of a Christian father is the call to lay down our lives for our children. To raise a godly seed, we must crucify our selfishness and become a living sacrifice for God. Jeremiah compelled the fathers of his day:

> "[L]et tears run down like a river day and night: give thyself no rest; let not the apple of thine eye cease. Arise, cry out in the night: in the beginning of the watches pour out thine heart like water before the face of the Lord: lift up thy hands toward him for the life of thy young children, that faint for hunger in the top of every street."[20]

Are we willing to pay the price? We can weep, pray, and intercede now while they remain under our roof, or we will certainly do it later when they turn their backs on God.

The root issue cannot be avoided. We can no longer attempt to conceal the fact that our own selfishness will destroy our children if we do not conquer it first. Jesus explained—and exemplified—this principle with His own disciples:

> "Verily, verily, I say unto you, Except a corn of wheat fall into the ground and die, it abideth alone: but if it die, it bringeth forth much fruit. He that loveth his life shall lose it; and he that hateth his life in this world shall keep it unto life eternal."[21]

It is our choice, brethren. We can give up this life and bear fruit in our children, or we can cling to this life and abide alone when our children leave the faith.

Our vision is beautiful, but it is not cheap. It will cost us everything, especially our pride. Gary Thomas writes "Once we have children, we cannot act and dream as if we had remained childless."[22] There is no such thing as an "instant" Christian home. Microwave home life will not get the job done. A few minutes of quality time will not suffice. The quality time theory is like believing in a fast-food Christian home. Our homes are not McDonalds; they are the training ground for the next generation of believers that will turn the world upside down with their faith in God.

An altar without sacrifice is an altar without fire. If we want our homes to be on fire for God, we must provide our own lives as the sacrifice for the altar. The situation is too serious for pretend Christianity. We must deny ourselves, take up our cross, and follow Christ, or betray our children into the hands of the enemy.

We must not settle for good children that turn out well and warm the pews faithfully every Sunday. We are called to raise world changers. We are called to raise champions for Christ. This calling has us in a corner that requires us to sacrifice all or abandon this vision altogether. Thank God. We love our children, and we cannot save them without a real relationship with our Father in heaven. Praise God for such a marvelous plan.

We must dedicate our whole life to dedicating their whole life to God. In four generations, it is highly likely that the only thing our descendents will know about us is that we had children and whether or not we passed our faith to the next generation. We must embrace our insignificance to the world. Our chances of being remembered for our job, our possessions, or our business are minimal at best. Embrace this insignificance and pursue with all your heart your relationship with the few people who will actually care that you existed—your family.[23]

Gary Thomas explains the vast likelihood is that the issue that is pressing on our minds, whether it's a business deal, sermon preparation, or the daily stresses of life, will be entirely forgotten by everyone, including us, within the year. We must take the time to push these things aside and spend time with our children.[24] Our children will stand on the back of our sacrifice.[25] How tall do we want them to stand?

Do our children really believe that we would lay our lives down for them? We believe this instinctively, but it is the child's perspective that will impact their salvation, not our own perspective.[26] In God's economy, people are worth more than anything else. Thus, Henrichsen writes, "To give your life for anything else is an investment in trivia."[27] A plaque written by an unknown author reads, "Empires fall, mansions crumble, cattle die, machinery rusts away, earthly pleasures fade away in a moment, but a child lives on and on in the lives of descendents and in those he influences all the way into eternity." What is the value of a child?

If we willingly sacrifice to be with our children and raise them as a godly seed, we will soon find that it was really no sacrifice at all. William Booth said it this way:

> "[I]f parents desire that their children shall be saved, and grow up to be of service to the Master, they must not grudge the pains and efforts and self-denial that the work may cost them. Moreover, in the long run, it will be found by far the easier course to the parent. That is, those who bend themselves to the task, sparing no amount of labour in the beginning, will find the task become easier and easier as the days go by, and on the whole will find far less wear and tear of both mind and heart in making Saints and Soldiers of their children than they would by indolently allowing them to have their own way and grow up in self-indulgence and sin."[28]

Perhaps the old hymn says it best, "Rise up, O men of God! Have done with lesser things. Give heart and mind and soul and strength to serve the King of Kings."[29]

Finally, the timing of sacrifice is essential. If we would sacrifice something for our children in their day of temptation and decision, let us sacrifice it now in their day of development and discipline. Even highly compromised fathers would sacrifice much to ensure faith when their child struggles in the day of decision. Just as David offered his own life in exchange for Absalom's, many fathers would pay any price to save a backsliding child. If we would surrender overtime, extra cars, credit cards, boats, promotions, careers, oversized homes, hobbies, sports, or entertainment to help our children choose right in the day of decision, let us do it now while we actually have the greatest influence on the choices they must one day face.

What will we give in exchange for our souls? What will we give in exchange for the souls of our children? If we would pray more in the day of decision, let us pray more now. If we would read more then, let us read more now. If we would communicate more then, let us communicate more now. If we would apologize more then, let us apologize more now. If we would sacrifice more then, let us sacrifice more now. Tomorrow may be too late.

1. Ezra 9:1-10:14
2. 2 Samuel 24:24
3. 2 Timothy 2:3-6
4. Gary Thomas, Sacred Parenting, (2004) p. 189
5. *Id.*
6. Rick Leibee, "Leader and His Youth" available at www.charitychristianfellowship.org/sermons/listing
7. Monte Swan, Romancing Your Child's Heart, (2002) p. 80
8. Walter A. Henrichsen, How to Disciple Your Children, (1981) p. 41
9. *Id.* p. 41
10. *Id.* p. 41
11. *Id.* p. 43
12. Steve Farrar, Finishing Strong, (1995) p. 47
13. *Id.* p. 47-48
14. *Id.* p. 50
15. Matthew 6:33
16. Matthew 19:13-15
17. I Timothy 6:9-10
18. Steve Farrar, Finishing Strong, (1995) p. 53
19. Charles Finney, "October 7, 1840 Letters to Parents—4" available at http://www.gospeltruth.net/children/401007_parents_4.htm
20. Lamentations 2:18-19
21. John 12:24-25
22. Gary Thomas, Sacred Parenting, (2004) p. 183
23. *Id.* p. 159
24. *Id.* p. 160
25. *Id.* p. 182
26. Monte Swan, Romancing Your Child's Heart, (2002) p 135
27. Walter A. Henrichsen, How to Disciple Your Children, (1981) p. 38
28. William Booth, How to Make the Children into Saints and Soldiers of Jesus Christ, (1888) available at http://www.gospeltruth.net/children/booth_training.htm.
29. "Rise up, O men of God!" Lyrics by William P. Merrill; Music by William H. Walter.

CHAPTER 21

THE FATHER'S RESPONSE: "STAND IN THE GAP"

The people of Israel assemble together near the border of the Promised Land. The long-awaited day has finally come. Moses is choosing a courageous leader from each tribe to go search out the blessings that await them in the land of Canaan.[1] As the names are revealed, the announcement spreads through the camp like wildfire. The tribe of Reuben sends Shammua. Simeon sends Shaphat. Issachar is represented by Igal. Benjamin sends Palti. The tribe of Zebulun sends Gaddiel. Dan is represented by Ammiel. Gaddi will go for Manasseh. Asher sends Sethur. Naphtali sends Nahbi. Gad is represented by Geuel. Ephraim will send Joshua, the son of Nun. Judah sends Caleb, the forty-year-old son of Jephunneh. These twelve men are the elite of Israel. Their feet will be the first to touch the Promised Land since the burial of Jacob.

To the man, the twelve spies are in awe of the blessings they see in Canaan. Each man discovers portions of the land that would provide a wonderful home for his tribe and their descendents. Yet, each man is fully aware of the bloodshed required to take possession of the land. Reuniting with each other shortly before returning to camp, they compare stories of all they have seen.

As the men stand to give their report to the people, the air is electric with excitement. Then, in one accord, ten men give a crushing report. The land is beautiful and more blessed than they had imagined, but there are giants in the land. The enemies are too big, too strong, and too fortified. To proceed would be suicide.

As thoughts of mutiny and insurrection spread through the crowd, Caleb shouts for order over the tumult. With a faith that giants could not shake, Caleb pleads with the people, "Let us go up at once, and possess it; for we are well able to overcome it." As Caleb struggles mightily to persuade the people, his ten companions shout him down:

> "We be not able to go up against the people; for they are stronger than we. The land, through which we have gone to search it, is a land that eateth up the inhabitants thereof; and all the people that we saw in it are men of a great stature. And there we saw the giants, the sons of Anak, which come of the giants: and we were in our own sight as grasshoppers, and so we were in their sight."

The crowd is clearly siding with the evil report.

Grieved, Joshua rises to stand at Caleb's side.[2] The two faithful leaders rend their clothes and desperately plead one more time:

> "The land, which we passed through to search it, is an exceeding good land. If the LORD delight in us, then he will bring us into this land, and give it us; a land which floweth with milk and honey. Only rebel not ye against the LORD, neither fear ye the people of the land; for they are bread for us: their defense is departed from them, and the LORD is with us: fear them not."

Their plea falls on deaf ears. The people are persuaded that they are grasshoppers before their enemies. They search for stones to forever silence the testimony of God's two faithful witnesses.

Suddenly, the glory of God appears before all. God's judgment is swift and final. Only Caleb and Joshua will ever see the Promised Land again. The ten spies, and all who believed them, will perish one by one in a forty year death march through the wilderness of the Arabian Peninsula.

For his faithfulness, Joshua will eventually be given command of the people of Israel. He will personally lead them in victory over the enemies that he had long ago prophesied would be bread before the people of God. For all time, the people of God will remember Joshua for his faithful leadership and service to God.

Caleb's testimony remains almost unrivaled in Scripture. For forty long years, he follows God fully, with a spirit completely different from his doubting peers.[3] God personally promises Caleb and his descendants an inheritance in the land. Caleb had given a faithful report despite the fact that the land he surveyed was infested with giants. In return, God promised that land to his family.

When the people of Israel cross over into Canaan, Caleb fights faithfully at Joshua's side. After fighting battles time and again on behalf of the children of those who sought to stone him, Caleb approaches Joshua. Looking into the eyes of an old friend, Caleb declares:

> "Thou knowest the thing that the LORD said unto Moses the man of God concerning me and thee in Kadeshbarnea. Forty years old was I when Moses the servant of the LORD sent me from Kadeshbarnea to espy out the land; and I brought him word again as it was in mine heart. Nevertheless my brethren that went up with me made the heart of the people melt: but I wholly followed the LORD my God. And Moses sware on that day, saying, Surely the land whereon thy feet have trodden shall be thine inheritance, and thy children's forever, because thou hast wholly followed the LORD my God. And now, behold, the LORD hath kept me alive, as he said, these forty and five years, even since the LORD spake this word unto Moses, while the children of Israel wandered in the wilderness: and now, lo, I am this day fourscore and five years old. As yet I am as strong this day as I was in the day that Moses sent me: as my strength was then, even so is my strength now, for war, both to go out, and to come in. Now therefore give me this mountain, whereof the LORD spake in that day; for thou heardest in that day how the Anakims were there, and that the cities were great and fenced: if so be the LORD will be with me, then I shall be able to drive them out, as the LORD said."[4]

Joshua gladly blesses Caleb with Hebron for an inheritance.

Armed with faith in God and a vision for the inheritance of his children, Caleb wages war on the giants of Hebron. His son-in-law fights faithfully by his side. In time, they vanquish the enemy and subdue the land. Yet, the faithfulness of Caleb was never selfish. When the fighting ceases, the leaders of Israel choose lots to determine where the children of Aaron will live. Caleb's lot is chosen. Ever faithful, Caleb gladly gives his city back to God as a home for the descendents of Aaron.[5] One more time, Caleb gives his best to God. Then, he leads his family farther into the mountain villages where they will lay a foundation for the generations to come.[6]

Fight in Faith for Your Children

Caleb stands out as one of the exemplary fathers in all of human history. David was a giant killer. Caleb was a "giants" killer. Caleb had the vision to fight battles for the next generation. Every foot of ground he gained came through battle and bloodshed. His children's children grew up there in peace and safety.

Our children will possess what we fight for. How much are we willing to fight? Will we turn away from this vision in unbelief like the ten spies and leave the battle for our children to fight? Or, will we stand in faith like Caleb, and so many who have followed in his footsteps, and leave our children an inheritance of victorious Christianity? God is looking for men who will fight battles for the next generation.

God needs men, especially fathers. He is seeking men who will stand in the gap.[7] The time to respond to our God-given call has come. To quote Paul, "[I]t is high time to awake out of sleep: for now is our salvation nearer than when we believed."[8] Our homes and our churches are in desperate need of men of character who beget other men of character. Throughout Scripture and history, the lack of spiritual men of character has been a judgment from God. We must hold back this tide.

The pastor cannot raise our children for us. The principal cannot raise our children for us. Even our wives cannot raise our children for us. The calling belongs to fathers. Leaders produce leaders. Mighty men of God produce other mighty men of God to follow after them. A second generation church should be a church full of godly men. A family tree dedicated to Christ should be full of godly men. If not, why not? Where is the breach? Brothers, we must not wait to build a godly home until it is too late. One day we may look back and realize that we missed the whole thing.

There are four great fears that prevent us from responding to the call. Men fear evil in the child, evil in the world, evil in the father, and failure in the church. All of these concerns are real, but none of them should prevent us from following the calling of God in our homes.

Many fathers avoid the pursuit of godly seed because they realize the evil in their children. Although our children are the potential sons and daughters of God, at birth they are the unrestrained spawn of Adam with an unregenerate soul, a carnal spirit, and an ignorant mind. This condition presents a very real challenge. However, this fact must not deter us. Indeed, this reality makes our calling even more important and holy. Andrew Murray writes:

> "[T]he work entrusted to us is holier than we know. This precious child, so delicate, so wonderfully made, so marred by sin already, and so exposed to its power, is of inconceivable worth. To take charge of a [. . .] soul, to train a will for God and eternity, makes us want to decline such a great responsibility. But we cannot."[9]

By God's grace, we are commissioned to take these children of Adam and guide through their transformation into the children of God.

Brothers, God must have leaders for the next generation. God's next great leader may be running around your house with a bad spirit, a dirty diaper, and a runny nose. Take care of that child. We're going to need him soon.[10]

Evil in the world is the second cause of great concern. The spiritual and natural turmoil occurring in the world causes many men to hesitate raising godly children. Some even question whether to have children at all. Yet, the survival of the church as we know it depends upon families raising godly children, even in the worst of times. We owe much to the great cloud of witnesses that have already run this race. We must pass the faith to another generation of young people prepared to represent Christ to the world. Their light will shine brightest in times of darkness.

Beyond the everyday problems afflicting this planet, we recognize that the systems of the world aggressively target our children. Our adversaries seek souls to devour. We cannot hide the fact that we are in a battle, and we dare not minimize the stakes. Not to realize we are in a conflict means one thing only—that the enemy has already knocked us unconscious.[11] Now is the time to wake up and get back in the fight with every ounce of energy we have left. We will not surrender, and we cannot retreat. Thus, we stand for righteousness in faith that the battle is the Lord's.

The third fear is the evil within us. To fully follow this vision and work with God as He seeks a godly seed in our homes, something within us must die. We possess a nature that can be traced all the way back to Adam. When Adam sinned, he betrayed God, failed his wife, and passed sin and death to all of his descendents. That same nature lives within us. We, too, are prone to betray God, fail our wives, and pass sin and death to our children. That fact gives us great cause for concern regarding our ability to fulfill the call.

We know that the vast majority of fathers around us are currently failing to produce a godly seed. Do we dare to think that we could join the heroes of the faith that have gone before us? Do we possess the inner strength necessary to fulfill the call? In a word, no. But we know who does. If we fully surrender ourselves to God, receive His Spirit, and follow His Word, we are able to do all things through Christ who strengthens us. We look unto Jesus, the author and finisher of our faith. By His strength, we can and will prevail. Like Joshua and Caleb before us, we are not ignorant of the giants in the land. Yet, we trust that God is leading us in this vision, and where He leads, He provides the strength for the victory.

The fourth great fear stems from the failure we see in the church. While we examined this issue previously, the fact that we have seen many young people abandon the faith has a demoralizing impact on many who consider this vision. Steve Farrar reminds us that the ten spies who failed were leaders in their tribes and likely spiritual giants among the people of God.[12] They were the best and brightest, the most elite that Israel had to offer. And ten of them failed. Only two finished strong. Because those ten men fainted in the day of decision, their wives died in the wilderness, their children endured forty years of failure in the wilderness, and an entire generation of the people of God suffered as a result of unbelief.[13]

In many ways, the same is true in our day. We are surrounded by those who would testify that certain defeat awaits us. The enemy has indeed slain many who have attempted to conquer this land before us. Nevertheless, we stand with Joshua and Caleb. The odds of failure are irrelevant and meaningless if we stand firmly in the covenant of God.

History has forgotten the names of the ten men who caused the hearts of the people to melt in unbelief. They perished in the wilderness with all the men who followed them. In contrast, Joshua and Caleb—God's two faithful fathers out of all of Israel—will be remembered for eternity. More importantly, they laid a foundation of righteousness and faith that supported many generations. Out of all Israel, only those two families could claim fathers that faithfully followed God from Egypt to Canaan. The time has come for us to leave that kind of legacy.

To summarize, we see four great reasons that fathers fail to raise a godly seed. First, God often does not have the father's heart. We cannot raise a godly seed until we fully surrender our lives to God. Second, many fathers do not have the child's heart. All the teaching, training, and disciplining of a lifetime cannot replace the heart to heart relationship between a father and his child. Third, sometimes we fathers have the child's heart, but we do not know what to do with it. The Bible is our guide for all the teaching, training, disciplining, and vision-casting for our children. Fourth, many times we fathers know what to do, but we refuse to consistently apply the truth to our lives. The cost of such inconsistency is unbearably high. If we know to do good and do it not, we will be held accountable.

Thus, God has brought us to a point of decision. We have an inescapable opportunity. The Lord who breathes this vision into our hearts will hold us accountable regardless of which decision we make. The almighty God is seeking a godly seed. Will we work with Him, or will we become His enemy? Charles Finney clearly explained the urgent response that is appropriate for our call:

> "Lay hold on the promises of God for [your children]. Search the Bible for promises. Lay your Bible open before you. Kneel over it, and spread out the case of your children before God. Begin with the covenant of Abraham, and understand that God made the covenant as well with the children as with the parents. And remember that an inspired Apostle has said, 'The promise is to you and to your children, and to as many as are afar off, even as many as the Lord our God shall call.' Take the promise in Isa. 44:3-5: 'I will pour water upon him that is thirsty, and floods upon the dry ground; I will pour my Spirit upon thy seed, and my blessing upon thine offspring; and they shall spring up among the grass, as willows by the water-courses. One shall say I am the Lord's; and another shall call himself by the name of Jacob; and another shall subscribe with his hand unto the Lord, and surname himself by the name of Israel.' Remember, that this promise was made more especially to the Church under the Christian dispensation, and respects the children of Christians, more especially than the children of Jewish parents. Throw your souls into these promises, and wrestle until you prevail."[14]

Let us lay hold of these promises and live them out in this present day.

Answering this call is not a "he-man effort of the flesh."[15] Answering the call requires an absolute surrender to and dependence upon God as He completes the good work that He has begun in us. We are not going to win this battle by luck, accident, compromise, or relaxation.

Victory demands vision. It demands a clear, strong, soul-igniting vision etched in the tables of the heart by the finger of God. Beyond that, the pursuit of godly seed requires a determination to diligently and consistently live out the elements of that vision in our homes. The call is going out. The trumpet is sounding. The time has come to answer the call.

---

1. Numbers 13
2. Numbers 14:6-10
3. Numbers 14:23-24
4. Joshua 14:6-14
5. Joshua 21:9-13
6. 1 Chronicles 6:54-56
7. Ezekiel 22:30
8. Romans 13:11-12
9. Andrew Murray, Raising Your Children for Christ, (1984) p. 288
10. Steve Farrar, Finishing Strong, (1995) p. 81
11. *Id.* p. 75
12. *Id.* p. 20
13. *Id.*
14. Charles Finney, "October 21, 1840 Letters to Parents—5" available at http://www.gospeltruth.net/children/401021_parents_5.htm
15. Steve Farrar, Finishing Strong, (1995) p. 28

Made in the USA
Monee, IL
08 July 2020